CONTEMPORARY PURITAN SALAFISM

Comparative Islamic Studies
Series Editor: Brannon Wheeler, US Naval Academy

This series, like its companion journal of the same title, publishes work that integrates Islamic studies into the contemporary study of religion, thus providing an opportunity for expert scholars of Islam to demonstrate the more general significance of their research both to comparatavists and to specialists working in other areas. Attention to Islamic materials from outside the central Arabic lands is of special interest, as are comparisons which stress the diversity of Islam as it interacts with changing human conditions.

Published

Earth, Empire and Sacred Text
Muslims and Christians as Trustees of Creation
David L. Johnston

East by Mid-East
Studies in Cultural, Historical and Strategic Co

Ibn Arabi and the Contemporary West
Beshara and the Ibn Arabi Society
Isobel Jeffery-Street

Notes from the Fortune-Telling Parrot
Islam and the Struggle for Religious Pluralism in Pakistan
David Pinault

Orientalists, Islamists and the Global Public Sphere
A Genealogy of the Modern Essentialist Image of Islam
Dietrich Jung

Prolegomena to a History of Islamicate Manichaeism
John C. Reeves

Prophecy and Power
Muhammad and the Qur'an in the Light of Comparison
Marilyn Robinson Waldman
Edited by Bruce B. Lawrence, with Lindsay Jones and Robert M. Baum

The Arabs and the Scramble for Africa
John C. Wilkinson

The Qur'ān
A New Annotated Translation
A. J. Droge

Forthcoming

Words of Experience
Translating Islam with Carl W. Ernst
Edited by Brannon M Wheeler and Ilyse Morgenstein Fuerst

CONTEMPORARY PURITAN SALAFISM

A Swedish Case Study

Susanne Olsson

SHEFFIELD UK   BRISTOL CT

Published by Equinox Publishing Ltd.

UK: Office 415, The Workstation, 15 Paternoster Row, Sheffield, South Yorkshire S1 2BX

USA: ISD, 70 Enterprise Drive, Bristol, CT 06010

www.equinoxpub.com

First published 2019.

A catalogue record for this book is available from the British Library.
ISBN: 9781781793398 (hardback)
          9781781794289 (ePDF)

Library of Congress Cataloging-in-Publication Data
Names: Olsson, Susanne, author.
Title: Contemporary puritan Salafism: a Swedish case study / Susanne Olsson.
Description: Bristol, CT: Equinox Pub. Ltd., 2019. Series: Comparative Islamic studies. Includes bibliographical references and index.
Identifiers: LCCN 2015046113 (print) | LCCN 2015046687 (ebook) | ISBN 9781781793398 (hb) | ISBN 9781781794289 (e-PDF) | ISBN 9781781794296 (epub)
Subjects: LCSH: Salafeiyah--Sweden. | Islam-Sweden. | Muslims--Sweden--Case studies.
Classification: LCC BP195.S18 O47 2016 (print) | LCC BP195.S18 (ebook) | DDC 297.8/1--dc23
LC record available at http://lcon.loc.gov/2015046113

Typeset by Forthcoming Publications Ltd

Contents

Acknowledgments

A number of people and institutions have influenced the process that brought this study into print. Above all, I wish to extend my gratitude to Professor David Westerlund, my former Ph.D. supervisor, who has always been very supportive and encouraging. I have also greatly benefitted from cooperating with Emin Poljarevic on the topic of contemporary Salafism, co-arranging panels at various conferences and receiving constructive comments on research drafts. Several scholars have been a part of a larger network on contemporary interpretations of Islam, who have been inspiring and helpful colleagues during the time I worked on this project: Jenny Berglund, Güney Dogan, Ulrika Mårtensson, Terje Østebø, Emin Poljarevic, Egdūnas Račius, Martin Riexinger, Mark Sedgwick, Leif Stenberg and Jonas Svensson. I would especially like to extend my gratitude to Göran Larsson who critically commented on the entire manuscript, which was very helpful and to which I am very grateful.

While working on this book I was employed at Södertörn University and I would like to thank all my former colleagues in the Higher Seminar in the Study of religions there for encouraging and constructive comments. I am also grateful for the support of my new colleagues and the constructive research environment in the History of Religions department at Stockholm University. I also wish to thank students and colleagues that I met at various conferences that have inspired this study through critical comments and discussions. I am also grateful to my friends and family, especially Lina, for putting up with me during the time I worked on this book.

The research behind this study was generously funded by the Swedish Riksbankens Jubileumsfond, to which I am very grateful. Riksbankens Jubileumsfond also funded an international workshop on contemporary Salafism at Södertörn University in 2013. I also wish to thank Helge Ax:son Johnson's Foundation, which supported conference participation related to the themes studied in this book.

Finally, and perhaps needless to say, all errors and unclear reasoning found in this study are my own creations.

Note on Transliteration and Terminology

In this study, Arabic terminology and phrases are explained the first time they occur. A brief glossary at the end of the book includes explanations of reoccurring terminology. Arabic words and phrases are transcribed in a simplified manner. Diacritic signs are omitted in order to simplify (except in citations), though long vowels are retained. Personal names are written as they are commonly written in English, without diacritic signs and long vowels. Some words that are commonly used in English are not transcribed according to these notes, such as Sunnah, Qur'an and imam. The following conventions have further been adopted:

- The letter *'ayn* is designated by: '
- The letter *hamzah* is designated by: '
- The letter *ta marbutah* is marked with an *-ah* ending, as in Sunnah and *ummah*, except in genitive constructions where *-at* is used.
- Arthur J. Droge's *The Qur'ān: A New Annotated Translation* is used when citing verses from the Qur'an, unless otherwise indicated.

Introduction

'My *ummah* will split into seventy-three sects. All of them are in the Fire
Except one sect.' He said: 'And which is it O Messenger of Allah?' He said:
'What I am upon and my Companions [*ashābi*].'[1]

Contemporary Salafism is a multifaceted global phenomenon. Several
groups and individuals present themselves as Salafis, while some reject
such an identification, even though they could be characterized as
Salafis from an analytical perspective. Some use 'Salafi' as a self-
description, even when the teachings followed do not cohere with the
scholarly definition of Salafism.

A puritan Salafi group in Sweden constitutes the empirical evidence
of this study, which seeks to address issues of authority and authenticity related to contemporary interpretations of Islam.[2] The focus is
on the official claims about what Islam is, or at least what it should be,
according to the confessional teaching of the group. The teaching is a
part of the group's 'mission' (*da'wah*) and 'program of action' (*manhaj*).

From the outset, it can be stated that being Salafi in contemporary
Sweden can make life difficult for participants, setting them apart from
mainstream Swedish society. Salafis are seen as visibly 'other'—not least
through their style of dress, which includes both female covering and the
male practice of growing a beard and wearing a head cap. Furthermore,
the official ideology promoted by the group's leaders makes them intel-
lectually 'other' in respect to major 'democratic questions', such as

1. From www.sunnah.com with slight modifications: *Jami' al-Tirmidhi* 2641,
   accessed February 10, 2014.
2. I follow the typology of Salafism elaborated by Wiktorowicz 2006, 217–221,
   which is further presented below. See also Olsson 2014.

gender issues, integration and segregation. One fundamental aspect that impacts on this particular interpretation of Islam is the actual situation of being minority Muslims, living in a society deemed to be 'fallen'. Although Salafis are a part of contemporary Swedish society, this group does not embrace the idea of becoming integrated and, therefore, devotes a lot of its time elaborating on how to live in ways befitting authentic Muslims among the non-believers (*kuffār*) of the impure surrounding that constitutes contemporary Sweden. Departing from this specific situation, we can note how the group formulates a view on what an authentic Islamic tradition is and how this tradition should be performed today.

Discussions among scholars today often explore the experiences of Muslims in a given part of Europe, examining issues relating to Islam's position within 'civil society' and 'public space'.[3] Islam can in many respects be regarded as an institutionalized religion in Europe, with many Muslims engaged in society. At the same time, some Muslims—voluntarily or otherwise—remain isolated. Many groups engage in confessional teaching in Islam, though this is an understudied area. A number of studies have sought to discuss various countries' official views on practicing and teaching *about* and *in* religion.[4] Education pertaining to religion currently gains more attention among researchers.[5] However, most studies have tended to focus on formal environments of education. In Sweden, researchers have generally dealt with 'free schools' that have a religious profile, doing classroom studies or problematizing the existence of free schools in a Swedish secular setting.[6] Only a few studies have examined confessional religious education, and even then, they are mainly focused on 'traditional' Islamic teaching or on Muslim-majority countries, whereas a very different situation exists in Sweden.[7] Notably, the focus of the present study is on confessional Islamic teaching in Sweden that is *not* bound by government control.

An often-heard comment is that confessional environments ought to be controlled in order to safeguard democratic values. In Sweden, this is already the case with schools, including free schools—regardless of their orientation. When this requirement is directed to confessional environments, for example mosques, it can be seen as a limitation of

3.   Asad 2003; Olsson 2009; Salvatore 2007.
4.   Van Bruinessen 2007; Daun 2004; Hefner and Zaman 2007.
5.   Berglund 2010; REDCo.
6.   See, for example, Berglund 2010.
7.   Eickelman 1978; Holger et al. 2004; Roald 1994.

the freedom of religion, a freedom which is granted and protected by law. Various countries have different rules regarding the freedom of religious expression, meaning that the experience of Muslims has to be treated on a country-by-country basis. Indeed, Muslims are affected by their national contexts. In Sweden, religious organizations that receive funding from the state are expected to live up to and promote democratic values. And yet, there seems to be an underlying suspicion that religious groups do not always do that—Muslim ones in particular. The topic of funding related to democratic values can be illustrated by an episode of the TV documentary series 'Uppdrag granskning' (Mandate Review). Aired on May 16, 2012, by Swedish National Television (SVT), 'Imamernas råd' ('The Advice of the Imams') documented what happened when two women, dressed in *niqāb*, went to several Muslim congregations in Sweden to ask imams for help. The pretext was that the husband of one of the women had beaten her, and so she approached the imam, asking whether or not she should report him to the police. The women were wearing hidden cameras and recorded each meeting. Some imams told the women that they should report the husband to the police, while some recommended the opposite. The documentary gained a lot of attention in the media. One issue raised was that some of the mosques that the women visited had received national funding and by law therefore should uphold democratic values, such as equality between men and women. This documentary indicates that there is a fear that Muslims say one thing in public and another in the in-group, and that Muslims therefore are essentially undemocratic.[8]

The close relationship between the Swedish Church and the state was changed in 2000, removing the exclusive position that the Swedish Church had held and thus relegating the old notion of a state church to history. This change did not cause much debate in Sweden and passed rather unnoticed. Sweden can be described as a country where

8.   On January 30, 2013, a follow-up documentary was broadcast by SVT, again as an episode of the Uppdrag granskning documentary. The episode, which had the title 'Tillbaka till moskéerna' ('Back to the Mosques'), sought to probe whether the mosques had become more 'democratic' since the last program was aired. See the documentary website: www.svt.se/ug. The Swedish Commission for Government Support to Faith Communities (SST) published a report in 2013 which focused on the need for training leaders of faith communities who arrived from other countries. The result was that this could only be done if it was based on the needs of society at large and anchored in the conditions of the religious communities (SST 2013).

secular and rational values are widespread.[9] The secular stance was also reflected in a government-initiated investigation, published in 2009, into the possibilities of creating a Swedish imam-education program. The report concluded that the state should not give its support since it should be neutral in questions pertaining to religion. Moreover, a person educated in such a state-sponsored program would not necessarily be accepted by the religious communities anyway.[10] Officially, Sweden promotes confessional neutrality, multiculturalism, and pluralism with equality and freedom of choice for all citizens being granted rights in the constitution. The national Education Act lists values such as democracy, integrity, equality, and solidarity that should be promoted in schools, including all free schools. Public schools have to be non-denominational and non-confessional by law. Free schools may give confessional education *in addition to* the compulsory curriculum and there are a number of schools which have an Islamic character in Sweden.[11]

Even though Sweden is a secular and liberal democracy, religion is present in public debates and in the public sphere. The presence of religion in public spheres is a challenge to a modernist ideology that holds that religion should be a private matter. This challenges religious traditions as well, mainly as regards how religion should be mediated, what should be mediated, and by whom. As Olivier Roy writes: 'The religious market—that is, the manipulation of Islamic symbols and legitimacy—also has a political dimension: who will speak for Muslims?'[12] John O. Voll argues that 'what we are seeing now in this crisis of authoritarianism is the battle for hegemony over discourse. If you can control

---

9.   The 'cultural map' produced by the World Value Survey project categorizes Sweden as having high scores in secular-rational and self-expression values. See http://www.worldvaluessurvey.org/WVSContents.jsp.

10. 'Staten och imamerna. Religion, integration, autonomi' (SOU 2009, 52). The theological departments of universities in Sweden successively strove to achieve more independence from the Swedish Church after the National Agency for Higher Education criticized confessional aspects in courses at university level. A change was then made by the theological departments, one that placed confessional training outside of universities, which are supposed to be secular institutions, into the hands of the Swedish Church. Academic credits are no longer given for confessional qualifications. In a similar manner, the SOU (2009, 52) argued that the neutrality of the state was a reason *not* to recommend the establishment of a state-supported imam education.

11. See Berglund 2010.

12. Roy 2004, 174.

the words, you can control the polity.'[13] This implies a question of who holds 'sacred authority' and how it is negotiated since more voices appear each day. However, related to this, we can note that there is no given 'orthodoxy' in Islam today. Traditional religious elites are continually questioned and many speak of a global contest of sacred authority, of which the local settings are, willingly or not, aware or unaware.

The first Muslim organization in Sweden was established in Stockholm in 1949, the Turk-Islamic Association in Sweden for the Promotion of Religion and Culture, by refugees from the Soviet Union.[14] Since then, the number of Muslims has increased and an estimated 350,000 to 400,000 Muslims live in Sweden today.[15] Around the middle of the twentieth century, Muslim immigrants had arrived in Sweden as labor migrants. In the 1960s this immigration pattern changed and many Muslims travelled as refugees or on the basis of family connections. These Muslims faced increasing unemployment and less economic welfare as compared to earlier immigrants, a situation that affected integration negatively. From this time, it seems that many Muslim migrants felt a profound need to practice Islam and with that to establish religious institutions. This may be explained by their being in a new and secular context, where religion becomes an active choice and where such questions as what it means to be a Muslim in Europe arise. This situation should not lead us to think, however, that migration caused all who arrived in Sweden to increase their religious commitment or practice. There are also examples of the opposite.[16]

The contemporary Muslim population in Sweden is heterogeneous, and there are large groups of Muslims with, for example, an Arabic, Turkish, and Bosnian background that are organized and have institutions such as mosques or cultural centres. There are also converts and other large minority ethnic groups, such as Somalis and Iranians, as well as many with Asian or Arabic backgrounds. There are currently six Islamic organizations in Sweden that receive state funding, and they are estimated to have 110,000 members. Of these, one has an ethnic Bosnian orientation and one is explicitly Shi'ite, while the other four

---

13. Voll 1997, 15.
14. Otterbeck 1998, 145–153; Larsson 2009, 482–483.
15. The number of Muslims in Sweden cannot be more than an estimated figure due to the fact that it is illegal to register peoples' religious identification. Moreover, defining what a Muslim actually is is also a complicated matter. Larsson 2009, 483.
16. Larsson 2009, 483–487.

are not specified and are directed to Sunni Muslims in a more general sense.[17] Turkish Muslims were the majority group until the 1980s, when Iranian and later Bosnian Muslims arrived. Today, there are several purpose-built mosques in Sweden, in addition to a number of 'basement mosques'. One of the purpose-built mosques, in the Stockholm suburb of Fittja, has been authorized to perform the call for prayer via the minaret since 2013.

In Sweden, there are Islamic interpretations and practices of different kinds. There are several Muslim interpretations of a liberal orientation in Sweden. The term 'Euro-Islam' is used by many designating a more liberal approach to Islam, and in Sweden it is sometimes called 'Blue-and-Yellow Islam', which alludes to the colours of the Swedish flag. Such interpretations often wish to define Islam as loyal to liberal and democratic values, seeking integration. This is likely what the non-Muslim majority prefers as well. Simultaneously, fundamentalist interpretations seem to have arisen, ones which reject majority culture and are often negatively positioned toward active citizenship and integration, which are considered a betrayal of authentic Islam.[18] Some promote implementation of Islamic law (*sharīʿah*) and argue that loyalty is only allowed to the Muslim community (*ummah*). Education is often following ideals and practices found in 'traditional education', where discipline, obedience, and memorization of texts are dominant aspects. There are reports indicating that fundamentalism is on the increase among some Muslims. Such reports, however, have received strong

17.   The Swedish Commission for Government Support to Faith Communities (SST, Nämnden för statligt stöd till trossamfund, www.sst.a.se) lists all organizations that receive state funding on their website. They also publish reports on religious minorities in Sweden, including both Shiah and Sunni Islam. See Larsson 2014a; Larsson and Thurfjell 2013.

18.   The term fundamentalist is often used to designate interpretations promoting violence; it often serves as a synonym for Jihadi ideologies. However, in this book, Salafism is a concept that indicates a fundamentalist stance towards Scripture. The term fundamentalism stems from a Protestant Christian interpretative tendency developed from the late nineteenth century, in response to modernism and liberalism within Christian interpretations, calling for a literal reading of the Bible and the inerrancy of the biblical texts. Hence, similarities with Salafi views on Scripture and interpretation are striking. See also the research by Martin Riesebrodt on fundamentalism, for example Riesebrodt 1993 and 2000. See also Larsson 2009, 492–494 concerning 'Euro-Islam' and 'ghetto-Islam'.

criticism from the research community because of the lack of empirical data, for example.[19] It nevertheless seems to be the case that fundamentalist groups are seeing an increase in the number of participants, this at the same time that liberal interpretations are evolving. The present study also offers an attempt to comment on possible reasons for the perceived growth of fundamentalism.

The increasing visibility and audibility of religion has developed gradually, but to many it seems to come as a surprise. This may be part of the reason why some minority groups (mainly Muslims) are being suspected of not being loyal to democratic ideals. When 'religion' does not stay where it was put (ideally), it becomes suspicious. Among the various voices speaking publicly about Islam, there is a prevalent Islamophobic attitude appearing—in some cases critical of all kinds of religion, except perhaps privatized religion. Right-wing people and so-called New Atheists criticize Islam (and religion in general) and speak as if Islam (and religion more broadly) had agency.[20] Muslims, on the other hand, are often portrayed as not having agency, being determined by Islam, seen as an ideology of violence and discrimination. If a Muslim argues that Islam represents something else, something peaceful or in line with democratic ideals, he or she is taken to have misunderstood what 'true' Islam is, or to be lying. The right wing in particular makes use of rhetoric based on the neologism Eurabia, which is promoted by right-wing and counter-*jihād* proponents. The argument promoted—in the form of a conspiracy theory—is that Muslims are seeking to take over Europe. The New Atheists are not that explicit, but do argue against multiculturalism in a similar manner. Other voices argue that 'true Islam' is peaceful and welcome in Sweden.[21] This reflects to a large extent public opinions about Islam as well. Those Muslims who appear to be democratic and 'Swedish', who do not dress in an overtly 'suspicious' way (i.e., looking too much like a Muslim), are readily accepted.

19. Fundamentalism in such reports, for example Ranstorp and Dos Santos 2009, focuses upon groups and individuals who promote violence as method. See also Gerle 1999; Gustafsson 2004; Holger et al. 2004; Larsson 2005, 2006; Otterbeck 2006.
20. See Olsson and Sorgenfrei 2011.
21. The interior minister of Sweden, for example, held that the Islamic State uses Islam in order to trick people into forming their religious affiliation, and that, as such, members of the group are not true Muslims. Sveriges Radio Website, http://sverigesradio.se/sida/artikel.aspx?programid=83&artikel=6098603, accessed November 16, 2015.

While it can be said that the general rhetoric in Sweden is suspicious of Muslims and Islam, and that, at the same time, right-wing extremism has not been considered as a real threat in Sweden (at least not until the terrorist attacks in Norway on July 22, 2011), there are indications that a potential change is taking place. In 2015, two people of immigrant background were killed in Sweden by a man inspired by extreme right-wing propaganda.[22] In addition, a right-wing party has been represented in the government (the Swedish Democrats) since 2010. Even though many would probably describe the Swedish climate as more positive, or perhaps naïve, compared to the neighboring countries Norway and Denmark, there is a general debate that is hostile, particularly to those Muslims who *look* Muslim, and here Salafi groups often become targets of criticism. 'They dress strange.' 'They promote and practice segregation.' 'They discriminate against women.' 'They are against democratic values.' Apart from values and attitudes, it is the *visibility* of religion that appears to be problematic. The concerns that arise almost automatically target Salafi Muslims, who represent an 'ultimate other' and are often suspected of being inclined towards violently.[23]

Minority Muslims

Strategies used by minority Muslims to preserve and develop a Muslim identity in a Swedish or European contemporary context are sometimes expressed in an active engagement with missionary activities in public space, aiming to Islamize society and expand the number of Muslims. In a European setting, Islamization relates to a large extent to the question of how to live as a believing and practicing Muslim in rather secularized surroundings. We have seen different Islamic interpretations develop where some are more accommodating to the surroundings than others. In the plethora of opportunities and possible lifestyles available, people have to make choices. One strategy is to reinterpret religion to adjust to the surrounding society, and a solution for some of a religious conviction seems to be to privatize faith and religious practice. We can also observe tendencies of protectionism and isolationism, where segregation and clearly defined borders between in- and out-group are

---

22. SVT website, http://www.svt.se/nyheter/regionalt/vast/har-ar-21-aringen-bakom-skolattacken, accessed November 16, 2015.
23. This has also been noted in studies on mosque-building in Sweden. When becoming visible and manifest, people react against religion. Karlsson Minganti and Svanberg 1995.

prevalent. The boundaries between such different strategies are blurred, but indicate different religious approaches to, or from, society. Muslims living as minorities find themselves in a dilemma, facing demands of integration or assimilation in some societies, while other Muslims may call for separation. Political scientist Andrew F. March views 'Muslim citizenship in non-Muslim liberal democracies *as a religious problem for believing Muslims*'.[24] There are many Muslims who do not necessarily experience a problem with being a Muslim and living and participating in a liberal democracy, but when discussed it is often in religious terms.

Today there is among many Muslims an emphasis on more univer-salistic language, freed from ethnic influences, advocating a universal interpretation of Islam uncoloured by culture. Thus, a separation between what is regarded as 'culture' as distinct from ('true') 'religion' is highlighted, and, moreover, a distinction between 'true Islam' and 'faulty Muslim practices' is common in insider rhetoric. Within this 'universalizing' trend, we find various kinds of attitudes to integration and segregation, so it is not possible to generalize the universalizing interpretations in this respect, claiming they are all liberal.

The above-mentioned 'Euro-Islam' refers to an understanding of Islam where cultural conformity is the predominating attitude or strategy chosen by Muslims. Euro-Islamic interpretations constitute an ideological development that can be characterized as 'cosmopolitan' and 'modern', as compared to many other local interpretations of Islam. It is noteworthy that individualism and privatization of religion are accepted to a large extent. Such interpretations can be characterized as attempts to form a religious identity apart from an ethnic or cultural identity. We can also observe the development of a particular minority jurisprudence (*fiqh al-aqalliyāt*) which shares traits with Euro-Islamic attitudes towards Islam.[25] However, this should not lead us to speak about European Islam in the singular, since this is merely *one* trend among contemporary European Muslims. A tendency within this interpretative trend is to remove what is regarded as 'culture' from 'true Islam', which is considered to be universal and possible to accommodate in all contexts. However, there is an ambiguity in terms such as 'universal' and 'local'. It could be argued that 'Euro-Islam' is as 'local' as, for instance, Turkish Islam, and that 'universal' Islam is that variety espoused by those who seek the establishment of a world-wide caliphate. The fact remains that

24.   March 2009b, 4; see also Olsson 2015b.
25.   On *fiqh al-aqalliyāt*, see Caeiro 2010; Fishman 2006; March 2009a and 2009b. See also Olsson 2015b.

proponents of 'Euro-Islam' speak of it as universal in the sense that it is adaptable to the conditions of the modern world.[26]

Euro-Islamic interpretations are rather liberal and accommodating, as compared to interpretations often called Salafi, which represent a fundamentalist and non-integrative stance to the surrounding society. Even though we can find similar arguments regarding what is 'true' and 'universal' Islam and what is a Muslim or cultural practice, differences appear regarding how textual sources are approached and the hermeneutic stances diverge, in that Euro-Islamic interpreters advocate more free reasoning and integration whereas Salafi interpreters have a more literal approach to the sources and are more selective when it comes to questions on integration. Both do, however, reject imitation of the juridical schools—i.e., the principle of *taqlīd*—and advocate new forms of authority and individual opportunity to access the Qur'an and Sunnah.[27]

Salafism has emerged as a framework from which contemporary Muslims in Europe draw inspiration and it has come to be regarded as correct or authentic Islam. Political scientist Jocelyne Cesari argues that it is difficult to decide what influence Salafi interpretations actually have, but that access to Salafi theology in minority cultures is a reason for its increasing popularity in Europe. In effect, even non-Salafis evaluate their practice from Salafi standards. Even if not all follow detailed so-called Salafi rulings, Salafism presents a standard image of what a good Muslim is. Salafi interpretations of Islam have an impact in Europe and affect Muslims regardless of their interpretative orientation. Cesari argues that:

> Although Salafi Islam is not the only interpretation of Islam existing in European society, it has indeed taken a central role in how Muslims deal with their religious tradition in the West. For example, in the mosques of France and the rest of Europe, most of the materials for religious teaching and proselytising follow the Salafi interpretation of Islam.[28]

26. Olsson 2009.
27. Olsson 2009. Sunnah is used as a designation of the tradition after Muhammad collected in large volumes. The six collections regarded as authoritative were compiled by Bukhari (d. 870), Muslim (d. 875), Abu Dawud (d. 888), al-Tirmidhi (d. 892), al-Nasa'i (d. 915), and Ibn Majah (d. 886). These volumes are used by the local group studied for this book. In Sunnah, thousands of narratives (*hadīth*, pl. *ahādīth*) are collected. The fundamental premise is that Muhammad is to be imitated in all respects, and the source for this is the Sunnah corpus. How Sunnah is perceived by the studied group, and Salafis in general, is thoroughly discussed in the present work.
28. Cesari 2005.

In general terms, Islam may be understood to function as an instrument of security and protection in the insecure and changing situations that people may experience in a minority situation.[29] Islam may also be understood as aggressive and expanding, promoting a view of a universal Muslim *ummah*.[30] Many contemporary Muslim interpreters question modernism, asking how they can live in a world where nothing is 'sacred'. In several contemporary interpretations of Islam, modernism or Westernization is often considered a cause of moral problems. Many are involved in questions concerning purity and simplicity in life with a basis in Islam, focusing on individual piety, which is a frame from which to understand many contemporary Salafi groups in Europe. Olivier Roy uses the concept 'post-Islamism' to characterize such contemporary apolitical Islamic tendencies that focus on piety. He discusses how globalization, Westernization, and the minority situation affect interpretations of Islam. Such interpretations are oriented toward the social and individual rather than the state or politics. In Roy's opinion, such interpretations regard religion and politics as two autonomous spheres.[31] Such interpretative positions are understandable in settings where Muslims live as minorities.[32] Post-Islamism, as Olivier Roy defines it, is a multifaceted phenomenon. It concerns issues related to the problematic matter of how an individual accommodates and/or co-exists with changes many see as part of (Western) modernity and still regards him/herself as an authentic Muslim who follows 'true Islam'. Many Muslims apprehend the situation as a decline of Islamic values in society, and simultaneously an increase of values related to consumer culture, as well as other non-Islamic ideals, values, and lifestyles. As this study will show, a very similar situation can be identified in Salafi-inclined interpretations in Europe today.

---

29. See Gellner 1992, 72. See also Kepel (1994a), who discusses re-Islamization from below in order to rebuild a strong identity in an alienating world.
30. Discussions of 'Muslim' problems such as Bosnia and Palestine also affect Muslim identity transnationally. See Eickelman and Piscatori 1996, 138ff. See also Olsson 2009.
31. Roy 2004, 3.
32. A problem with Roy's position is that he separates religion from religiosity and does not reflect upon the problems this separation involves. His view on religion is determined by a Christian outlook, with a focus on institutions and faith issues. In this respect, he seems to have an essentialist view of religion and speaks, for example, about 'religion itself' and 'genuine religious practice'. Roy 2004, 29, 124. Such an approach to religion has been extensively criticized in Asad 1993.

Integration and Segregation

Religion was to a large extent absent from the international relations discourse prior to the Iranian revolution. Earlier, conflicts were understood to occur primarily between nation states. More recently, however, culture and religion—an important issue that transcends national borders—has come more into focus. Muslim integration is a crucial question in contemporary academic research. The global situation after September 11, 2001, has caused this topic to be embedded in a war-like language, where the 'war on terror' targets Muslims as a special case, victimizing them. This language influences views on integration, as if such integration constitutes an extraordinary situation.[33] This meta-narrative of Islam constitutes a particular challenge that affects public opinions about Islam and Muslims and impacts on identity formation among Muslims themselves. It is a language of power-relations where Islam is stigmatized and reified.[34] Mahmood Mamdani, in *Good Muslim, Bad Muslim*, refers to this as 'cultural talk' that identifies Islam as a unified ideology to which Muslims conform, creating an antinomy between Islam and modernity.[35] Underlying 'cultural talks' about Islam are sets of dichotomies, such as the West versus Islam, secularism versus religion.[36]

Drawing on Talal Asad, Jocelyne Cesari considers traditions as conglomerations of discursive practices that influence believers' viewpoints on what is correct and meaningful.[37] Islam, existing within and interacting with Western democracies, unfolds as a multiple phenomenon that must not be generalized. This setting has also led Muslims to an individualized and less public form of Islamic observance.

> The secularization of Islam is seen in the transformation of individual religious observance, as well as the acceptance—by the vast silent majority—of the separation between public and private space respective to each society.... Through their words as well as their actions, Muslims in the West contribute to the imaginary of contemporary Islam.... Participation in the Islamic imaginary is given concrete expression in a variety of disparate religious practices and mobilizations.... The most visible of these

33. Cesari 2004, 3.
34. Cesari 2004, 21–42.
35. Mamdani 2004.
36. See also Cesari 2010a, 1–2. We should also note that this also appears in, for example, religious interpretations as well, such as in the group studied here, which will become apparent below.
37. Cesari 2004, 5–6; Asad 1993.

practices have to do with participation in radical or proselytizing trans-national movements such as Salafi or Wahabi Islam. These groups promote a defensive or reactive identity.[38]

Considering the seeming growth of Salafism in Western contexts, an explanation can certainly be found in the socioeconomic conditions of segregation. Dissociation from the dominant culture can be understood as a strategy to reclaim a stigmatized identity, elaborating the disadvantages into positive attributes.[39] A reactive identity-formation can be the result of hostility, prejudice, and stigmatization of Islam, which may lead to an intensification of a person's attachment to Islam, making it the central point of identification. This must not necessarily be accompanied with an increase in religious observance. 'Instead, it is essentially a way to establish personal identity in relation to the outside environment and the discrimination it presents'.[40] Such reactive identity-formations may downplay ethnicity and focus on a pan-Islamic identity. From such an analytical angle, Islam becomes a tool of political resistance, which may function as a 'siege mentality'.[41]

The social scientist Amel Boubekeur has explained the emergence of Salafism in Europe as functional and based on a rejection of European values. According to Boubekeur, 'The emergence of Salafism in Europe must be interpreted as the refusal of an excessive politicisation of Islam according to European standards, and a critique of the integration of values seen to be foreign to Islam, such as democracy and citizenship, into Islamic heritage'.[42] She argues that a diversification of Islamization in Europe can be observed, growing since the beginning of the 21st century, where Salafism is a recent actor competing with 'traditional' actors such as the Muslim Brotherhood and Tabligh.[43]

In Europe, most Salafi groups seem to reject violent means or revolutionary activities and, in many cases, they avoid political engagement, focusing instead on purification from innovation and on promoting Islamic education.[44] The focus is on piety, purification of belief and of practice, and striving to establish an Islamic consciousness:

38. Cesari 2004, 6.
39. Cesari 2004, 24–25.
40. Cesari 2004, 42.
41. Cesari 2004, 42, 44.
42. Boubekeur 2007, 34.
43. Boubekeur 2007; see also Amghar 2007, 39.
44. However, there are Swedes who have travelled to the Levant to join the Islamic state. See Larsson and Björk 2015. Sweden also experienced terror attacks in 2010 and 2017. See Hernroth-Rothstein 2014.

This means bringing an Islamic conscience back to Muslims, by returning to a religious practice purified of all additions subsequent to the last koranic revelation and to the apostolate of the Prophet. Through preaching, a new social movement would be created to lead to a world order in which Islam is accorded a pre-eminent place. Pious Salafis are thus not primarily concerned with politics but rather with the correction of belief and religious practices.[45]

Salafis who oppose political participation argue that such participation would contradict what they consider to be true Islam. Democracy, understood as *shirk* (associating something with God), leads to heresy (*kufr*), since it is not based on divine commands.[46] Withdrawal as a strategy is often advocated. This may explain why many such Salafis would not participate in demonstrations regarding 'Muslim issues', why they do not negotiate with the state, why they do not seek state-funding, and why they do not choose not to be active participants in non-Muslim systems.[47]

To participate in this way would mean implicitly recognising an identical status between Islam and the problems of society: withdrawal is thus preferable to all forms of participation. This attitude vis-à-vis European societies is confirmed by the fatwas of the Saudi theologians, who make emigration (*hijrah*) to a Muslim country a religious obligation for any practicing Muslim living in the West.[48]

Notably, though Salafis strive to uphold such a segregationist stance, due to their position of non-violence, no direct confrontation with the surrounding society is considered.

Sociologist Samir Amghar elaborates on such non-political Salafism as well as those who are politically inclined and promote *jihād*. He argues that: 'Although deprived of all organizational synergy and distanced from each other by mutual ex-communication, the various streams of the Salafist movement have common ideological foundations and myths

---

45. Amghar 2007, 43.
46. *Shirk* is considered the major sin. It negates the view on their only being one God, all-mighty and powerful. It is often translated as 'giving God a partner', in the sense of limiting God's might and power. To accept democracy would mean to accept something that is not ordained by God, according to a Salafi understanding.
47. Amghar 2007, 44–45.
48. Amghar 2007, 45. A *fatwa* is a legal ruling.

that structure their political imagination—all things that it shares with Islamists'.[49] Amghar notes that a similarity between Salafis and Islamists is found in the notion that Islam cannot be reduced only to ritual practices. Rather, Islam is seen as a holistic system. They both reject a divide between the secular and the religious. Moreover, both present themselves as a solution to the problems of European society. Amghar argues that the difference between Salafism and Islamism is that the latter is based on activism of groups with a precise political vision and project, often organized as political parties or social movements. Salafis, rather, promote a 'messianic utopia', as compared to Islamists,[50] and are above all concerned with the idea of a 'religious threat', not a political one. The mythological 'imaginaire' is founded on decadence.

> Islam is, according to this myth, in decomposition and Muslim identity is becoming lost in the haze of Western hegemony. For Salafists, as for Islamists, the decay of irreligious youth hastens the end time. Muslim society and Muslim minorities in the West have entered a state of generalised anomie (disregard for divine law and values), in particular the product of divisions between Muslims that only Islam can combat. Salafist political mythology also emphasises an apocalyptic millenarian dimension: the end of the world is near, numerous signs of the prophetic tradition announce its imminence, and it will be preceded by a holy war, between Muslims and non-Muslims, where Islam will triumph over evil as incarnated by the West.[51]

Samir Amghar notes that the moral decline that the Salafis strive to combat is explained by them as resulting from a betrayal of what they regard to be the true message of God. However, Amghar also considers this explanation a product of conspiracy ideas, which are used to explain the present weakness of Muslims. He states that,

---

49. Amghar 2007, 46-47.
50. Amghar 2007, 47 note 25. It may be argued though, in line with Amghar, that Salafis have not been inclined to develop political programs to any large extent, but this is likely to change. Note that Amghar's text was published in 2007, before the Islamic State announced a caliphate in the Levant and before the political party al-Nour was established in Egypt after the revolution of 2011. See also Poljarevic 2016 for a discussion on Salafism and utopia.
51. Amghar 2007, 47–48.

Behind this plot are the West and the Jews who have concocted a plan to keep Muslims dominated and prevent Islam from developing. In this ideological representation, Islam is the only power able to overthrow Western imperialism and dominance that is manipulated by an occult power for which the Jews are responsible.[52]

The success of Salafism among certain groups in Europe can be explained, according to Samir Amghar, partly on the basis of the failure of political Islam. Salafis accuse Islamists of representing *hizbiya* (partisan instrumentalization of Islam), which fragments the *ummah*, thereby creating *fitnah* (upheaval) and further weakening Muslims.[53] According to Amghar, 'This movement [the Salafi] now appears to be an "Islamist variant", seductive for those groups that are marginalised and excluded from all political participation'.[54] Amghar holds that Salafis do find an opportunity to engage in political participation, whereas Jihadis advocate political violence and others advocate more or less political indifference.[55] Amghar's functionalist approach to contemporary European Salafism leads him to see three political functions of Salafism in general: the protest, tribune, and elective functions. The political function of protest is the oppositional nature of Salafism, criticizing the social and political systems and other religious choices. Salafis do not (usually) present a precise political project. The tribune function develops from the political function. Salafism becomes a tribune of malcontents that other groups cannot accommodate. Hence, Amghar traces the emergence of Salafism to a failure of political representation in Europe. Salafism becomes a 'rebellion' where Islam affirms the self in opposition to the surrounding society with its dominating values. The elective function is the Salafi notion of belonging to an elite, a chosen group which shall realize God's will on earth. In this manner, they are an avant-garde movement: 'As actors in a story defined by God, Salafists take care of those Muslims not yet touched by divine grace'.[56]

52. Amghar 2007, 48.
53. Amghar 2007, 50.
54. Amghar 2007, 49.
55. Amghar 2007, 49–50. This may be a conclusion drawn on the particular situation in France, where Madkhali Salafism seems to be widespread.
56. Amghar 2007, 51. This book does not probe much into background causes to Salafism. Many studies propose feelings of exclusion as a cause. Research has also shown that many jihadis typically do not have traditional religious education that can be used to explain radicalization. Rather, 'what inspires the most lethal terrorists in the world today is not so much the Qur'an or religious

Contemporary Interpretations

Islamic movements are involved in the struggle for meaning and values. Even if a sociological explanation of empirical reality and perceived chaos is considered to be a reason for the development of an interpretation, we cannot ignore the problem of 'meaning'. Jacques Waardenburg states that 'it is precisely Islam that is used as an instrument and symbol to express and articulate protest, resistance, and struggle'.[57] This concerns the *function* of religion, and therefore it is important to contextualize interpretations in order to understand why a certain *function* and *meaning* is ascribed to 'Islam'. However, the meaning, it must be admitted, may have a religious meaning for the insider—even though other non-religious meanings can be attached to it from an outsider's point of view.

> In fact, most Islamic struggles are waged through society and cultural discourse rather than state institutions or government decision-making bodies. Such efforts challenge dominant cultural codes and create networks of shared meaning about the proper functions of society, groups, and the individual.[58]

Writing about 'born-again' Muslims, Oliver Roy understands their identity as part of a modernist trend of 'the culture of the self'. In a sense, these Muslims 'are staging their own selves, often to the verge of exhibitionism, which is also part of the expression of an exacerbated individualism'.[59] Roy further discusses his view that individuals today are transformed into actors, staging themselves.

> What is reconstructed here is not only religion itself, it is the self itself, in some sort of permanent representation and staging of the self. Believers (and especially converts and born-again Muslims) act in such a way as to stage their own faith: a sort of 'exhibitionism' is often manifested among many neofundamentalists, who use deliberate markers of their own religious identity (specific dress and also terms, usually Arabic ones, frequently occur in their speech—brother, jazakallah [May Allah reward you], bismillah [In the name of Allah], and so on). This stress on the

teachings as a thrilling cause and call to action that promises glory and esteem in the eyes of friends. Jihad is an egalitarian, equal-opportunity employer: fraternal, fast-breaking, glorious and cool.' Atran 2014. See also Atran 2010.

57. Waardenburg 2002, 368.
58. Wiktorowicz 2003, 16.
59. Roy 2004, 193.

individual and interest in the self is quite modern. Many non-Muslim sects (such as Hare Krishna) transform individuals into actors who perform their faith using the street as a stage. The individual has to be 'constructed'. This construction is based on a set of markers with little content but with high differentiation value (from beards to toothbrushes). Because it addresses individuals in search of the self, neofundamentalism has a strong appeal for disfranchised youths. It gives sense to generational conflicts.[60]

For example, deculturalization of Islam, sacralization of individual experience, and ignorance of traditional authority all focus on a voluntary religiosity—everything is devoted to the 'promotion of the individual'.[61] Islamic revivalism, he argues, and the modernist trend of the culture of the self, go hand in hand.[62]

> The melding of a modern analytical approach with a Koranic moral conception of norms is typical of the synthesis between modern objectivisation of the self (the basis of the concept of psychology) and an ethical and moral lecture on Islamic norms. Web sites also offer 'Islamic' goods, fashion, books, perfumes and other products. We are back to Islamo-business, for which there is a demand that fits with a modern consumer society. Ethics are called upon to regulate this fully accepted consumer society. An entire industry is developing to 'Islamise' this way of life.[63]

Bryan S. Turner describes piety movements as culturally creative:

> They involve either a new emphasis on religious practices or the invention of practices that are then claimed to be orthodox, or more exactly orthoprax. Piety tends to have a radical impact on the everyday world of believers by encouraging devotees to change their habits or in the language of modern sociology to transform their habitus or their dispositions and tastes towards the material world. Piety is about the construction of definite and distinctive life styles of new religious tastes and preferences.[64]

60. Roy 2004, 267–268. The quotation refers to a Western setting, where Muslims are a minority. As discussed above, Roy's essentialist views regarding religion appear in formulations such as in this quotation where he writes about 'religion itself'.
61. Roy 2004, 268–269. This does not fit too well with the material used in this book. It is not an ignorance of traditional authority, but a rejection of it and a continuous struggle to claim and foster interpretative authority.
62. Roy 2004, 193.
63. Roy 2004, 194–195.
64. Turner 2008, 2.

In his discussion on piety, Turner relates it to virtue and argues that an open display of piety is often perceived as inauthentic: 'To show piety publicly is to destroy it, and hence piety must be subtly insinuated and suggested by indirect comparisons with those lacking in religious virtue'.[65] Thus, as Tong and Turner put it:

> [I]ndividual acts of piety have to be seen and understood within a wider social context and within a deeper historical framework. For example, the modernisation of the everyday world (or habitus) in Islam is articulated through acts of piety that create post-traditional life styles—religious or pious life styles that are in competition with tradition, with the secular habitus of other Muslims and with other religious traditions.[66]

The secular character of European societies influences how individuals perceive Islam, causing more individualized and secularized versions of Islam to develop.[67] Jocelyne Cesari notes that three types of Muslim identity-formations can be observed within this trend: (1) those adhering to a privatized version of Islam; (2) non-practicing, who identify as Muslims on an emotional or ethical basis; and (3) fundamentalists, embracing a totalizing version of communal Islam.[68] The third type is the primary focus of the present work. Totalized interpretations of Islam are 'integralist' in their approach to tradition, in the sense of religion being regarded as a complete way of life. It is not possible to generalize about such totalized interpretations. There are degrees to how totalization is expressed, verbally and in practice:

> Paradoxically, fundamentalism can be said to have a postmodern quality, in that it often proceeds from the deliberate rejection of worldliness and its excesses. In other words, fundamentalism is, more often than not, a freely chosen identity, not something imposed by the community, tradition, or the family. A puritan and separatist version of Islam is appealing to many young people, and in certain cases can even be a response to cultural and social ghettoization.[69]

---

65. Turner 2008, 3.
66. Tong and Turner 2008, 43.
67. According to Cesari 2004, 45: 'To be Muslim in Europe or the United States means to lose one's relationship to Islam as a cultural and social *fait accompli*, and instead to open it up to questioning and individual choice'.
68. Cesari 2004, 46.
69. Cesari 2004, 53–54.

Among many fundamentalist Muslims, a meta-narrative binary underlies the development of interpretation and practice, where 'the West' is associated with negative aspects and 'Islam' becomes the positive pole of identification. A fundamentalist community may be seen as the means of escape when faced with the prospect of living in an impure environment. Salafism is attractive to many Western youths, giving concreteness and legitimacy to their stance and rejection of the world surrounding them. With their avowed goal being the recreation of what they deem to be a true Islamic lifestyle, as informed by the example of the Prophet Muhammad, Salafis focus on wholeness and purity, resulting in time-consuming adherence to detailed rulings that are expressed in each aspect of life.[70] Dress codes, as expressions of reactionary views on women and gender segregation, are the most easily observable outcomes of such a fundamentalist stance.[71] The imposition of firm rules related to style of dress can be understood in various ways. On the one hand, it can be something that creates and upholds an identity. Yet, on the other hand, dress codes can also be used by people as a means of discipline. Among other things, the veil can be regarded as a fashion garment.[72] However, it is important to see the symbolic aspect of the veil as well. A veil may have a normative and symbolic dimension: 'At a symbolic level, women wearing the veil highlight the specific ethos of the community in which they live and function: these are pious people who disapprove of public displays of sexuality, particularly when connected with women'.[73] In the case of Salafis, men too wear distinctive clothing (notably long shirts) and grow a beard, also making them visibly 'other'.

Jocelyne Cesari, following Khaled Abou El Fadl, argues that in such fundamentalist interpretations, 'Islamic tradition has degenerated into a self-satisfied and morally arrogant theology, and Islam itself is detached from its historical, national, and political contexts and turned into a kind of universal and absolute orthodoxy'.[74] She continues:

> The self-assurance of Salafism is grounded in a binary and ahistorical reading of scripture. The result is an overriding puritanism that overcompensates for humiliation with a self-righteous arrogance, and in which

70. This would correspond to a maximalist position. See Lincoln 2003.
71. Cesari 2004, 54.
72. One example is the *hijāb*, which has developed into a regular fashion item. 'ChaDior' is a concept that has been used in Iran, for example, to allude to the typically Iranian female dress *chador*. Roy 2004, 271.
73. Cooke 2002, 153–154.
74. Cesari 2004, 100, referring to Abou El Fadl 2001.

good Muslims are constantly contrasted with the western, democratic, secular, depraved and immoral Other. When this arrogance is combined with the call for war against the Infidels, the conditions for both radicalism and a warlike attitude come together as one.[75]

Salafis are fundamentalists, often conservative and puritan, and their influence seems to be growing in Europe. Fundamentalists, according to Cesari, are

> those who base their religious observance on the direct reading of Islam's source texts, the Qur'an and the Hadith. Such a return to the original texts often does go hand in hand with a conservative or puritanical interpretation, as demonstrated by the growing popularity of Jamaat-Islamiya in England and the United States, or the inspiration many young Muslims are finding inspiration [*sic*] in the Tabligh and (in the European suburbs) the teaching of leaders such as Sheikh Albani.[76]

The insider strategy of differentiating so-called authentic Islam from Muslim culturally coloured practices gives rise to an essentialist approach that reifies Islam.

> The attempt to re-constitute Islam separately from its local cultural manifestations is stimulated by an essentialism that seems to mirror the culturalist differentialism of non-Muslims' stereotypes. Both treat Islam as an autonomous subject that 'says' certain things, for example, what Islam 'says' about Muslim girls and wearing *hijab*. However, whereas cultural differentialism assumes a transparent relationship between Islam and the behavior of actual Muslims, young Muslims themselves contend that 'Islam' is quite different from the way in which some Muslims currently (ab)use it.[77]

The present study also seeks to explore this strategy. Specifically, it focusses on a group of puritan Salafi Muslims who advocate a program of action (*manhaj*) that promotes segregation and avoidance of the impure surrounding society. This work looks at those seen by Salifis as 'others': those considered impure or non-Muslim or Muslims practicing and/or promoting a faulty Islam—compared to their view of what constitutes authentic Islam. Identity construction is central to 'othering' and a lot of effort is put into focusing on the construction of a group identity which

---

75. Cesari 2004, 100.
76. Cesari 2004, 180. Nasir al-Din al-Albani (1914–1999) is one of the most promim nent scholars referred to by many contemporary Salafis.
77. Jacobsen 2005, 159–160; see also Jacobsen 2011.

is presented as normative with established values and behavioural codes. The identity construction is elaborated through a definition of who the 'others' are, and stereotypical images of 'others' are frequent. Othering in practice consists of societal polarization and distancing from those not belonging to the in-group, based on intergroup attitudes and aversion. Othering refers to identity-formation processes, where groups define identity as opposed to other groups, marking differences and delineations from them, formed in a dialectical opposition. The other is considered inferior and is delegitimized, disliked and mistrusted. Such othering in practice leads to social exclusion. Othering is a concept that overlaps with other social psychological terms and processes, such as stereotyping, prejudice, and discrimination.[78]

Quintan Wiktorowicz stresses that most studies on Islamic activism have been descriptive and focused on ideology, structure, and goals of specific actors or the history of a particular movement.[79] He presents the various perspectives that have dominated the study of Islamic activism and argues that it is important to combine these perspectives. Early Social Movement Theory (SMT) was highly functionalist and explained the development of social movements with a socio-psychological approach based on the assumed existence of anomie and despair. Some scholars highlighted socio-economic factors as principal causes, while others referred to cultural imperialism. Imperialism is also a common explanation used by Muslim interpreters themselves. Contemporary SMT, on the other hand, attempts to combine several perspectives. In contrast to earlier socio-psychological approaches, which often saw the subject as irrational, more recent theories regard social movements as rational, organized manifestations of collective action.

> Movements are [in SMT] not seen as irrational outbursts intended to alleviate psychological distress, but rather as organized contention structured through mechanisms of mobilization that provide strategic resources for sustained collective action.[80]

Within SMT, the notion of core framing tasks is considered important in order to understand how movements transform and mobilize people into participants and activists. This perspective is helpful in order to see the rationality of a movement, to avoid the sole focus on psychological needs, and to show creative strategies for coping with the perceived

78. Canales 2000; Çelik et al. 2016; Jensen 2011; Johnson et al. 2004; Olsson 2017.
79. Wiktorowicz 2003, 3.
80. Wiktorowicz 2003, 6–10.

situation. Core framing tasks imply that a movement constructs frames that: (1) diagnose a condition that needs to be remedied; (2) offer a solution to the problematic condition; and (3) 'provide a rationale to motivate support and collective action'.[81] These frames are important in that they reflect 'the cultural and ideational components of contentious politics [and] translate grievances and perceived opportunities into the mobilization of resources and movement activism'.[82] In my study, this 'simple' step-by-step strategy of the core framing tasks will be identified and used to explain how the group's teachers build up motivation for their cause.

81. Wiktorowicz 2003, 15–16.
82. Wiktorowicz 2003, 19.

Tradition and Authority

Sacred traditions sometimes tell of a golden age in the past. They preserve glimmers of the glorious age and establish beliefs, practices, and institutions to help people cope with the 'iron age' of the present. At other times, traditions anticipate the attainment of a glorious future age, which they portray in prophecies. And sacred traditions often address past and future together. In all three cases, a view of time as something that can be recapitulated, or at least held in synoptic vision long enough to lend perspective on the present, underlies the concept of sacred tradition. The work of seizing time through myth or prophecy explains the critical importance of memory in religious traditions. Memory defies time and change. 'Remember!' is the first commandment of tradition.[1]

My study aims to connect to some on-going, interrelated theoretical fields prevalent in the contemporary discipline of the history of religions in order to illuminate the group in this study. In the following, the most important of these will be discussed. My study relates to tradition in a wide sense and focuses on how tradition is understood, negotiated, and contested, and how tradition is constructed as authentic in order to fit a specific historical context, a context where specific interpretations and practices are rendered authentic and authoritative. In elucidating the insider's 'normative' view of 'tradition', and how such a view is constructed, the interrelated concepts of 'authenticity' and 'authority' are the most relevant points on which to focus. With such

---

1.   Valliere 2005, 9268. This citation, taken out of context, may lead readers to assume Valliere has an essentialist view on sacred traditions, but this is not the case. The word 'tradition' should be read as though within brackets. Thanks to Kristoffer af Edholm for alerting me on this possible reading.

a focus, we need to engage how loyalty and belonging are constructed and understood by social actors. Religious traditions are constructed within specific historical contexts. As Berkey aptly puts it, religious traditions are 'contingent upon the circumstances and viewpoints of those who claim it as their own'.[2] This sociological insight also makes it relevant to discuss the construction of 'orthodoxy' and, consequently, to problematize the use of such a concept (and related concepts) as historically situated.

Tradition and Orthodoxy

> It is a common human phenomenon that tradition and reason may oppose each other, mainly because tradition causes continuity, and hence stability, while reason causes change, and hence instability. Tradition is usually traced back to a great authority such as the teachings of the great ancestors, while reason is based on personal efforts and does not submit to external authority.[3]

The Salafi interpretation in focus in this study is part of a contemporary Islamic landscape. This landscape consists of divergent and conflicting interpretations, where there is no given authority. We can observe the almost daily emergence of new kinds of interpreter and new variants of Islam.

'Orthodoxy' refers to the authoritative interpretation of a religious tradition, and in Islamic history, 'orthodoxy' has been understood by a majority of Muslims to be equivalent to *taqlīdic* Islam. The concept *taqlīd* indicates an acceptance of imitation of the juridical schools, and an idea of a codified authentic truth that is unchanging and universal:

> Change is the way of the world but language, and especially sacred language, often claims an unearthly timelessness. Hence a formula or a title at the heart of a tradition is especially prone to be idealized. It easily remains unchanged even when the understanding of the object being referred to has, in effect, become something quite different.[4]

To establish what 'orthodoxy' is from an outsider perspective is not possible, but we can discern how something has been understood as being 'orthodox' in various times and places in history and try to understand

---

2. Berkey 2001, 96.
3. Abrahamov 1998, vii.
4. Gaffney 1994, 27.

why a specific interpretation has been upheld as authentic and representing truth. When considering 'orthodoxy', we must acknowledge the changing and conflicting nature(s) of 'orthodoxy' in specific historical situations. This implies that 'orthodoxy' relates to power relations, where claims for sacred authority may support different ideas of what constitutes 'orthodoxy':

> Orthodoxy as a social phenomenon is not a 'thing' but rather a process. For theological doctrines to become established as orthodox, they must find a place in the constantly changing net of social relations and institutions that constitute society. This is a two-way process: ideas can reconfigure these relations and institutions, but the social context also actively receives ideas and promotes, channels and/or suppresses them. Thus the history of orthodoxy cannot be simply a history of ideas, but a history of how, in particular situations, claims to truth came to be enshrined in social practices, such as rituals, and in institutions, such as 'the community of scholars'.[5]

'Orthodoxy' is established through social practice and is not something given. It is an on-going process that is negotiated and changed depending on the historical situation. Moreover, 'orthodoxy' is constantly subject to interpretations. What constitutes Islamic 'orthodoxy' is continuously contested and there are no given criteria for how it should be constituted and no organized institution that can establish what it is. Therefore, 'the question arises whether we can speak here of official religion at all and, if so, what may be the criteria of calling something "official Islam" with a recognized leadership'.[6] In the contemporary setting, interpreters who challenge 'orthodoxy' create a multitude of Islamic traditions, who in their turn cause reactions and increase the fragmentation of the Islamic landscape.

> All discussions emerge from a tradition, or in due course, create their own tradition. Even when a specific tradition, or the very idea of tradition, is contested or challenged, a new interpretative tradition is created, and in due time that tradition forms the basis for new presuppositions.[7]

5.   El Shamsy 2008, 97.
6.   Waardenburg 2002, 94. He concludes that 'normative' is a better concept to use than 'official'. Waardenburg 2002, 97–101. This lack of a given authoritative centre is also discussed by Kingston 2001.
7.   Abou El Fadl 2001, 124.

Traditionally, the Islamic scholars, the *'ulamā'*, and representatives of *taqlīd*, have been in an authoritative position to decide how to understand the word of God. Such authoritative positioning is now more contested than ever, both by Muslims that we could define as being 'traditionalists' and by those of a liberal or rationalist-oriented stance:

> Thus, 'traditional' (as opposed to 'traditionalist') Islam refers to the attempt of the ulama and the majority of Muslims who accepted their authority to preserve and conserve the status quo. 'Traditionalist' Islam refers to the counter-tendency to renew and revitalize the status quo, usually from within, by criticizing present interpretations and practices with reference to an idealist past. 'Rationalist' Islam refers to the historical impulse of the Mu'tazili mutakallimun [dogmatic theologians] in particular (but kalam [dogmatic theology] more generally) to articulate the message of Islam within any given age's contemporary intellectual and social trends.[8]

Richard C. Martin and Abbas Barzegar define 'orthodoxy' as 'the exercise of power through the production of knowledge in interpretive institutions, in book publishing, and in local communities that remain connected to the larger Muslim world through specific means of communication'.[9] They argue that 'orthodox religion at any given moment in history is the result of the historical evolution of competing popular religious ideas and practices'.[10] It is understandable, therefore, that interpretations of Islam outside the frames of 'orthodoxy' have effects on the Islamic landscape at large, and that they affect general views of 'orthodoxy' as well as those who work within the frames of a certain understanding of 'orthodoxy'.

Traditionally, Islamic education has been dominated by oral transmission, where students have been expected to learn by heart through listening to recitations from a teacher. Thus, the authoritative transmission of knowledge has been based on a person-to-person system.

---

8. Martin and Woodward 1997: 14. Mu'tazilah is a theological current that develeoped in the eighth century, one which promoted a dogmatic theology where reason was used as a method. Mu'tazilis argued that the Qur'an was created, which contradicted the view of God's speech as eternal, and they promoted a metaphorical understanding of the attributes of God and argued for the free will of humans, in a manner which others perceived as opposing the view of God as almighty.
9. Martin and Barzegar 2010, 185.
10. Martin and Barzegar 2010, 188.

Reading was not considered sufficient for the gaining of knowledge.[11] However, this system of oral transmission is rapidly changing. *'Ulamā'* began to accept printed material, a change that gave people the opportunity to gain direct access to written texts, thereby undermining the authoritative position of teachers. These transformations in the interpretative process inevitably resulted in the development of interpretations stemming from outside traditional religious elite circles, thereby increasing the contestation of sacred authority.[12] In the words of historian Francis Robinson, 'They will form their own conclusions and pursue what their conscience dictates. Thus, the individual human conscience, that most uncomfortable bedfellow for all forms of authority, began to work its way more fully in the life of Muslim societies'.[13]

Contemporary 'orthodox' institutions and representatives of authority are facing serious challenges. The dissolution of 'place', caused by processes of globalization and migration, influences—and the 'dislocation' furthers—the contemporary setting of contested authority where new interpretations increase. Dislocation, or deterritorialization, affects minority Muslims who may feel a need to establish new approaches to authority and revelation. Furthermore, new media bring new voices that contribute to the objectification and fragmentation of Islam.[14]

Religious authority is challenged from 'within', that is, by other Muslims. Simultaneously, authority is also challenged from 'without', by modernity and a global flow of ideas influencing perceptions of Islam.[15] The conflict of religious authority thus fragments contemporary Islam and transforms it into an ambiguous and ever-changing field. Consequently, there is an on-going conflict regarding 'sacred authority' within the world of Islam.[16] What one *can* say with certainty about 'orthodoxy' is that it is about power. When discussing it, we need to understand it in its historical setting and as affected by societal changes. What is considered 'orthodox' depends on person and context. However, we can also note that the juristic communities have functioned as a (challenged) source of identity and authority throughout history. They

---

11. Robinson 2009, 343, 339-343.
12. Robinson 2009, 345-350; see also Olsson 2015a.
13. Robinson 2009, 350.
14. Martin and Barzegar 2010; Roy 2004; on objectification, see Eickelman and Piscatori 1996.
15. Eickelman and Piscatori 1996, 37-45; see Zaman 2002 for an excellent analysis of how the religious elite responded to changes.
16. The concept 'sacred authority' is used by Eickelman and Piscatori 1996. See also Wiktorowicz 2005a.

have been considered the ultimate expression of Islamic 'orthodoxy'— and, hence, authority. 'Orthodoxy' has been constructed in a specific social and institutional environment, into which *'ulamā'* have been socialized, influencing ideas on authenticity and authority.[17] Many interpreters today challenge the tradition of *taqlīdic* Islam. However, even those who reject it usually relate to it in their attempts to legitimize their own interpretation as authentic. We can also note that many interpreters, even of a lay background, employ interpretative styles and methods used by *taqlīdic 'ulamā'*.[18] This is also the case in the group being discussed in the present study, which will be demonstrated below.[19]

'Works in Movements'

From an outsider perspective, there is no centre, or (given) 'orthodox' Sunni Islamic interpretation, but still, there is the notion of text constituting the core of Islam:

> It is certainly true that Sunnī Islam does lack a formal institutional and hierarchical structure of authority. There is no authoritative center other than God and the Prophet, but God and the Prophet are represented by texts. In effect, it is the text that stands as the authoritative center in Islam.[20]

With this citation, the focus turns explicitly to the written word. Sunni Islam does not have a formal structure of authority in praxis, and to speak of an authoritative centre in Islam, one must therefore turn to the basic texts.[21] The view of God as the ultimate authority causes the texts to become the centre of Islam, and texts are used and interpreted in various ways. Even though it seems like lived or practiced religion is a growing field of study among scholars of religion, it is important not to forget that texts constitute an important part of contemporary lived religion, that they influence the lives and thoughts of people. If we consider interpretations and practices referred to as Salafi, then this function of texts for everyday life is certainly a striking feature.

17.   El Shamsy 2008, 97, 100–115; see also Olsson 2015a.
18.   Martin and Barzegar 2010, 196.
19.   See also Olsson 2015a, 2015b.
20.   Abou El Fadl 2001, 11.
21.   Abou El Fadl 2001, 11.

Revelation is represented by texts (the Qur'an and Sunnah), and texts are necessarily interpreted by humans. In the following citation, Sunnah is described as a 'symbolic construct' that gains its meaning from the juristic culture. It is important to remember this 'symbolic' aspect when analyzing the authority of the Sunnah as revelation.

> In fact, the very idea of the *Sunnah* or *hadīth* is inseparable from the creative practice of the juristic community. If one speaks about the *Sunnah* or *hadīth* in the contemporary age, one is necessarily speaking about a symbolic construct that obtains its meaning and normative power from the juristic culture.[22]

The Qur'an and Sunnah are constantly being (re)interpreted, but there is an insider idea that their meanings are nevertheless permanent. Khaled Abou El Fadl shows that, as 'works in movement', they can support various interpretations, both those inclined to the juristic principle of imitation and those prone to interpretation (in various ways), as this study will further illustrate.

> The Qur'ān and *Sunnah*, to borrow Umberto Eco's expression, are 'works in movement'—they are works that leave themselves open to multiple interpretive strategies. This does not mean that they are open to any interpretation, but that they are capable of supporting a dynamic inter-pretive movement. If the *Sharī'ah* is going to have a continued relevance through a variety of contexts and ages, Islamic law must embrace the idea of an active movement in the construction of meaning.[23]

The work of contemporary Muslims attempting to gain an authori-tative position must strive to conform and answer both the new global situation and the actual historical situation of the participants they seek to address; in the case of my study, the participants constitute suburban Swedish Muslims.[24]

Texts such as the Qur'an and Sunnah are important sources used by many interpreters today, and we can note that texts are used *functionally* and as sources of authority. 'The text has the ability to play both a

22. Abou El Fadl 2001, 97.
23. Abou El Fadl 2001, 146.
24. 'Participants' is a collective noun used for all those who attend the group's activities. There is no formal membership, and some participants may have attended just one meeting or lecture, while others may have attended most activities.

restraining and negative role in the determination of meaning, and an active and positive role in the evolution of interpretive communities.'[25] As an example of such functionalization, it has been the 'ulamā' within taqlīdic Islam who have issued fatāwa, the primary expression of Islamic authority. However, an increasing number of Muslims are issuing fatāwa, even without formal religious training.

> Within this context of interpretive pluralism, Muslims often rely on the reputation of religious authorities as a heuristic device to ascertain the authenticity and validity of a religious ruling, something seen as critical for social movement frame alignment. Religious authorities can include community leaders, mosque imams, and self-taught charismatic leaders, or trained Islamic scholars—anyone perceived as knowledgeable about Islam.[26]

Wiktorowicz argues that those who participate in this interpretative field are playing critical roles as intermediaries between sacred texts and everyday religious practice of individuals. They function as 'cultural brokers', interpreting the texts in order to conform to rapid changes.[27] However, we must note that Muslims are not obliged to follow a specific legal ruling, fatwa. There are no formal institutions that can function as a controlling organ. Hence, it is up to the individual to decide if he or she will follow a specific fatwa.[28] This has certainly always been the case, at least theoretically, but it is accentuated today where more fatāwa are available and an awareness, or objectification, of Islam has increased among large sections of Muslims. Moreover, as we have seen already, there is no clear answer to the question as to who is an Islamic scholar.[29] Wiktorowicz argues that the term 'scholar',

25. Abou El Fadl 2001, 125.
26. Wiktorowicz 2005a, 25.
27. Wiktorowicz 2005a, 25.
28. Roy 2004, 175. This also appears in fatāwa issued today, which have to be taken into consideration by those issuing a fatwa. See, e.g., Roy 2004, 276.
29. Wiktorowicz 2005a, 25–26. This aspect is important to keep in mind. Many fatāwa that are produced do not have large societal consequences, but may only affect the individuals who ask the question. However, when acted upon, some fatāwa may indeed have global effects. Compare, for instance, the fatwa by, among others, bin Laden from 1998. The fatwa is signed by Usama b. Muhammad b. Ladin, Ayman al-Zawahiri, amir of the Jama'āt al-Islamiya (Egypt), Rifa'i Ahmad Taha, of the Jama'āt al-Islamiya (Egypt), Mir Hamza, Jami'at al-'Ulama'-i Pakistan (Pakistan) and Fazlur Rahman, amir of the Harakat al-Jihadiya (Bangladesh). See Cook 2005, 173–175, for a translation

represents subjectively derived community recognition about an individual's capacity to render informed, accurate religious interpretations. For the seeker, then, evaluations of reputation are influenced not only by perceptions about knowledge but also other characteristics, like charisma. (Wiktorowicz 2005a, 26)[30]

This is even more acute today, when authority is contested by the existence of people without formal religious training entering the field, acting like defenders of the truth, requesting a position of authority. Anybody may be *apprehended* as a scholar. As long as somebody listens to what he or she says and accepts it to be an expression of true Islam, the person may be seen as having gained an authoritative position.[31]

Defining Islam

I think it important to assert [...] that there is an Islamic tradition, a set of ideas, symbols, and interrelated texts and practices which may have a normative (although contested) force.[32]

[N]o society can completely immunize itself from historical change, and even those that purport to represent timeless and permanent social and cultural arrangements are themselves subject to evolution, even if that evolution is obscured by the ideology of permanence.[33]

What is regarded as authentic Islam? Can Islam be reinterpreted and adjusted to the surrounding context? Such questions are important to

into English. The *fatwa* was first published in Arabic, on p. 3 of the London-based newspaper *al-Quds al-'Arabi*, February 23, 1998. A scanned copy of the original article is found at http: //www.library.cornell.edu/colldev/mideast/fatw2.htm, accessed November 23, 2011.

30. Wiktorowicz 2005a, 26.
31. For a more thorough discussion on *taqlīd* and *ijtihād*, see Olsson 2015b. The discussion shows that the *taqlīd*ic position was never was completely codified, and that the rejection of interpretations and the production of *fatāwa* (*iftā'*) never stopped. See also the influential article 'Was the gate of ijtihad closed?' (1984) by Wael B. Hallaq, which refutes the perspectives of Joseph Schacht and William Montgomery Watt, that has dominated Islamic Studies regarding the issue of Islamic law and the juridical schools. Rather, the contemporary scholarly literature on *fatwa*-issuing emphasizes *fatāwa* as instruments of doctrinal creativity and change, analyzing how unchanging doctrines adapt to new circumstances. See Agrama 2010.
32. Berkey 2001, 7.
33. Berkey 2001, 94.

probe into since the Muslim population is growing in Europe along with increasing problems of Islamophobia and segregation. Secular ideologies dominate European majority cultures, but religion seems to be increasingly important in public space. There are many, both Muslims and non-Muslims, who elaborate between the fictive polarized discourses of 'Islam' and 'the West'. In viewing such discourses as social reality, these discourses have an impact on how people relate to religion and the surrounding society, thereby shaping perceptions of 'authenticity'. This process creates an 'in-betweenness', a standing between 'Islam' and 'the Western', and it is this standing that effects identity formation and the construction of in- and out-group.

One important issue of this study is religious change; that is, how issues of authenticity and renewal of Islamic tradition are understood and negotiated. Questions on authority are necessary to consider, since one manner of establishing what is authentic tradition is to determine what is the authority behind such a claim. Here, as we shall see, textual sources and the ways that they are understood and approached are foundational.

From the above, it ought to be clear that there is no Islamic 'orthodoxy', but rather discourses leading to or contesting 'orthodoxy'. However, one argument is that there is nevertheless a 'core' to Islam constituted by revelation (the Qur'an and Sunnah), even though there is no agreement as to its interpretation. Considering the contemporary situation of multiple interpretations of Islam, Jocelyne Cesari builds on Talal Asad when she argues:

> In these conditions, research on Islam in the West must take into account the ways in which Muslims embrace current definitions of the Islamic tradition and how they define themselves amid intense debates that dominate the current struggles to authorize a 'correct' form of Islam.[34]

This is not the least important in the case of the empirical material of this study, where the group strives hard to authorize a specific form of Islam well aware that there are many conflicting interpretations that they simultaneously must reject.

A religious tradition, considered as a discourse, is a 'frame of reference' in that any word's meaning or a practice is bound by the discursive context where the word or action is embedded. Nothing can exist as meaningful entities outside of discourse. Islam, or any religious tradition, is a conglomeration of discursive practices. Such discursive practices allow

---

34. Cesari 2009, 164.

followers of a religious tradition to decide what is true and meaningful, indicating that what is regarded as meaningful to them may vary between and within individuals and historical situations.[35] As such, 'tradition can be a product of considerable creativity and subjective expression, rather than merely habit and passive replication'.[36] Understood as a discursive field, Islam is continually influenced by crises of authority, critical moments which can be traced back in time. With globalization and influences from the Western world, Muslims have responded in various ways to such cultural and historical changes. On a societal level, political, financial, and educational systems have been changed and, simultaneously, religious tradition and traditional religious authority have been challenged by developments in the modern world. Following Asad, a religious tradition can be understood as a 'discursive field', indicating that the aim of academic scholars ought to be to understand how knowledge is produced and what are the institutional conditions for the production of knowledge. Given such historical formations, it is not surprising, therefore, that various definitions of 'Islam'—or 'authentic' Islam—have arisen. To use such a discursive understanding of a religious tradition avoids essentialist understandings, including views of religion as an agent, which calls for an avoidance of expressions such as 'Islam says' or 'according to the Qur'an'. Instead, a discursive understanding acknowledges that 'Islam' is all about human interpretations. Islam can thus be said to be an arena constituted of various processes of *becoming* Islamic, or becoming understood as being Islamic, since the processes belong to the discursive tradition which we call Islam, with the 'core' of this tradition being revelation. These processes include artifacts, ideas and practices *understood* as something established and having a history. Approaching Islam as a discursive tradition helps us understand how people define and create a past and a future related to a contemporary idea or practice. In this respect, Asad writes that discourses,

> relate conceptually to a past (when the practice was instituted and from which the knowledge of its point and proper performance has been transmitted) and a future (how the point of that practice can best be secured in the short or long term, or why it should be modified or abandoned), through a present (how it is linked to other practices, institutions, and social conditions).[37]

35.   Asad 1993.
36.   McGuire 2008, 63.
37.   Asad 1986, 14.

The discursive tradition of Islam can be used in order to legitimize a specific interpretation of Islam and to authorize various artifacts, practices, and ideas as being Islamic. A discourse-centred approach enables us to understand how language, interacting with Islamic textual sources, particularly the Qur'an and Sunnah, 'authorizes' certain artifacts, ideas, and practices and *makes* them Islamic. Hence, a 'practice is [considered to be] Islamic because it is authorized by the discursive traditions of Islam, and is so taught by Muslims—whether by an 'alim, a khatib, a Sufi shaykh, or an untutored parent'.[38] Any practice can thus be *given* an Islamic meaning, or understood as inhabiting Islamic meaning, and then become part of the discursive tradition of Islam.[39]

Tradition can in this sense be understood to be a conglomeration of discursive practices and ideas that form the basis for believers to determine what is correct and meaningful. To combat the essentialist assumption that meaning is constructed as a unified system, extending from the international through the national to the local level, Islam should instead be envisioned as a conglomeration of context-specific discursive practices.[40] Henceforth, the empirical material of this study can be regarded as productions by people bound by discourses that must be seen in connection to institutionalization of Islam, normative views on expertise, and various other traditions found within the discursive Islamic field, and we must acknowledge the specific minority position of the studied group in order to understand the orientation of the proscribed ideology promoted by the group's leaders.

An illustrative discussion related to this is found in Asef Bayat's study on Islam and democracy, in which he shows how meaning is socially constructed and related to power. An argument in his book *Making Islam Democratic* 'is that sacred injunctions are matters of struggle, of competing readings. They are, in other words, matters of history; humans define their truth. The individuals and groups who hold social power can assert and hegemonize their truths.'[41] It follows that what Islam 'is' depends on interpretations. Meanings are constructed, and

38. Asad 1986, 14–15.
39. For a critical comment on this view on Islam as a discursive tradition, see Schielke 2010, where he argues that 'there is too much Islam in the anthropology of Islam'. As I understand it, his criticism is that such close attention is paid to Islam that anthropologists become blinded by it, resulting in other motivations and causes in people's everyday life practices being lost from view.
40. Cesari 2009, 16.
41. Bayat 2007, 4.

'religion' is interpreted, hence the 'making' in the title of Bayat's book. As Bayat aptly puts it: 'In a sense, religious injunctions are nothing but our understanding of them; they are what we make them to be'.[42] The question whether Islam is democratic, therefore, is not merely an intellectual, but also an ideological issue:

> The question is not whether Islam is or is not compatible with democracy or, by extension, modernity, but rather under what conditions Muslims can *make* them compatible. Nothing intrinsic to Islam—or, for that matter, to any other religion—makes it *inherently* democratic or undemocratic. *We*, the social agents, determine the inclusive or authoritarian thrust of religions because, from this perspective, religion is nothing but a body of beliefs and ideas that invariably make claims to authentic meaning and a 'higher truth'.[43]

Thus, a religious tradition is a human construction, transformed by social agents in various historical situations, upholding or transforming notions of 'truth' and 'authority'.

Moreover, within the broader field of Islamic Studies, a focus on lived religion seems to have increased, a development which is partly due to the promotion of a non-essentialist view of Islam. The argument is that it is important to avoid generalizations and to study a limited number of Muslims and their practices and narratives about Islam. This is certainly a significant field of study. However, one can regret that textual studies are not regarded by many as equally important as the study of lived religion. Even though Asad's notion of Islam as a discursive field rejects scholarly essentialist understandings of Islam, we need to acknowledge that there is an 'Islam out there', to which Muslims, and others, relate. Such an acknowledgement does not mean that Islam is universally or essentially defined in any sense. As Asad also argues in his rejection of universal definitions of religion: 'My argument is that there cannot be a universal definition of religion, not only because its constituent elements and relationships are historically specific, but because that definition is itself the historical product of discursive processes'.[44] It is not the case that Asad, or Edward Said for that matter, intended for us to become ethnographers studying lived religion in order to avoid an Orientalist or essentialist position. Rather, what they addressed is

42. Bayat 2007, 5.
43. Bayat 2007, 4.
44. Asad 2006, 29.

the scholarly perspectives and assumptions that cause us to understand what we study in specific, and faulty, ways. We need to call for an increased interest in analyzing texts *as a part of* contemporary lived religion. This has been discussed by Cesari in an article regarding Western research in which she discusses the ethnographic dominance in studies of lived religion:

> The problem is that it is not possible to treat Islam as a mere artifact of anthropological study because Muslims identify with Islam.... Like it or not, anthropologists and social scientists have to work with the universalist claims of Islam to a certain extent because Muslims themselves make such claims and continually calibrate their practices to them. In fact, references to what is right or wrong, just or unjust, possible or not possible within Islam are largely determined by sources and materials that anthropologists have unfortunately excluded from their domain of research. Although I agree with Abu Lughod that it is a healthy impulse to study a religion through what its practitioners say and do, it is by no means sufficient because the debates about the nature of Islam and what it means to be a Muslim themselves shape people's actions and discourse. Islamic texts and sources are both polyvocal and contradictory, and there are dialogues between texts and practices as well [as] discussions that are internal to the domain of practice.[45]

Moreover, it is also important to comment on how the material of this study is approached. The material is considered as part of the official—constructed—ideology of the group. It is not considered as necessarily an expression of the belief held by the teachers. As Bruce Lincoln reminds us, 'since the beliefs themselves remain inaccessible, one can never be certain about the relation between beliefs and expressions (although one can often make educated guesses)'.[46] It is important for us to keep this insight in mind throughout this study, since it cautions us not to pretend that we are unveiling any true beliefs of the group's participants. The assumption is that what is said in lectures is a part of the official ideology and that it constitutes norms about what one *should* believe or do.

---

45. Cesari 2009, 16.
46. Lincoln 2005, 66 note 3. In this sense, Lincoln studies the document left behind in the car of Muhammad Atta, who took part in the attacks on September 11, 2001. Lincoln 2003. See also Olsson and Stenberg 2015.

In the following sections, our discussion will turn to the issue of authority and tradition. One purpose here is to highlight the position of the texts, especially the Sunnah in contemporary Islam, as a background for understanding the strivings within the studied group to uphold the Sunnah as the main source of authority and imitation.

Some Thoughts on Tradition

> A belief or practice in any field of culture may be said to be a tradition to the extent that it is received from the hands, lips, or the example of others rather than being discovered or invented; that it is received on the assumption that the authors and transmitters are reliable and therefore the tradition valid; and that it is received with the expressed command and conscious intention of further transmission without substantial change.... Tradition, purporting to embody a fixed truth from an authoritative source, demands faithfulness and obedience.[47]

This study is not an attempt to establish a definition of tradition. Tradition, in the sense of 'handing over' and what is being handed over, is used as a wide concept. Tradition in Islam is often associated with the Sunnah ('tradition') of Muhammad and the first and second generation of Muslims, the 'pious predecessors'.[48] The Sunnah functions as a guide

---

47.   Valliere 2005, 9267.
48.   The term 'pious predecessors' is used throughout this study. It is sometimes referred to as 'pious' or 'righteous forefathers', but since women are also included, the term 'predecessor' is more suitable. These include the first and second generation of Muslims. The role of the pious predecessors is always underscored by Salafis. For example, Fawzan states: 'The best of the generations is that in which Allah's Messenger (*salla Allāh 'alayhi wa sallam*) was raised, followed by those who came after them, and then followed by those who came after them. These are the best generations. And the best of the preferred generations are the companions (*rādī Allah 'anhum*) [May Allah be pleased with them].' Fawzan 2012a, 199. The predecessors usually include the first three generations of Muslims and are regarded as having a pure understanding of Islam, while later generations are accused of innovation. The predecessors include the companions of Muhammad, the *sahābah*, and their followers (*tābi'ūn*), who did not meet Muhammad, including the next generation (*tābi'u al-tābi'īn*). Ibn Hanbal, who is regarded as the last 'follower', is included in this group. Later reformists are also seen as important, and regarded as following the example of the early predecessors; these include Ibn Taymiyah and 'Abd al-Wahhab. See Wiktorowicz 2005a, 111–112. Among contemporary Salafis, the Hanbali Ibn Taymiyah is used as a main source of authority. Some of Ibn

to belief and practice. However, the concept of 'tradition' is not only limited to the Sunnah, but also to how religious authority is established, and what is regarded as 'orthodox' in various respects, including hermeneutic stances and epistemological views on how to establish authority.

Eric Hobsbawm's views on 'invented tradition' have gained a lot of attention and criticism, where he defines the concept as such:

> 'Invented tradition' is taken to mean a set of practices, normally governed by overtly or tacitly accepted rules and of a ritual or symbolic nature, which seek to inculcate certain values and norms of behavior by repetition, which automatically implies continuity with the past. In fact, where possible, they normally attempt to establish continuity with a suitable historical past.[49]

Hobsbawm's definition of 'invented tradition' establishes that there is reference to a historic past and a stress on continuity, but he also highlights that this reference is largely factitious. In his view, 'invented traditions' ought to be seen as a response to the modern situation: 'It is the contrast between the constant change and innovation of the modern world and the attempt to structure at least some parts of social life within it as unchanging and invariant, that makes the "invention of tradition" so interesting for historians...'[50] An 'invented tradition' is considered in a functional manner, where Hobsbawm argues that it gives 'any desired change (or resistance to innovation) the sanction of precedent, social continuity and natural law as expressed in history'.[51] In this sense, it is an ideological construct that uses the past to impose

Taymiyah's students are frequently mentioned as well in Salafi circles, such as Ibn Qayyim al-Jawziya, al-Dhahabi (d. 1348), and Ibn Kathir (d. 1373), who wrote *al-sīrat al-nabawiyah* which is used by many Salafis. Another frequently mentioned scholar is Ibn Rajab al-Hanbali (d. 1393), a *tafsīr* expert and student of Ibn Qayyim al-Jawziya. Some scholars from other traditions are also frequently used, like the Egyptian Shafi'i scholar Ibn Hajar al-Asqalani (d. 1448), who wrote *fath al-bārī*, a commentary of Bukhari's collection. Among contemporary scholars we can note particularly al-Albani (d. 1999), Ibn Baz (d. 1999), and Ibn 'Uthaymin (d. 2001). The student of al-Albani, Rabi' al-Madkhali, is also often referred to and 'Uthaymin's student Muqbil bin Hadi al-Wadi'i (d. 2001) and Salih Fawzan. The latter is one of the most important scholars used in the local group.

49. Hobsbawm 2013a, 1.
50. Hobsbawm 2013a, 2.
51. Hobsbawm 2013a, 2.

a sense of invariance. 'Invented traditions', in Hobsbawm's understanding, belong to three overlapping types, where they: (1) establish or symbolize social cohesion and group membership; (2) establish or legitimize institutions, status, and authority; and (3) socialize, inculcate beliefs, values, conventions and behaviour.[52] For historians, an 'invented tradition' indicates a symptom or evidence of problems we otherwise may not see: 'It is the historian's business to discover them retrospectively—but also to try to understand why, in terms of changing societies in changing historical situations, such needs came to be felt'.[53] Moreover, 'invented tradition' is a topic that sheds light on our relation to the past. An 'invented tradition' uses 'history as a legitimator of action and cement of group cohesion. Frequently, it becomes the actual symbol of struggle.'[54]

'Tradition' has been debated and the academic use of the term has been criticized since it risks leading us to analyze the use of 'tradition' merely as a nostalgic strategy to feel more at ease in the modern world. Saba Mahmood argues:

> It is fashionable these days to interpret any invocation of tradition, any claim to continuity with the past, as a nostalgic event, an 'auratic' gesture that under the disillusioned (or hyperrealist?) modernist gaze crumbles to reveal the illusory character of such forms of (be)longing.[55]

Saba Mahmood is critical of Eric Hobsbawm's definition of 'invented tradition'. However, Hobsbawm also presents the example of the farmers' revival around 1900, where the use of folkloristic themes, such as folk dances and regional dress, were used. He does not analyze this as a 'nostalgic longing for the old-time culture' but rather as a demonstration of the farmers' class identity and a strategy to distance themselves from other classes, thus rejecting the notion of 'nostalgic longing'.[56] However, Mahmood also criticizes the interpretation of usages of 'tradition' as a strategy of legitimization, which is highlighted in Hobsbawm's discussion on tradition. Mahmood argues:

---

52. Hobsbawm 2013a, 9.
53. Hobsbawm 2013b, 307. This particular citation concerns the 'invention' of tastes and fashions that are 'created', or 'manipulated', depending on needs in certain groups—for example, in popular entertainment, youth culture, or in the creation and legitimacy of a political ideology.
54. Hobsbawm 2013a, 11.
55. Mahmood 2005, 113.
56. Hobsbawm 2013a, 2–3 note 9.

Another related version of the same argument, commonly used within the social sciences and humanities, suggests that a claim for the traditional status of a practice is a particularly modern mode of asserting its legitimacy: this mode uses the past as a reservoir of symbols, idioms, and languages to authorize political and social projects that are in fact quite recent in origin.[57]

The notion of 'invented tradition' has been used to explain the legitimization and authentication of new modes of thinking, ideas, and practices, which does not necessarily have a historical basis—but they may nevertheless be understood to have such by religious insiders. Saba Mahmood problematizes such analyses and draws on the Foucauldian concept of 'discursive formation', which may be defined as:

a field of statements and practices whose structure of possibility is neither the individual, nor a collective body of overseers, but a form of relation between the past and present predicated upon a system of rules that demarcate both the limits and the possibility of what is sayable, doable, and recognizable as a comprehensible event in all its manifest forms.[58]

In this respect, Saba Mahmood refers to Talal Asad's discussion of Islam, presented above, as a 'discursive tradition' that would refrain from value judgment when using 'tradition' in various ways. Mahmood wishes to avoid the idea that 'tradition' is invented and, if Islam is to be considered an Asadian 'discursive field', this can be avoided, she argues. Moreover, her discussion on 'tradition' reveals the importance of the sacred texts within the discursive tradition Islam:

Asad suggests that Islam is best regarded as a 'discursive tradition' whose pedagogical practices articulate a conceptual relationship with the past, through an engagement with a set of foundational texts (the Quran and the hadith), commentaries thereon, and the conduct of exemplary figures. Tradition, in this sense, may be conceived as a particular modality of Foucault's discursive formation in which reflection upon the past is a constitutive condition for the understanding and reformulation of the present and the future. Islamic discursive practices, in this view, link practitioners across the temporal modalities of past, present, and future through pedagogy of practical, scholarly, and embodied forms of knowledges and virtues deemed central to the tradition.[59]

---

57. Mahmood 2005, 114.
58. Mahmood 2005, 115.
59. Mahmood 2005, 115, referring to Asad 1986, 14.

It follows that an Islamic discursive tradition is not static. Rather, it is 'a mode of discursive engagement with sacred texts, one effect of which is the creation of sensibilities and embodied capacities (of reason, affect, and volition) that in turn are the conditions for the tradition's reproduction'.[60] Saba Mahmood explains that such an understanding of tradition privileges a central question: 'how is the present made intelligible through a set of historically sedimented practices and forms of reasoning that are learned and communicated through processes of pedagogy, training, and argumentation?'

> By emphasizing the practical context through which foundational texts gain their specific meaning, Asad shifts from an understanding of scripture as a corpus of authoritatively inscribed scholarly opinions that stand for religious truth, to one in which divine texts are one of the central elements in a discursive field of relations of power *through which* truth is established. Thus the process by which a particular interpretation of a canonical source comes to be authorized depends not only upon one's knowledge of the scholarly tradition, but also upon the practical context of power relations (including hierarchies of age, class, gender, and knowledge) under which textual authority is invoked.[61]

Sabah Mahmood sees 'subject formation as a means of understanding how a particular discourse establishes its authority and truth within a historical moment'.[62] Informants in her study explained activities as conforming to traditional Islamic practices, drawing on their perception of Islamic history and notions of Islamic piety: 'Yet, while certain continuities with earlier practices were evident, it was also clear that the modern adaptations of classical Islamic notions did not mirror their historical precedents, but were modulated by, and refracted through, contemporary social and historical conditions'.[63] Mahmood refers to Charles Hirschkind's study on the ethics of listening to further illuminate her point. Hirschkind's analysis comments on the difficulties in practicing historical forms of knowledge today:

> Hirschkind argues that the fractured space and temporality of modernity do not simply efface older forms of perception and knowledges, as [Walter] Benjamin seems to suggest [with his notion of 'invented tradition'], but

60. Mahmood 2005, 115.
61. Mahmood 2005, 116.
62. Mahmood 2005, 116.
63. Mahmood 2005, 116–117.

that these aspects of modernity also make possible the retrieval and maintenance of traditional practices and perceptual regimes, giving these practices a renewed life and novel form. Indeed, one of his points is that the adoption of what are termed 'modern' ways of being do not signify a wholesale replacement of preexisting sensibilities, but are structured by, and embedded in, ongoing historical traditions.[64]

What social actors claim as tradition may be, knowingly or unknowingly, a strategy to authorize and authenticate a certain version of Islam. We should not simply consider it as an invention of a tradition that never existed. That would turn us into scholars making value judgments on whether our informants are right or not, which is not a suitable task for historians of religion. Understanding Islam as a discursive tradition, following Asad, helps us avoid making value judgments and, furthermore, illustrates the process by which various versions of Islam are created and upheld. Islamic Studies scholar Jan Hjärpe evoked the metaphor of a 'basket' to highlight the contemporary setting of interpretative fragmentation and to explain how religious traditions can continue to attract people even within such moments of fragmentation. A religious tradition is like a basket, but everything in it is not on display simultaneously. Religion, understood functionally, can be used by people and, depending on their needs, they will be able to find something in the basket to support them.[65] The 'same thing' that people pick up may of course be understood very differently in various historical settings.

Sacred Authority

As a system of symbols, religion may represent eternal truths but such revelation was received, constituted, and canonized at some founding moment and it continues to be handed down through a changing world for the sake of mortals who inhabit its diverse parts at different times. A creed may be viewed as immutable, but the way its language is understood, organized, and acted upon in concrete circumstances inevitably varies. Exactly how believers react to this diversity, and indeed, the degree that they are aware of it, forms yet another dimension of religion as a force of both segmentation and integration.[66]

64. Mahmood 2005, 117.
65. Hjärpe 1997.
66. Gaffney 1994, 29.

Muhammad Qasim Zaman discusses authority in his book *Modern Islamic Thought in a Radical Age*, where he mainly uses modernist interpreters as examples of the modern conflict of authority. Nevertheless, his arguments are useful for a discussion on religious authority and contestation in general. Zaman understands authority as 'the aspiration, effort, and ability to shape people's belief and practice on recognizably "religious" grounds'.[67] This is a wide definition, but useful in order to cover various aspects of authority. In his work, Zaman highlights three considerations concerning authority and modern Islam that also bring useful insights into the issue of religious authority at large. The first consideration is to acknowledge such authority as imagined, as compared to how it works in practice—these are two different things and there is a significant disjunction between them.[68] Moreover, Zaman calls for the need for contextualization in order to understand claims to authority:

> Second, and closely related to the foregoing, although particular individuals, texts, ideas, and institutions may, and often do, put forth claims to authority in the abstract, the meaning and scope of any such claims are necessarily tied to the specificities of their context. Even the most authoritative of a religious tradition's texts not only constrain but are constrained by how people will understand them in their particular contexts.[69]

Such an approach means that authority is best regarded as a *relational* concept. The third consideration is that authority is a matter of unrelenting contestation, specifically that 'it is hard to imagine authority without challenges to it'. Zaman continues:

> So far as claims to authority are concerned, the significance of contestation lies rather in reminding us that authority is not a stable endowment but one that is always exposed to implicit or explicit challenge and that it waxes and wanes in response to the pressures bearing upon it. Conversely, in speaking of contestation, it is not necessary to think of elaborate formal debates among intellectual heavyweights trying to beat each other in pursuit of public acclamation or royal patronage. These too have survived the medieval courtly cultures for whose entertainment they were sometimes organized, however.[70]

67.   Zaman 2002, 29.
68.   Zaman 2002, 30.
69.   Zaman 2002, 31.
70.   Zaman 2002, 33.

Contestation 'is as integral to the life of a tradition as it is to claims to authority'.[71] Zaman refers to Alasdair MacIntyre's work on tradition and contestation, specifically MacIntyre's highlighting of internal debates:

> A tradition is an argument extended through time in which certain fundamental agreements are defined and redefined in terms of two kinds of conflict: those with critics and enemies external to the tradition who reject all or at least key parts of those fundamental agreements, and those internal, interpretative debates through which the meaning and rationale of the fundamental agreements come to be expressed and by whose progress a tradition is constituted. Such internal debates may on occasion destroy what had been the basis of common fundamental agreement, so that either a tradition divides into two or more warring components, whose adherents are transformed into external critics of each other's positions, or else the tradition loses all coherence and fails to survive. It can also happen that two traditions, hitherto independent and even antagonistic, can come to recognize certain possibilities of fundamental agreement and reconstitute themselves as a single, more complex debate.[72]

Zaman also shows how a tradition is constantly negotiated and changed, and even how defenders of a tradition make changes to it. Moreover, he demonstrates that 'internal critics' do not necessarily challenge everything in a tradition. Zaman notes that internal critics usually defend a certain aspect of a tradition in criticizing another aspect and that a defender of a specific tradition does not blindly imitate past authority. He shows how internal critics do not criticize all aspects of a tradition, since 'their goal typically is to defend certain aspects of that tradition by critiquing others'.[73] Sometimes it may be difficult therefore to distinguish the often-fluid boundaries between internal and external critics and defenders of a specific tradition. As for religious authority, internal criticism is also defined by the context. In trying to understand criticism in its context, we may hope to understand the significance of it and what it means to adherents of a specific tradition in a particular historical setting. Internal criticism is relational, because it is internal. According to Zaman,

71. Zaman 2002, 34.
72. MacIntyre 1988, 12, cited in Zaman 2002, 34.
73. Zaman 2002, 34.

Implicitly or explicitly, it seeks to reconfigure how different facets of the tradition relate to one another. And like their rivals, a tradition's internal critics stand in a close self-described relation to earlier authorities, although these are not always the authorities that have carried the greatest weight in that tradition.[74]

This aspect of 'internal critics' will also become apparent in the analysis of the empirical material below.

The Position of Sunnah

A sense of tradition as normative is a basic element in all religious systems, whether or not formal concepts of tradition exist. When formal concepts appear, they may be broad or specialized, depending on their function in the system and the degree of differentiation among the sources of religious belief and practice. Often the sense of tradition as normative is expressed by a broad collective reference to authoritative teachers or compendia: 'the fathers,' 'the elders,' 'the sages,' 'the poets.' An evolution from broad to specialized concepts can sometimes be discerned.... In Sunnī Islam, by contrast, the formal concept of tradition, the *sunnah* (custom, example) of the Prophet, became more specialized as a result of the formation of a closed collection of traditions—the six books of *ḥadīths*, or stories of the Prophet, compiled in the third and fourth centuries AH (ninth and tenth centuries CE) and eventually accepted as authoritative throughout Sunnī Islam.[75]

The Sunnah is, alongside the Qur'an, at the very centre of authority in Islamic traditions. The perspective upheld on the Sunnah as an important part of 'tradition' in most interpretations of Islam up until today is a sign of its central position in the contestation of sacred authority. The Sunnah is a major expression of the golden history of Islam, and is considered a part of divine revelation. It is upheld as a source of knowledge containing facts about the deeds and sayings of the Prophet, which is *the* role model to imitate.[76]

In every 'founded' religious tradition, maintaining proximity to the founder has been an important source of legitimacy and authority, just as arguments about how to establish that proximity have been a source

74. Zaman 2002, 35.
75. Valliere 2005, 9268.
76. One principal use of biographical texts is to provide inspiring examples to be imitated. This pertains to biographies of Muhammad (*sīrah*), but also the Sunnah. See Khalidi 2009 on the image of Muhammad in various sources.

of conflict. In the Islamic tradition, the word *sunnah* has been the focal point of such issues. A word with a very old history in the Arabic language, *sunnah* comes from a root that is concretely associated with honing or molding, with something firmly rooted, like a tooth (*sinn*). *Sunnah*, by extension, came to mean habitual practice, customary procedure or action, norm, standard, or 'usage sanctioned by tradition'.[77]

The Sunnah has been described by Daniel Brown as 'the fulcrum on which the central debates over religious authority turn'.[78] The Sunnah is at the very centre of conflicts where Muslims debate its relevance and how to approach it.[79] The Sunnah is important as it is considered to be a sacred source, offering a connection to the early era and the time of the Prophet Muhammad: 'For most Muslims, sunna is a symbol of the link with the Prophetic era, the representation of the Prophet in the here and now, a concrete embodiment of the need that Muslims have felt in every generation for continuity with an ideal past'.[80] The idea of continuity with a tradition may function to strengthen group identity and to motivate specific actions, built on a specific understanding of the past.

> All religious traditions construct pictures of their own formative periods. The pictures are built up over time by the retrospective projection of religious ideals onto the history of the tradition. Such pictures must not be accepted as literal descriptions of the formation of a tradition. Their function is to stress the unity and continuity of tradition, whereas the critical history of any tradition in the formative period never fails to reveal breaks, conflicts, and a diversity of views and practices.[81]

Understandings of tradition may thus function as legitimizing forces. Images of a 'sacred' or 'golden' past portray how the present can become a part of this time. Below I offer an attempt at explaining how and why the Sunnah is used and understood. My hope is that it will shed some more light on the issue of the importance of the Sunnah today.

When we consider the interpretative conflicts that we can observe today, it can be said that they are largely shaped by a view of early Islamic history and sources, where the Sunnah is at the centre, as well

---

77. Waldman 2005, 8852.
78. Brown 1996, 3.
79. 'The problem of sunna has become the most important dimension of a modern Muslim crisis of religious authority, occupying a central place in Muslim religious discourse' (Brown 1996, 1).
80. Brown 1996, 2.
81. Valliere 2005, 9274.

as shaped by the development of Islamic doctrine and jurisprudence and their authority. Brown correctly identifies 'Two recurring questions [that] run under the surface of modern discussions of sunna and define the modern Muslim crisis of religious authority. The first is "How does God speak?" and the second "Who speaks for God?"'[82]

The first question is concerned with revelation, prophecy, and how to know God's will. The second question concerns what it is that places the contestation over the place and authority of the Sunnah into focus. Of course, the first question is relevant in the definition of the Sunnah as revelation holding a status comparable with the Qur'an. The Sunnah as the collection of the Prophet's deeds and sayings brings it authority. Moreover, authority is also given to the Sunnah due to the view of the Sunnah as being revelation. This means that the Qur'an is not the only revelation.[83] The distinction made is that the Qur'an is considered the literal word of God, whereas the Sunnah embodies or models the 'correct' meaning of that literal word; thus, they are interdependent moments of revelation. There are those who disregard the Sunnah corpus and reject or reinterpret its authority—most notably Qur'anists, among whom the Egyptian Ahmed Subhy Mansour (b. 1949) is most prominent.[84] However, this is *not* the case with contemporary Salafis, where it is more a question of how the corpus of the Sunnah is to be approached *and* used. This includes how it can inform the life of contemporary Muslims—that is, how the Sunnah should be put into practice. In this way, the ideological production of the group studied is a challenge to the traditional authority of *taqlīdic 'ulamā'*. It is not a rejection of the importance of the Sunnah, but rather a strengthening of its authority, with the purpose of making people imitators of Muhammad, but not giving them a position to interpret the Qur'an in their own right. In this manner, they can claim to be the protectors and defenders of authentic tradition. As Brown puts it, they 'find in sunna both their source of authenticity and their chief means of asserting their independence and flexibility *vis-à-vis* a religious establishment which they see as inflexible and out of touch with reality'.[85]

Daniel Brown, reflecting the 'tradition-as-legitimacy approach', argues that to understand why the Sunnah is such a universal legitimizing tool, we need to consider the place of prophecy in Islam and, furthermore,

---

82. Brown 1996, 133.
83. Abrahamov 1998, 4.
84. Gallab 2015.
85. Brown 1996, 134.

we need to recognize that 'in times of uncertainty and flux, it is natural for Muslims to look for guidance to the one era of certainty and stability, the time of the Prophet'.[86] This perspective explains why the Sunnah is of such importance today. The Sunnah brings a sense of continuity with the past, linking the founding period of Islam to a current historical situation that is changing and challenging religious tradition.

> Consequently, sunna gains tremendous stature as a source of religious authority and as the source of continuity with the past, with the whole of Islamic history, but especially with the time of the Prophet. Dealing with sunna, whether by using it selectively, rejecting it, or reinterpreting it, is therefore essential to any effort by Muslims to adjust to changed circumstances.[87]

Muslims holding various ideological positions *use* the Sunnah to gain legitimacy. Thus, they all demonstrate that an appeal to the example of the Prophet is the only way to justify the given claim or interpretation/application as authentically Islamic.[88] This use of the Sunnah is an expression of the importance of the 'core' of Islam with the sacred texts functioning as markers of identity and authenticity. Brown demonstrates that this struggle over the Sunnah is not a simple matter of tradition versus modernity, or reason versus revelation. Regardless of the particular position they espouse, many, if not most, interpreters attempt to show how they are in accordance with the Sunnah. Even interpreters with a rationalist leaning show a scripturalist position. Hence, the importance of the Sunnah within the contemporary Islamic interpretative discourse ought not to be underestimated. Daniel Brown argues: 'Discussions about Sunnah should be understood as battles internal to the tradition over the right to interpret that same tradition'.[89] Brown rejects the dichotomy of modernity versus tradition and argues that 'tradition is not an enemy of change, but the very stuff that is subject to change. Tradition both changes and may be used to justify change; it can, in fact, be revolutionary.'[90] Even though tradition is described as having dynamism, Brown also shows how tradition can be used to defend against what is seen as innovation, for example, certain values felt to be threatened by 'innovation':

86. Brown 1996, 138.
87. Brown 1996, 138.
88. Brown 1996, 138.
89. Brown 1996, 139.
90. Brown 1996, 2.

Alternative uses of tradition are thus a major battleground; there is fierce competition to control the process by which the content of tradition is defined, and for modern Muslims, sunna has become the bitterest point of conflict. Thus, the modern problem of sunna arises out of the conflict among Muslims over the definition and content of the authentic tradition, and over the method by which that tradition is to be defined.[91]

Brown suggests that 'we should instead imagine tradition as a beam of light, refracted by the prism of modernity. A tradition emerges from the prism of modernity as a multi-colored spectrum of responses.'[92] Hence, tradition is changed through, or because of, modernity, even though understood as unchanging by insiders. Those participating in the debate over Sunnah are

> engaged in an ongoing process of *rethinking* the traditions in which they participate. Some, of course, deny any connection with the tradition, and others deny that their activity can be called 'rethinking,' preferring to see it as the revival or preservation of some ideal and unchanging model. Nonetheless, even the most radical opponents of tradition are not departing from the tradition, but molding it and seeking to lay claim to the authenticity it bestows. Likewise, even the most conservative defenders of tradition cannot help but reshape the very tradition that they seek to preserve unchanged.[93]

Brown's comment here is illustrative of Islam as a 'discursive field' and of how various interpreters may conceive of what they are doing differently, based on how they apprehend 'tradition'. The comment also shows the interconnectedness between concepts such as 'tradition' and 'authenticity', and considers the uses of tradition as strategies of legitimacy and relates tradition to modernity. The comment further shows though that there is no static tradition and that even those who claim to preserve a tradition participate in its change. Tradition is thus always in flux and in a state of 'becoming'.[94]

In this chapter, we have seen that issues pertaining to authority and authenticity are very much at centre stage. They are interconnected and cause the need to elaborate on what the past is, especially

---

91. Brown 1996, 3.
92. Brown 1996, 3.
93. Brown 1996, 3-4.
94. Thanks to Philip Laurence Tite for commenting on this, using the metaphor of a prism, where tradition is viewed via the lens/es of modernity, and that tradition is not static but always in flux and in a state of 'becoming'.

the 'golden era', and how social actors gain access to the past. As a source of legitimacy and authenticity, the past, represented by the words of the Sunnah, takes an unprecedented position among Salafis today and, therefore, the struggle over the definition of the Sunnah ought not to be disregarded when probing into the fragmented field of contemporary Islam. What tradition 'is' depends on who we ask. In the case of Salafis, tradition is the Sunnah, and the Sunnah represents the Prophet Muhammad and the pious predecessors who shall be imitated. The analysis below will consider this view of tradition related to the theoretical issues addressed above.

Material and Outline

The theoretical issues discussed above will be returned to throughout the empirical chapters. These theoretical issues function both as a background and as explanatory discussions that are brought up to contextualize, in a wide sense, the group being studied within the conflicting interpretative landscape that we call Islam. Since these are theoretical issues that are focused on in the study, the material that is chosen addresses them in different ways. A large number of lectures have therefore been excluded since they address other topics.

In my study, I address the teachers as 'teachers', rather than use their real names or pseudonyms. The reason for this decision is that I want to approach those involved in teaching as a unity in order to discover the official stance of the group. The teachers, therefore, speak 'with a single voice' and conform to a specific version of Islam, which they then spread to participants. The local teachers are active and lecture on a frequent basis and they can be regarded as the core of the group. In presenting such 'official' views, I want to strengthen the anonymity of the teachers by making no distinction between who was the lecturing teacher. Each speaker is referred to simply as 'the teacher', representing the official ideology of the group.[95] Some teachers seem to be more 'popular' than others, and I have mainly used lectures given by them. The first meeting was with one of the popular teachers, who gave several of the lectures

95. The lectures used stem from four teachers. One of them focused more on the themes in focus in this book and his lectures are therefore given priority. It seems that this teacher relied on and referenced Fawzan extensively, which explains why Fawzan's teachings feature heavily in this book. In all of the numerous lectures, I did not come across any disagreements between the teachers. As such, I do not find it problematic to treat the four teachers as having one voice, expressing the official dogma of the group.

used as material below. I have also omitted the name that is sometimes used for this group for the sake of anonymity.[96] The group also produces study material, which I have also omitted for the same reason. In some cases, I use published material that teachers refer to extensively during lectures. Again, to be clear, this is material used by the group, but not produced by it. I comment on how it is used (i.e., interpreted) by the teachers.

This study thus concerns the official ideology of the group mainly drawn from lectures. Regarding the teachers, this study only uses material presented by the *local* teachers, not guest lecturers. I have excluded mentioning some Islamic scholars that are often mentioned as authoritative by the group or who have been invited as guest lecturers. International guests invited to Sweden to give guest lectures are also not mentioned, nor are their lectures used in my study. In the group, these guest lecturers are presented as *'ulamā'*, representing authentic Islamic teaching. In most cases, they came from renowned Islamic institutions in the Arab world, speaking Arabic in their lectures, which were often translated into Swedish by one of the local teachers. The reason for these methodological decisions is to preserve the anonymity of the group and the individuals participating in it. It can be noted that the international guests normally addressed similar topics to those dealt with by the local teachers, meaning that the omission of their lectures does not represent a skewing of the subjects encountered in group lectures. At the same time, the very existence of visits by international guests illustrates that there are transnational connections and that this specific puritan Salafi discourse is similar to many others. What differs between the guests and the local teachers is the striving by the local teachers to illustrate how the teaching is relevant in a *Swedish* setting and how to relate to specifically Swedish issues or happenings in Sweden or Scandinavia.

In the next chapter, I present an outline of what most Salafis today would see as the main creed of Salafism. As will be seen, the creed is common among different factions, but the view on *manhaj* (program of action) varies. I introduce Salafi Islam in general, outlining the main theological stances of Salafi Islam, including ideas on *manhaj*. I also

96.   There a   logies
      in Swed   alafi
      environ   n
      this stu
      on the

probe into explanations to the appeal of Salafism today among minority Muslims. Following this chapter, it will be apparent that while creed is understood similarly among various Salafi Muslims, there is a great deal of diversity with regard to the 'program of action'. Chapter 3 thus functions to contextualize the local group that will be studied in the more empirical chapters.

Chapter 4 introduces the local puritan group, their activities, and the main theological teaching promoted in the local group. Moreover, views on education and authority are addressed along with the main views on practice and the aim of the local group to produce pious individuals. This chapter briefly outlines how the group functions, specifically who attends lessons and who teaches those lessons, and it includes some basic information about their creed (*'aqīdah*).

Chapter 5 deals with the perspective of jurisprudence prevalent in the local group. Here, the view on *sharīʿah*, *fiqh*, and the juridical schools are presented in order to place the group in the larger interpretative setting, a setting where hermeneutical stances and views on authority are in focus. This chapter also addresses the view on sources and methods as well as figures in early Islamic history, the 'golden past'.

Chapter 6 addresses how the group defines the 'program of action' (*manhaj*). This question does not only engage detailed information about how to perform rituals such as daily prayer, but also defines what character traits individuals should conform to through such activities. Such aspects of the 'program of action' will be mentioned in the analysis, but the focus will be on wider concerns about how the group is to relate to the surrounding society and, furthermore, how such decisions on in-group/out-group relations are authenticated. The program of action of the group identifies 'the call to Islam', *daʿwah*, as a central Islamic action, which concerns how the group presents their Salafism as a way of life, where *daʿwah* is considered a main zeal and the 'commanding of right and forbidding wrong' is a major demand.

Finally, Chapter 7 concerns the establishment of in-group and out-group identification and how the in-group is to relate to such 'others', be those 'others' other Muslims or non-Muslims. Such intergroup boundaries rest upon differing views on 'the West' and Sweden. Important key concepts, such as infidelity (*kufr*), *jihād* (struggle), and accusations of unbelief (*takfīr*) are analyzed with the notion of being 'the saved group' (i.e., the immediate contrasts between the in-group with 'others', those 'others' being defined as not authentic or as innovators). The chapter concludes with a look at their view on segregation and emigration (*hijrah*).

The Epilogue to this book briefly summarizes the findings of this study and comments on them in relation to the theoretical issues discussed in the present chapter, namely, issues concerning tradition, authority, and authenticity.

* * *

Throughout the following chapters reference will be made to the many lectures given by the teachers of the group. During these lectures I took notes, on which many of my conclusions are based. In order to protect the anonymity of the local Swedish group that allowed me to observe their activities, I am unable to give further details regarding the times and locations of the lectures. A perusal of the following list, however, gives a good indication of the types of topics treated by the various teachers who spoke to the group:

Lecture 1: Steadfast.
Lecture 2: Meaning of Life.
Lecture 3: *da'wah*.
Lecture 4: Islam.
Lecture 5: Family.
Lecture 6: The Contemporary Situation.
Lecture 7: The Arabic language.
Lecture 8: The Saved Group.
Lecture 9: *ahl al-sunnah*.
Lecture 10: *ummah*.
Lecture 11: The Strangers.
Lecture 12: *Zuhud*.
Lecture 13: *nawāsib*.
Lecture 14: Knowledge.
Lecture 15: *salah*.
Lecture 16: The 73, sects 1–3.
Lecture 17: Leaders 1–3.
Lectures (several): Jurisprudence.

salafi islam

This chapter will briefly introduce some of the main traits of Salafism. The local group on which the present study focusses is Salafi oriented and illustrates how a certain interpretative attitude to Islam unfolds in a local context.[1] This chapter also shows the textual focus that is emerging among many contemporary groups. It will briefly present some basic characteristics of contemporary Salafism. More specific discussions on terminology and creed will appear in the empirical chapters below when necessary. This chapter serves to outline a general definition of Salafism and to introduce creed, which will not be given much focus in the empirical chapters. The reason, as this chapter will illustrate, is that while Salafi views on creed are quite similar, views on 'program of action' (*manhaj*) differ markedly. One of the aims of this study is to problematize the use of terminology and specifically the term Salafi, which is used rather indiscriminately today among both Muslims and non-Muslims. Therefore, a comparison to Wahhabism is made, one which also addresses the question of Salafi stances on Islamic jurisprudence and the Sunni juridical schools. The chapter ends with a comment on the appeal of contemporary Salafism, which may be used as an explanation of the appeal of the particular group in focus in this study as well.

The term Salafi is used by both Muslims and non-Muslims today. It does not refer to a homogenous outlook on life or practice, nor does it entail merely one interpretative stance. Salafism ought to be seen as an

---

1.   Calling them 'the local group' does not mean that they are active only in just one locality, geographically speaking. The group has activities in various suburbs and cities, and they have transnational connections as well. These latter connections are not discussed in this study.

umbrella term framing fragmented and contradictory attitudes towards Islam, but with some characteristics in common. Muslims using it as a self-designation claim authenticity based on a return to the sources. By outsiders, it is often used in a negative sense, referring to reactionary and conservative Muslims, and often to violence and terrorism. As a self-description, it is related to the term *al-salaf al-sālih*, referring to the first generations of Muslims, the 'pious predecessors', and a claim to follow their example.

The interpretative strategy is characterized as a return to the texts of the Qur'an and Sunnah to guide beliefs and actions. Salafis do not accept imitation of the codified jurisprudence in the established juridical schools (*taqlīd*).[2] Sometimes, Salafis call themselves *ahl al-hadīth*, the people of the *hadīth*, to underline the importance of Sunnah as a source, and there is an aspiration to imitate the behaviour and practice of Muhammad in detail. Whether or not the latter is possible, it is still held as the ideal.

Salafism is a contemporary Islamic project, which is concerned with identity issues to a large extent, and of creating legitimacy for certain kinds of authority. The movement has social implications, which by extension may have political effects. In relation to the political side of Salafism, Bernard Haykel argues that:

> Salafis are first and foremost religious and social reformers who are engaged in creating and reproducing particular forms of authority and identity, both personal and communal. Indeed, Salafis are determined to create a distinct Muslim subjectivity, one with profound social and political implications.[3]

Consensus (*ijmā'*) is an important aspect of Islamic traditions. It is not immediately clear what is meant when referring to it. It has been defined by Muslim scholars in five ways: (1) the majority of Muslims; (2) leading Muslim scholars; (3) the companions of Muhammad; (4) all Muslims when agreeing on a certain matter; and (5) all Muslims when agreeing on a certain leader.[4] Salafis usually accept the second or third, or both, definitions, which is also the case with the group in focus. Moreover, a feature of Salafism is also 'negative' attitudes, where innovation (*bid'ah*) is rejected. A main characteristic of Salafism is a literalist approach to

2.   Wiktorowicz 2005a, 119.
3.   Haykel 2009, 34–35.
4.   Abrahamov 1998, 5.

the Qur'an and Sunnah and one aspect of the prohibition of innovation is the rejection of metaphysics,[5] which is expressed in literal readings and rejection of metaphorical understandings of revelation.

The Salafi view on the Qur'an and Sunnah is that they are normative. Salafis do not acknowledge that human understanding of the texts changes depending on historical situatedness. The texts should be read in a way that is decontextualized. They are seen as universalistic, since the program of action (*manhaj*) and the content of faith (*'aqīdah*) are seen as never-changing and should at all times be adhered to and imitated.[6] The use of logic and human reason is seen as unnecessary since the sources are regarded as self-explanatory. 'Approaches that are guided by human logic will necessarily fall foul of human desire, which will lead to the selective and biased extrapolation of religious evidence to support human interests rather than religious truth.'[7] This means that they try to avoid interpretation of the texts and cannot be said to advocate *ijtihād* in the sense of independent reasoning. Salafis use other scholars' works as sources, as long as these are considered to follow the authentic Salafi *manhaj* and *'aqīdah*—which may vary among the different Salafi groups. When the teaching of scholars is employed, the Qur'an and Sunnah are always used in conjunction.

Salafi Theology

It is possible to generalize Salafi theology since Salafis share a rather common creed (*'aqīdah*). Salafis reject early rationalist theological tendencies of Mu'tazilah and Ash'ariya since Salafis argue that knowledge must come directly from the textual sources.[8] Theologically, metaphori-

---

5. Abrahamov 1998, 9, 23–27. The term *bid'ah* is generally translated as 'innovation'. What innovation is considered to be may differ, though. In principle, from a Salafi perspective, if something is not based on the example of the Qur'an and Sunnah, as well as the pious forebears, it may be considered *bid'ah*. See also Rispler 1991 and Maribel 1992.
6. Duderija 2010, 76. See also Duderija 2011.
7. Wiktorowicz 2006, 210.
8. Haykel 2009, 35–36 note 6. See also Wiktorowicz 2006, 210–211. Ash'ariya developed as a reaction to the Mu'tazili rational theology, denying some of its main dogmas, such as the Qur'an being created and that attributes of God ought to be understood metaphorically. However, the Ash'ariya maintained that rationalism was to be used in order to understand Scripture and to develop dogma, a position that can hardly be accepted within Salafi circles.

cal reading is avoided and God's attributes are accepted literally. Salafis argue that the divine attributes are a part of *ghayb*, which is understood to be a domain beyond what humans can perceive and sense. Therefore, they must not be understood metaphorically. Hence, if the Qur'an describes God in human terms, for example that God has hands, as in 'Surely those who swear allegiance to you swear allegiance to God—the hand of God is over their hands' (Q 48:10), a Salafi must accept that he has hands, even though they are not understood to be like human hands, but speculations should be avoided. Humans cannot understand the attributes of God fully, but they are still regarded as real.[9]

To preserve God's unity (*tawhīd*) and reject any association of power with something or somebody besides God, i.e. an act of *shirk*, is a central creed. The doctrine of *tawhīd* is elaborate, but will not be repeated at length here. It is understood as strict monotheism, where God is seen as the sole creator, of supreme and unique existence. This creed underlies the Salafi rejection of ideological systems created by humans. Salafis regard all deeds as acts of worship if they are in line with God's will. If not, they are seen as deviant behaviour, being interpreted as submission to something other than God.[10] The strict interpretation of *tawhīd al-ilāhiya*, the oneness of God, leads Salafis to regard saint worship and all forms of intercession as *shirk*. The verse 'And that the mosques (belong) to God, so do not call on anyone (along) with God' (Q 72:18) is used as a proof, for example.[11] *Shirk* is mentioned numerous times in the Qur'an:

> Surely God does not forgive (anything) being associated with Him, but He forgives what is other than that for whomever He pleases. (Q 4:48)

> Certainly they have disbelieved who say, 'Surely God—He is the Messiah son of Mary', when the Messiah said, 'Sons of Israel! Serve God, my Lord and your Lord. Surely he who associates (anything) with God, God has forbidden him (from) the Garden, and his refuge is the Fire. The evildoers have no helpers.' (Q 5:72)

> [T]urning to Him (in repentance). Guard (yourself) against Him, and observe the prayer, and do not be one of the idolaters. (Q 30:31)[12]

---

9.   Wiktorowicz 2001, 114–115.
10. Wiktorowicz 2006, 209.
11. Wiktorowicz 2001, 115.
12. Wiktorowicz 2001, 115–116. Citations are from Pickhtall's translation.

Innovation (*bid'ah*) is rejected, and Salafis claim that all that Muslims need is to be found in revelation. That which has no support in revelation is considered an invention.[13] Another important question pertains to how one should relate to those considered innovators.

> Just as the source of the truth is adherence to unchanged and definite principles, so the source of deviation and innovation is adherence to different, changeable principles. And contrary to the following of the traditionists, there is a clear opposition to the innovators which takes various forms.<?>

Those who do not share this view are seen as threats to Islam, and various opinions exist among Salafis as to whether such people should simply be avoided or whether they should actively be criticized and objected to, verbally and/or physically. As Binyamin Abrahamov, Professor of Islamic theology, notes, one *hadīth* that is brought up by many today discourages people for sitting with innovators: 'Whoever helps an innovator helps to destroy Islam'.<?> This attitude leads to various ways of rejection and avoidance, and may even lead to segregation and advocacy of emigration.

Salafism and Wahhabism

The revivalist movement Wahhabi Islam is often related to Salafism in media and research.<?> This comparison is misleading but it constitutes an illustrative example of the political consequences a Salafi creed may have. A comparison between the two also explicates the characteristics of Salafism. In the opinion of Ibn 'Abd al-Wahhab (1703–1792), those who did not adhere to his version of *tawhīd* were unbelievers (*kuffār*) or apostates (*murtadd*). He considered it his right to excommunicate (*takfīr*) non-adherents, which, in his interpretation, legalized the use of *jihād* against them.<?> Such a polemic attitude is also found among some Salafis today.

13.   Wiktorowicz 2001, 116–117; 2006, 210.
<?>.   Abrahamov 1998, 9.
<?>.   Abrahamov 1998, 9. Compare the various prohibitions mentioned above about sitting with people who are not regarded as scholars.
<?>.   See, for example, Fattah 2003; Schwartz 2007.
<?>.   Meijer 2009, 3–5.

Wahhabism emerged as a revivalist movement aiming to purify Islam; only later on, after increasing contact with the West, did it come to be understood as a rejection of Westernization, though with the acceptance of technology.[18] An illustrative example of tensions found within Salafism, and compared to Wahhabism, is found in the interpretation made by Nasir al-Din al-Albani (1914–1999). He exposed 'flaws' within 'Wahhabi Salafism', showing how it followed *taqlīd* through the Hanbali juridical school; as such, it could not be regarded as authentic Salafism. Al-Albani focused on the study of Sunnah and criticized Wahhabis for not turning directly to the sources but taking the route around the Hanbali *madhhab*. Roel Meijer comments that this was a radical position in Saudi Arabia. Al-Albani also accused the Muslim Brotherhood of neglecting religious knowledge (*'ilm*), giving priority to

18.　Other so-called Salafis who emerged, mainly in Egypt in the twentieth century, led by the revivalist Islam of Muhammad 'Abduh and Jamal al-Din al-Afghani, responded more positively to the West, where they found positive models for development, ones not considered contradictory to the overriding goal of returning to the Islamic sources. Meijer 2009, 7. Rashid Rida is an exception, since he later on in his life developed a more positive position towards Wahhabism and its scriptural and literal view. Henri Lauzière (2010), in his brilliant article 'The Construction of *Salafiya*', gives an excellent analysis, showing how there is no evidence that the modernists mentioned here used the term Salafi as a self-designation and also that there are no medieval sources using it as a noun, thus questioning claims of a long and historical continuity or origin. Moreover, Lauzière notes how Louis Massignon (d. 1962) used the term, which led to the common view that the Egyptian modernists were Salafis, causing a terminological confusion that has since been widespread and taken for granted among scholars. This insight has also led scholars to note that contemporary Salafism is radically different from the modernist movements. This brought about the need for a revised terminology, leading to such neologisms as neo-Salafiya or Salafism turning into Wahhabism, which is a misleading use of terminology. Hence, for sake of clarity, the Egyptian modernizers should *not* be placed under the category Salafi in a typology. This latter kind of so-called Salafism is not represented in the empirical parts of this book as it falls outside of the definition of Salafism used. Besides, the commonplace practice of naming this Egyptian modernist Reform Movement Salafism is misleading and is above all a creation of scholarly imagination. Contemporary Salafism is associated mainly with Sunni anti-rationalist Purists who do not have much, if anything, in common with the liberal reformers of the twentieth-century Egypt. The idea of returning to the sources may look similar at first sight, but, upon closer scrutiny, it is not.

politics.[19] Al-Albani wished to preserve the hierarchical system of transmitting knowledge personally between a teacher and student, which Meijer sees as a basic organizational structure among Salafis, which, he argues, can be seen as a strategy designed to keep them out of control of the state.[20]

Another area of tension concerns the creation of in- and out-groups. Salafi self-understanding can be related to the term *al-walā' wa al-barā'*, loyalty and disavowal, which has caused sectarianism.[21] Other Muslims can be targeted, if defined as *kuffār*. According to many Salafis, a true believer must show enmity towards such people. It is not enough to passively dislike such people.[22] A 'hostile othering' of non-Salafis is also a possible reason for the appeal of Salafism.[23]

Another example is the practice of *hisbah*, commanding the right and forbidding the wrong (*al-amr bi al-ma'rūf wa nahy 'an al-munkar*), used by Wahhabis to control and regulate religious observance. This principle has also been utilized by Salafis in their struggles for purity and for political demands.[24] It was also used by early Wahhabis to 'correct'

19. Meijer 2009, 9, 21–24; see also Haykel 2009, 42–45.
20. Meijer 2009, 9. See Lacroix 2009 for a presentation on al-Albani's impact on contemporary Salafism.
21. In Shi'ite theology, the term *tawallā* is used to denote the love one should have for the relatives of Muhammad (*ahl al-bayt*), based on Q 42:23, and *tabarra'* denotes disassociation with those defined as enemies of *ahl al-bayt*. See also Landolt 2015 for an overview of the term *walāyah*.
22. The radicalization of the phrase *al-walā' wa al-barā'* led some Wahhabi scholars to reject even the Saudi state since it did not distance itself from foreigners and non-Muslims, such as Juhayman al-'Uthaybi, who led the occupation of the Grand mosque in Mecca in 1979, and Abu Muhammad al-Maqdisi, who accused the Saudi state of apostasy because of its relations to the West. In doing that, Maqdisi legitimized *jihād* against the state based on Salafi reasoning. Meijer 2009, 10–11. Meijer mentions Bin Baz, the then grand *muftī* of Saudi Arabia, who gave the order to refrain from greeting non-Muslims and to cultivate hatred for them.
23. Haykel 2009, 37. Another aspect where Salafism seems to be influenced by Wahhabism is the condemnation of Shi'ah Islam as heresy, based on the Shi'i veneration of the Imams and their rejection of the so-called rightly guided caliphate that Sunni Muslims accepted. Meijer 2009, 11. See also Steinberg 2009. This particular feature will not be thoroughly discussed in this book, but mentioned in connection to 'othering' in general. See also Olsson 2017.
24. Meijer 2009, 11–12. The word *hisbah* is also used today to designate 'morality police' in Arabic.

those considered deviant.[25] Roel Meijer writes concerning contemporary Salafism that it leads to endless interpretations due to the time invested in doctrinal disputes:

> Another aspect related to the inner contradictions of the doctrine of Wahhabism/Salafism [...] is its tendency to fragment. It stands to reason that the strong emphasis on doctrinal purity and the literalist bent that Salafism has inherited from Wahhabism inevitably leads to internal disputes, splits and fragmentation. [...] Salafis spend a considerable amount of time and energy on doctrinal disputes. Although Salafism claims that its doctrine is transparent, its quietist and activist interpretations lead to endless interpretations.[26]

Meijer continues:

> Salafism's strong points, such as clarity, empowerment, quietism, activism, and universalism are undermined by its countervailing forces: rigidity, fragmentation, political dissolution and localism. As it is being reduced to a toolbox, it will increasingly be hijacked by other issues, such as the politics of identity in Europe, the anti-imperialist movement in the Middle East and Asia and sectarianism in countries like Iraq and Lebanon.[27]

Thus, Meijer's analysis of contemporary Salafism reduces it to a toolbox, which risks being hijacked by identity issues, sectarianism and anti-imperialism. The notion of identity politics in Europe can also be noted in the local group that is the focus of this study.

al-walā' wa al-barā'

One strategy found among Salafis is the promotion of *takfīr* against others, which is employed as a method which makes differences clear between various Salafis as well as non-Salafis. *Takfīr* is used to accuse others of being sinners or infidels, and various responses to those regarded as sinners of some sort are advocated. *Kufr* usually refers to unbelief in God and the Prophet Muhammad. It is divided into two levels, where major *kufr* refers to denial of God and Islamic teachings. A person committing lesser *kufr* is considered to be a believer, though one

25. See Hurvitz 2002. In Sweden, there have been media reports on morality police in suburban areas. See Bangstad 2011 for a discussion on the Norwegian situation.
26. Meijer 2009, 12.
27. Meijer 2009, 29.

who does not appreciate what God has provided. Apart from *kufr*, other concepts are also used.[28] *Mushrik* refers to polytheists. It designates a person who is regarded an apostate, *murtadd*. Apostasy, *irtidād* or *ridda*, means going from apostasy into unbelief, i.e. explicit denial of what is considered Islamic truths.[29] This concept of apostasy was used from the eighth century in legal discourses regarding apostasy.[30] The mainstream Sunni view has been that God judges whether a person is an apostate or not. This view goes back to the first caliphate, where Kharijis argued that sinners ought to be excluded from the *ummah*, and that it was their right to perform *takfīr* in this world.[31] The opposing opinion, held by the Murji'ah, considered that only God could judge if a person was a sinner and that punishment therefore should be postponed until the day of judgment. Such an opinion has been the prevalent opinion among theologians throughout history, probably as a means to control the use of *takfīr* in order not to upset societal stability.[32] Nevertheless, to accuse

28. Adang 2002a, 2002b; Hawting 2002.
29. Griffel 2000, 48–50, 99; Amir-Moezzi 2002, 420–421.
30. Hallaq 2001, 119–127.
31. See Griffel 2000, 13 for a discussion on *takfīr*. Kharijis, or khawārij, designates a group that originated in the first civil war, referring to a group of people who withdrew their support of the caliph 'Ali following his arbitration with Mu'awiya, and who claimed the right to punish him for being a sinner. It is presently often used as a derogatory term for groups and individuals who claim the right to perform *takfīr*.
32. We find several verses in the Qur'an regarding apostasy (see Hallaq 2001), for example: 'Or do you wish to question your messenger, as Moses was questioned before? Whoever exchanges belief for disbelief has indeed gone astray from the right way' (Q 2:108); 'Surely those who disbelieve and keep (people) from the way of God—they have gone very far astray' (Q 4:167). These verses merely talk about going astray. In other verses the message we find is more severe: 'Do not let those who are quick to disbelieve [*al-kufr*] cause you sorrow. Surely they will not harm God at all. God does not wish to assign to them any share in the Hereafter. From them (there is) great punishment' (Q 3:176); 'How will God guide a people who have disbelieved after having believed, and (after) they have borne witness that the messenger is true, and the clear signs have come to them? God does not guide the people who are evildoers. (Q 3:86) Those— their payment is that on them (rests) the curse of God, and the angels, and the people all together. (Q 3:87) There (they will) remain—the punishment will not be lightened for them, nor will they be spared (Q 3:88)—except for those who turn (in repentance) after that and set (things) right. Surely God is forgiving, compassionate. (Q 3:89) Surely those who disbelieve after their believing, (and) then increase in disbelief—their repentance will not be accepted. And

someone of being guilty of *kufr* (*takfīr*) has longer historical roots, but it has become more commonplace today in mainstream Salafi discourse, where such accusations are part of the method (*manhaj*) and are linked to the idea of excommunication, *takfīr*. However, not all Salafis advocate a hostile othering of such 'sinners'. Some merely advocate separation from them.

The phrase *al-walā' wa al-barā'*, 'allegiance/loyalty and disavowal', is often used by contemporary Salafis in support of the opinion that a Muslim should avoid *jāhili*-societies since loyalty should only be to other Muslims, and infidels should be met with open hatred.[33] The phrase is used in a variety of ways today, but it is generally used to define in- and out-groups. Joas Wagemakers argues that it can be used 'as a bulwark against successful integration into society' in the West.[34] This will be returned to more explicitly below to outline how the local Salafi group under study perceives it.

The phrase is important for *takfīr*, which functions as a delimitation of people into 'us' and 'them'. David Cook explains that it 'enables radical Muslims to assert control over the definitions of who is and who is not a Muslim and it forces those who would wish to challenge that control into silence or into being characterized as "non-Muslims"'.[35] Joas Wagemakers has analyzed *al-walā' wa al-barā'* from a SMT perspective and presented the usage of the phrase as a way of 'framing', which defines people into us and them. He notes that a 'frame' does not equal 'ideology', the latter being a detailed system whereas the former is

---

those—they are the ones who go astray. (Q 3:90) Surely those who disbelieve [*kafarū*], and die while they are disbelievers [*kuffār*]—not all the world's gold would be accepted from (any) of them, even if he (tried) to ransom (himself) with it. Those—for them (there is) a painful punishment. They will have no helpers' (3:91). Among Salafis there is also a differentiation between people aware of the truth who violate the rules knowingly, and those who do it out of ignorance (Wiktorowicz 2001, 123). The latter is not defined as a *kāfir* based on the following verse: 'But God only turns (in forgiveness) to those who do evil in ignorance, (and) then turn (in repentance) soon after. Then God will turn to them (in forgiveness). God is knowing, wise' (Q 4:17). The act of associating something with God, often held to be an unforgivable sin, is mentioned in the Qur'an as well: 'Surely God does not forgive (anything) being associated with Him, but He forgives what is other than that for whomever He pleases. Whoever associates (anything) with God has forged a great sin' (Q 4:48).

33. Devin et al. 2009, 50–51; Wagemakers 2009.
34. Wagemakers 2009, 82.
35. Cook 2005, 141. See also Devin et al. 2009, 50.

broader, vaguer version of belief systems to mobilize and promote ones cause.[36] The phrase has been used by Salafis as a 'pious instrument' in order to reject innovation. Salafi interpretations focus on piety and purity and stress the importance of avoiding contacts with non-Muslims for purity reasons and the risk of distortion of loyalty (*al-walā'*). For this reason, disavowal (*al-barā'*) of others is an obligation. This does not necessarily entail an aggressive method of disavowal. Wagemakers notes that the concept is hardly used outside of Salafi circles,[37] which may indicate that it is useful for a specifically Salafi viewpoint today.

The Appeal of Salafism

Roel Meijer discusses possible reasons for the appeal of Salafism today. He argues that Salafism has a capacity to empower people and to change identities. Making use of 'postcolonial' language, his analysis argues that the downtrodden and discriminated are turned into the saved or chosen group (*al-firqat al-nājiyah, tā'ifat al-mansūrah*), with privileged access to truth. The term 'the saved group' refers to *ahādīth* reporting that the *ummah* will be divided into 73 groups and only one of them will be saved from the fire. It is reported that Muhammad said that there will be a small group of Muslims holding the truth until Judgment day.[38] This teaching is accepted by the Swedish group studied for this book; it defines itself as belonging to 'the saved'. Next, some of those *ahādīth* used in Salafi groups are cited.

36. See also Larsson and Björk 2015 (in Swedish) for a report on radicalization and joining violent groups.
37. Wagemakers 2008.
38. These two terms are frequently mentioned in Salafi texts. The following citation is taken from a Salafi website summoning the *ahādīth* commonly used: 'Indeed the people of the Book before you split into seventy-two sects. And this nation will split into seventy-three sects, seventy-two are in the Fire and one in Paradise.' And in another narrative, 'All are in the Fire except one. It was asked: Who is that one? He replied, "That which I and my Companions are upon"' [Jami at-Tirmidhi (5/62) and Mustadrak al-Hakim (1/128)]. 'There will not cease to be a group from my Ummah victorious and steadfast upon the truth, those who abandon them will not harm them, until the command of Allah comes about' [Sahih Muslim (6/52–53) and Sunan Abu Dawud (2/202)]. 'The Victorious Group is the Saved-Sect, there is no difference because it consists of one reality' (Shaykh Abu Usamah Saleem Ibn 'Eed al-Hilaalee).' http://athariyah.webs.com/thesavedsect.htm, accessed January 11, 2012.

It has been narrated on the authority of Mughira who said: 'I heard the Messenger of Allah [*salla Allāh 'alayhi wa sallam*, May Allah exalt and bring peace upon him] say: A group of people from my *ummah* will continue to be triumphant over the people until the Command of Allah overtakes them while they are still triumphant'.[39]

It has been narrated on the authority of Jabir b. 'Abdullah who said: 'I heard the Messenger of Allah *sas* [*salla Allāh 'alayhi wa sallam*, May Allah exalt and bring peace upon him] say: A group of people from my *ummah* will continue to fight in defense of truth and remain triumphant until the Day of Judgment'.[40]

Narrated Al-Mughira bin Shu'ba: 'The Prophet *sas* said: "Some of my followers will remain victorious (and on the right path) till the Last Day comes, and they will still be victorious"'.[41]

Narrated 'Abdullah bin 'Amr that the Messenger of Allah *sas* said: 'What befell the children of Isra'il will befall my *ummah*, step by step, such that if there was one who had intercourse with his mother in the open, then there would be someone from my *ummah* who would do that. Indeed the children of Isra'il split into seventy-two sects, and my *ummah* will split into seventy-three sects. All of them are in the Fire Except one sect.' He said: 'And which is it O Messenger of Allah?' He said: 'What I am upon and my Companions [*ashābi*]'.[42]

Abu 'Amir al-Hawdhani said: Mu'awiyah b. Abi Sufiyan stood among us and said: Beware! The Apostle of Allah *sas* stood among us and said: Beware! The people of the Book before were split up into seventy-two sects, and this community will be split into seventy-three: seventy-two of them will go to Hell and one of them will go to Paradise, and it is the majority group.[43]

39. From sunnah.com with slight modifications: Sahih Muslim 1921a, accessed February 10, 2014. The phrase *salla Allāh 'alayhi wa sallam* is abbreviated *sas*.
40. From sunnah.com with slight modifications: Sahih Muslim 1923, accessed February 10, 2014.
41. From sunnah.com with slight modifications: Sahih al-Bukhari 3640, accessed February 10, 2014.
42. From sunnah.com with slight modifications: Jami' al-Tirmidhi 2641, accessed February 10, 2014.
43. From sunnah.com with slight modifications: Sunan Abi Dawud 4597, accessed February 10, 2014.

The view of being the saved group is 'proved' through the Sunnah and it empowers Salafis in the struggle against opponents, real or imagined, which varies depending on the geographical boundedness of the individual. 'Salafis are therefore able to contest the hegemonic power of their opponents: parents, the elite, the state, dominant cultural and economic values of the global capitalist system as well as the total identification with an alien nation which nation-states in Europe impose.'[44] Salafis, argues Meijer, focus on doctrinal purity rather than politics and have therefore 'been able to empower individuals by providing a universal alternative model of truth and social action (even in its passive form of rejecting existing religious, cultural and political systems)'.[45] Salafism may invoke a sense of superiority in its adherents, claiming a superior morality aiming to purify all levels of society. It is a claim to hold superior religious knowledge through the return to the sources, and with that a rejection of *taqlīd* and all forms of 'folk-Islam'. Displaying a profound concern with boundaries, they have a distinct appearance, visible in dress-codes. Such symbolic behaviour reinforces a sense of separateness in creating boundaries between 'us' and 'them', as does 'time-management', since daily life is framed by ritual observance.[46]

Another trait often associated with Salafism is deculturalization. Quintan Wiktorowicz argues that Salafis are 'agents of a globalised Islam' as their interpretation intends to transcend local cultures, 'eliminating culturally produced innovations'.[47] Bernard Haykel's analysis illustrates that the attraction of Salafism most likely is *not* found in their de-territorialization or their 'fundamentalism', but rather in the textual authority they promote. The Salafis' conviction of having realized the truth and their ability to provide textual proofs thereof likely contributes to the appeal of Salafism.[48] Haykel argues that such appeal can be explained by the Salafi view that

44. Meijer 2009, 13.
45. Meijer 2009, 13.
46. Meijer 2009, 16; see also Haykel 2009, 35. See Gauvain 2013 for a detailed ethnographic account of Egyptian Salafis, mainly related to purity.
47. Wiktorowicz 2006, 210.
48. Haykel 2009, 36–37. Haykel also criticizes Olivier Roy, who does not define 'Salafism', and who argues that deterritorialization is important for Salafi success, without noting that Salafism is rooted in many Arabic countries where it is not possible to call them deterritorialized. Besides, such an approach is not very helpful in explaining why Salafism was so popular before the era of mass globalization, and why, furthermore, Salafism is not only a modern phenomenon.

religious knowledge can be acquired easily; to become a scholar is not an impossible feat; and Muslims are endowed with agency, and indeed are duty bound, to acquire this knowledge for themselves through a personal effort. Acquisition of religious knowledge is a personally empowering and salvific process for every legally competent Muslim.[49]

Another aspect that may attract people is the Salafi focus on the Muslim community, the *ummah*, in distinction from many Islamists who are more nationally or regionally oriented in their work. Salafis are often quietists, but activists in the sense of urging participants to conduct *da'wah*, and in calling for *al-walā' wa al-barā'* and *takfīr*. Roel Meijer argues that contemporary Salafis benefit from the ambiguousness of doctrinal varieties, which allows flexibility and makes it possible to adapt to various surroundings, for example in supporting or rejecting political regimes.[50]

The growth of Salafism in Europe has led to what Roel Meijer calls a 'conversion' of Muslims who construct a new identity, not based on their parental culture or the dominant culture of the nation state. Second-generation Muslims, it is claimed, are transformed into superior human beings having access to truth, while previously having been humiliated and marginalized.[51] Becoming a Salafi is, in Meijer's *Global Salafism*, a psychological solution to an identity problem in a contemporary world in turmoil, where Salafism gives directions and answers.

Quintan Wiktorowicz writes that the Salafis' divergence 'lies in the inherently subjective nature of applying a creed to new issues and problems. This is a human enterprise and therefore subject to differing interpretations of context.'[52] While it would be easy to demonstrate Qur'anic verses that are not easily understood—and it should be noted that Salafis do not deny that difficulty in understanding exists—to do so points only to the reason why the *ahādīth* are so important, functioning as guides for the understanding of the Qur'an. In fact, the *ahādīth* are

49. Haykel 2009, 45.
50. Meijer 2009, 13–14.
51. Meijer 2009, 14. From a postcolonial perspective it may be possible to see a local environment producing spaces of subaltern signification. It is a place where people can affirm specific sets of identities and subject positions and in this way also threaten—or be perceived to threaten—dominant discourses in society, even though it is not necessarily done in public. This is likely a reason why many seem to fear a Muslim growth in society as well.
52. Wiktorowicz 2006, 214.

so important that some Salafis describe themselves as the *ahl al-hadīth*.[53] The differences between Salafis are understood by Wiktorowicz to be based on how they understand the problem they approach, which is often based on context. Moreover, in drawing analogies to the past, the present is understood in a specific way and seen as comparable to earlier periods in Islamic history.[54]

According to Quintan Wiktorowicz' typology, Salafism is divided into:[55] (1) Purists, who focus on nonviolence, purification, and education; (2) Politicos, who wish to adopt the creed for politics, noting that God is the only legislator and calling for social justice; and (3) Jihadis, who are more militant, calling for a change through violence and revolution. 'All three factions share a common creed but offer different explanations of the contemporary world and its concomitant problems and thus propose different solutions. The splits are about contextual analysis, not belief.'[56]

Salafi intolerance towards different theological opinions is founded on their idea that only one view can be correct.[57] Textual authority has also prevented the development of scholarly authorities within Salafism, even though some scholars are often given a high position. Bernard Haykel argues that Salafis are 'relatively open, even democratic' as an interpretative community.[58] Learning (*tarbiya*) is a main part of Salafi work since a Muslim, ideally at least, must learn about Islam in order not to deviate.[59]

Since Salafis do not agree on a specified hierarchy of certain scholars, or a given 'orthodoxy', allegiances may change, which creates a competitive stance between groups. This situation is exacerbated by the fact

53. Wiktorowicz 2006, 214.
54. Wiktorowicz 2006, 216.
55. Roel Meijer places the political character of Salafism within a typology of various Salafis, who are: (1) quietist and discrete; (2) covert, in the sense of calling for quietism but still acting politically; and (3) openly activist, coming closer to Islamism, for example in the *Sahwah*-movement. Meijer 2009, 17; see also Haykel 2009, 48. The local group studied here would fit into the first type. As Lauzière (2010) argues, the modernist reform movement of the twentieth century, including 'Abduh and Afghani, are left out in this typology for reasons mentioned above, which are thoroughly discussed in his article.
56. Wiktorowicz 2006, 208.
57. Haykel 2009, 38–42. See also Wiktorowicz 2006 for a more thorough presentation of the common creed among Salafis.
58. Haykel 2009, 36.
59. Wiktorowicz 2006, 212.

that only *one* truth can be accepted. 'The lack of centralized leadership in the Salafi movement thus creates a fluid dynamic vulnerable to fragmentation and intramovement disagreements.'[60]

Bernard Haykel illustrates that the concept of *manhaj* is important because it details how Salafis should live. This is a modern contemporary usage, and Haykel links it to al-Albani, who made use of the Qur'anic verse: 'So judge between them by what God has sent down, and do not follow their (vain) desires (away) from what has come to you of the truth. For each of you We have made a pathway and an open road. If God had (so) pleased, He would indeed have made you one community' (Q 5:48). This can be understood as a call for Muslims to reject affiliation with any group, including political ones. However, there are also Salafis who reject al-Albani's interpretation, arguing that it is obligatory for Muslims to actively engage in rejection of associationism of any sort, which they claim pertains to *shirk*. Thereby, political engagement *may* be seen as part of the Salafi *manhaj*.[61]

As a final comment in this chapter, considering the designation Salafi to characterize contemporary Islamic interpretations and practices, the term needs to be reflected upon critically. In Europe and elsewhere, several groups participating in missionary activity (*da'wah*) may conform to the ideal of returning directly to the sources, and advocate a literal reading of the texts, where Muhammad is *the* role model and, thus, reject imitation of other authoritative readings, creating new forms for and hierarchies of authority. However, a return to the sources is something that many Muslims advocate today, calling for a reinterpretation of the textual sources on various grounds. Such a move does not necessitate Salafi identification. We can, for example, observe explicitly political interpretations advocating *ijtihād* in the sense of independent reasoning, drawing directly upon the Qur'an and Sunnah, rejecting imitation of the juridical schools. We have Euro-Islamic interpreters who advocate independent reasoning in order to adapt Islam to the particularities of various European nation-states. There are feminist interpreters who may argue that God's will as expressed in the Qur'an should not be understood in the detailed rules but rather as expressed in a general divine demand for justice and equality. Such reasoning enables feminist readers to interpret the text more metaphorically and

---

60.   Wiktorowicz 2005b, 214.
61.   Haykel 2009, 47–48. Compare the development of the political party al-Nour after the 2011 revolution in Egypt. That would equate to the type of Politico Salafism of the typology used in this book.

as historically situated, and in many cases to reject prophetic narratives as fabricated. This, simultaneously, leads to the rejection of the traditional evaluation that is found in the juridical schools, and with that the rejection of the schools themselves.[62]

All of this illustrates the problem of using rigid categorizations and typologies in the history of religions, even though they are useful when trying to understand what we observe in the world of religion. Somebody may have the outward appearance of being a Salafi on the basis of a long beard or the wearing of the face-veil, the *niqāb*—these being outward symbols promoting conservative gender roles based on the Sunnah and the Qur'an. However, looking more carefully into strategies of interpretation, it turns out that only some aspects ought to be defined as distinctively Salafi, while others should not. A man who appears to be Salafi may actually turn out to praise reason and logic as main Islamic traits in some respects. In such a case the secular scholar of religion will encounter definitional problems. However, the construction and deployment of terminology and typologies is strategically useful if we wish to understand and explain differences and similarities between things; as such the argument cannot be a broad-brush one of simply rejecting typologies or ceasing to define terminology. The fact is that terms such as Salafism and *da'wah* are often used in unclear ways. There are many groups who conform to the 'image' of Salafism, in terms of dress-code and so forth, but who do not follow the creed, or *manhaj*, or adhere to characteristic views of interpretation and sources. That Salafism attracts many people today may then not lie in the fact that creed and *manhaj* are agreed upon, but may in part be about identity and the need to make a visible stand against something that is opposed.[63] However, in the following, we will enter a field where a group of self-identified Salafis is in focus. Here, it is not merely the outer and visible forms of Salafism that are important; instead, we are dealing with a coherent outlook on life, one that is being formulated and lived out in a contemporary Swedish setting.

The term Salafi has also been differentiated in various ways by various types by scholars, which indicates not only that it encompasses a variety of interpretations, but also that scholars have experienced a need for more precise definition. There is a need to avoid generalization, and to understand various religious phenomena in context—locally, nationally,

---

62. Olsson 2009, 2015a; Svensson 2000; Martin and Barzegar 2010.
63. Olsson 2012. See also Cesari 2005.

and globally—in order to understand why religious traditions continuously develop and why religious interpretations often refuse to fit into the typologies we create and to conform to the terminological definitions we use as scholars of religion. If we were to follow the terminology of Wiktorowicz, the group focussed upon in this study would be placed in the category of Salafi Purists.

The above presentation of Salafism and some of the key concepts and phrases used will be returned to in the empirical chapters below. There, an attempt is made to characterize the local group and to define what kind of Salafi interpretation is promoted therein.

The Local Puritan Group

The group visited for the purposes of this study was a Puritan Salafi group engaged in teaching, giving series of thematic lectures, presenting a distinct Salafi perspective, and performing *da'wah*. They do not receive any public funding, which I later learned was a conscious decision. The reason for this is that they do not want to be monitored or controlled, thereby giving them the freedom to express whatever opinions they see fit. The group focuses mainly on ethics, ritual behaviour, and faith issues, but also addresses themes such as terrorism and other pressing issues for minority Muslims. Some issues initially struck me as entirely illogical, perhaps even picky. They were exhaustingly detailed. Why would people take such an interest in whether it is permissible to pluck eyebrows or not? Why do they have to spend so much time on issues such as explaining that a person with a tattoo is cursed?[1] How come such things are regarded as relevant to such an extent that they spend hours talking about them? At the same time, I was very impressed by the skills of the teachers. I envied their command of Arabic. They spend years studying, which enables them to find a textual source as a back-up for every minute argument they make. They showed a vast knowledge of scholars from various times and places, who were constantly referred to as authorities. Impressed—and probably a bit jealous as well—I decided to probe deeper into their view of Islam and how they argued for their position as Salafis in contemporary Sweden. Being quite familiar with more liberal Islamic groups and voices that express so-called Euro-Islamic versions of Islam, the contemporary Salafi discourse struck me with full force and moved my imagination. The way they dealt with sources and their ways of teaching were particularly intriguing and piqued my interest. And so it was, with a touch of a bad conscience, I found myself

1.   See Larsson 2011 for more information about tattoos in Islam.

thinking about them as being 'more Islamic' than 'others'—a sense of wonder that I have observed in other people engaging in the study of the Islamic interpretations and practices of Salafi teachers and students.

The *da'wah* in this particular group, as in so many others characterized as Salafi, is often in the style of presenting material that is true to the text, repeating what is written, avoiding individual interpretations, confirming a specific truth. However, there were also comments on how the things discussed were relevant in people's lives, and, successively, I began to think about this as a strategy to construct a method enabling participants to live a Salafi life in Sweden. This life is understood as something more than 'merely' being able to recite the Qur'an in perfect Arabic, more than reading and memorizing the texts selected by the teachers. It included action, walking and breathing Salafism in every step on the straight path towards Heaven—which successively turned out to be a long and winding road to many who decided to walk it. Reaching the gates of Heaven requires time and effort and, in order to get there, participants must follow a multitude of detailed rules and live up to certain ideals. The teachers are the ones helping participants gain access to the path leading them Heaven. So, the participants must listen, comprehend, and then practically implement the knowledge that is transmitted to them. A Salafi does not take a break from being Salafi. Being Salafi is what gives the participant's life on earth meaning and direction. As such, members of the group must constantly follow the program of action (*manhaj*) advocated by the teachers, who claim to present—and represent—the tradition of the rightful predecessors. This is also noted by the Saudi shaykh Salih al-Fawzan (b. 1933), who is held in high esteem as a religious authority within the group in focus. Fawzan also has an official position in Saudi Arabia as a member of the Permanent Committee for Islamic Research and Issuing of Fatwas (*al-ri'āsa al-'āmma lī al-buhūth al-'ilmiya wa al-iftā'*).

Fawzan is used as a source in many of the lectures used as material in this study. He argues that faith (*'īmān*) linguistically means a

> firm belief that is accompanied by confidence which is not shaken by doubt. [...] As for the technical meaning of *'īmān* it is belief of the heart, speech with the tongue and deeds by the limbs. It increases through obedience (to Allah) and decreases through disobedience (to Him). There will be no *'īmān* except by combining all of these things. So whosoever believes with his heart without believing with his tongue is not a believer.[2]

2. Fawzan 2012a, 194–195. Here, Fawzan rejects the position of Murji'ah, who argued that faith with the heart would be sufficient. He argues too that faith

Here, we can notice the stress on action. It is not enough merely to believe. Moreover, Fawzan utilizes medieval sources to support his opinion. In the group, Fawzan's comments on the Hanbali al-Hasan ibn ʿAli al-Barbahari's (d. 941) treatise *Sharh al-Sunnah*, 'explanation of the Sunnah', is used. Barbahari was active in ʿAbbasid Baghdad and he wrote with a sense of urgency and anxiety of loss of 'authentic Islam'. According to Barbahari, Muslims were straying from the Sunnah, and so he wrote *Sharh al-Sunnah* in order to lead them back to the right path. He wrote in a historical time which saw various interpretations of Islam flourishing, not least dogmatic theology, which he utterly rejects in the book. Baghdadi's struggle must be analyzed with an appreciation for ʿAbbasid Bagdad, as well as the events following the *mihnah* and the many interpretations of Islam that flourished, all of which caused fragmentation. He called for an immediate and fundamentalist return to revelation (the Qurʾan *and* Sunnah). 'Othering' can be seen as central to his treatise, serving to delineate what true Islam is. Barbahari agitated against those who, in his view, were committing innovation (*bidʿah*), which included Shiʿites, Sufis, and dogmatic theologians (*mutakallimūn*), but also 'ordinary Muslims'. He was a charismatic leader who conducted a pietistic struggle to transfer his moral vision onto society. Ultimately, his efforts brought about an eruption of violence, one that led to his subsequent murder.[3] *Sharh al-Sunnah* is used to this day by many groups, and in the local case under discussion in this book, it is used alongside the commentary of Fawzan, who is held by the group to be a leading

with the tongue alone is the faith of hypocrites. However, Fawzan shows a somewhat lenient attitude, declaring others apostates. If someone claims to be Muslim, he or she should be considered a Muslim: 'However, whoever commits one of the nullifiers of Islam; we are required to judge him as being an apostate. If he repents, it is better, otherwise he should be killed as a defence for the religion. This is the first thing that legalizes the blood of a Muslim.' Fawzan 2012a, 312–313. Moreover, Fawzan argues that the *ahl al-sunnah* is moderate and does not declare someone a disbeliever unless it is based on a proof. Fawzan 2012a, 463. Nullifiers are explained in Fawzan 2012b, 85–91 as being statements, actions, beliefs, and doubts that contradict what is true Islam.

3. See Ibn al-Athir 1965–66. *al-Kāmil fī al-taʾrīkh, taʾlīf, ʿIzz al-Dīn Abi al-Ḥassan Abi al-Karam Muḥammad bin Muḥammad bin ʿAbd al-Karīm bin ʿAbd al-Wāhid al-Shabtānī al-maʾrūf bi Ibn al-Athīr* (Dar Sadir li al-tibaʾah wa al-Nashr, 1965–66, 13 vols.) by the historiographer Ibn al-Athīr (1160–1233) presents (in vol. 8) the role of Barbahari during the conflicts in ʿAbbāsid Baghdad. See also Michael Cook 2000 and 2003.

shaykh, one who is regarded as an authority in all matters. The local teachers use and frequently refer to his work. Barbahari's treatise is used by Fawzan in order to stress the importance of a correct *manhaj*:

> How many are those who claim to be on the *Manhaj* (methodology) of the *Salaf* (righteous predecessors) but do not follow it precisely because they do not know their *Manhaj*, and they think that this action or saying (of theirs) is from the saying or action of the *Salaf*. So it (their following) would not be precisely. It is therefore essential that you learn the way of the *Salaf* if you wish to follow their *Manhaj*. And this book is one of the books that will describe and explain their way to you.[4]

The *manhaj* is considered to be that which distinguishes the righteous from others. Fawzan is very critical of those who do not live according to the *manhaj* he promotes, which is the most basic criteria for defining in-group and out-group:

> (Nowadays) everyone claims to be upon the Qur'an and *Sunnah*; what distinguishes between us and them? That which distinguishes between us is the *Manhaj* of the righteous predecessors. This is because the righteous predecessors were those who understood the Qur'an and *Sunnah* and lived by them. So we are following the righteous predecessors. This is the distinction between us and the people of misguidance and deviated sects.[5]

Moreover, Fawzan connects this to the rejection of following desires, which, in his view, is afflicting many Muslims today:

> You should establish your *Manhaj* upon the Qur'an and *Sunnah*. Do not establish it upon your desires or upon the sayings of so and so, or upon the Manhaj of a party or the *Jamā'ah* [group, association] of so and so. Do not establish it upon such. Establish it upon the Qur'an, the *Sunnah* and the *Manhaj* of the righteous predecessors.[6]

As we shall see, these views are in various ways embraced and expressed in the group's teaching.

4. Fawzan 2012b, 93.
5. Fawzan 2012b, 101. Here, he also refers to the 73 sects. Translations of Fawzan use 'sect'. In the group I studied, the word 'sect' is also used (Swe. sekt), both in reference to themselves as 'the chosen sect', but also regarding others considered sects in a negative sense. I use the word 'group' when referring to the group's view on itself as chosen, to avoid the negative connotations that the word 'sect' has; 'sect' will, however, be retained in all citations. Where 'the saved/chosen sect' is mentioned, it is to be understood in a positive sense.
6. Fawzan 2012b, 107.

Continuous reflection on issues of continuity and change, inventions and reinventions of tradition, the approach to the textual sources, and the handling of interpretational issues that had practical impacts on everyday life, ultimately led me to think in greater detail about issues of authority and loyalty. My impression was that some local teachers were seen by those who frequently attended lectures as embodying and representing 'sacred authority'. I contacted one of the teachers, expecting that he would consider me an ignorant unbeliever and refuse to meet me. I believe that my anticipated rejection was based on an earlier, failed attempt to establish contact with another group of Salafis who engaged in translating texts from established Salafi scholars into (faulty) Swedish. On that occasion, after a public lecture that I attended, I noticed a man from the group moving among the attendees. To me, he looked like the architypal caricature of a Salafi. Wearing a long beard, his clothing did not go one inch below the prescribed measure; had it done so, he would have been consigned to the firey depths of Hell for eternity.[7] The man refused to look at me as he actively tried to give out short texts to targeted individuals, all male. Eventually—and with clear reluctance—he agreed to hand over a copy of his text to me. After corresponding with members of this group, and sending them a copy of one of my articles—one they had specifically asked for—I was met with a wall of defeaning silence. I can only assume that something in my article somehow offended them.[8]

Resuming my search for a Salafi group with which to engage, and following a chain of e-mail and SMS exchanges, a teacher of the local group called me and agreed to meet me. He did not seem to care who I was or what I wanted; he simply said, 'Sure, we can meet. Can you come

7. This idea is widespread in Salafi groups, which explains the length of the clothing of many men. It is based on a narration where Muhammad said 'The part of an Izar which hangs below the ankles is in the Fire'. Bukhari no 5787. An *izār* is a waist cloth, similar to a sarong.

8. The article was 'Apostasy in Egypt: Contemporary Cases of *hisbah*', in *The Muslim World* 98/1 (2008): 95–115, and dealt with how the concept of *hisbah* has been used historically and its contemporary transformation and use in some Egyptian law-cases, focusing on the case against Nasr Hamid Abu Zaid as well as that against Nawal al-Sa'daawi. In my opinion, the article is not controversial at all. Later on, the group contacted me and informed me that they had read several of my articles and found that I had made many mistakes. They offered to meet me to inform me about my mistakes, with a view that I could correct them. They asked if they could send a bill, to which I responded negatively. We never did meet.

to my place, then?' In the days that followed, via SMS, we set the time and place for our meeting. We met around a week later in his private home.

The Teacher

The teacher lived in a nice, quiet area with friendly people, many of whom were clearly of immigrant background. The neighbours directed me here and there around the entire area until, finally, I managed to reach the door of the apartment building—a full half-hour late. I needed to call the teacher as I had not been given the number of his apartment. There was no turning back. As the door to the apartment opened, no hand was stretched out to greet me. I expected that. Nevertheless, the teacher immediately struck me as a very friendly and hospitable person. He looked as I had expected him to look, with a beard, and dressed in a long, beige-coloured shirt. And then I noticed the Adidas hoody he was wearing over the top of his long shirt, and the Adidas jogging bottoms he was wearing underneath. I couldn't help finding that somewhat peculiar. I also noticed a picture of Hello Kitty as I made my way into the living room. It struck me that, from a Salafi perspective, having such a picture would not normally be considered 'correct'. The teacher offered me something to drink after informing me that his wife and children had had to go out unexpectedly and that he expected to join them soon. I was glad and relieved that he hadn't cancelled our meeting. While he made coffee, I sat on a sofa in his living room. Books with ornate, golden titles filled the room—all the books you could ever wish for if you are interested in that kind of Islam. I read the titles on the spines of the books that surrounded me. I felt somewhat awkward, as though I was sneaking around, prying at his private things—even though I hadn't moved from the sofa! The teacher probably didn't know that I read Arabic. Virtually every book in his library was in Arabic. I noticed large collections of *ahadīth* and may commentaries, such as *Fath al-bārī* and Nawawi's *riyād al-sālihīn*, and also a large collection of *fatāwa* by well-known *'ulamā'*.

I stayed for around an hour and a half in his nice, welcoming apartment, filled with an enviable (and valuable) collection of books. A lap-top computer was in front of the teacher. Some nicely folded prayer rugs and some oriental-looking candles caught my eye. An oriental rug was on the floor, but there were no pictures on the walls. There was, of course, hardly enough room on the walls, what with all the book shelves. Even so, I assume that the lack of pictures had something to do with the Salafi belief that such things are forbidden.

During our discussion the teacher told me that he had studied for several years, specializing in *hadīth*. The *da'wah*, he informed me, was done in his spare time, which, with a full-time job and a family with small children, wasn't plentiful. He told me that he learns a lot from teaching Islam to others and that working working alongside others sometimes helps to spread the load.

The teacher told me that his role, on occasions, involves him acting as a therapist. People come to him and ask him about private matters, and he tries to answer and help them. He explained that many young people trust him as an authority, as do people who are older than him, once they realize that he knows what he is talking about. When he referred to himself as an authority he looked a bit embarrassed. He noted that knowing all his books by heart was not enough in itself. This knowledge must be transformed into a lifestyle, into everyday life and ritual practice. What theology is may be interesting in itself, he noted, but it also has practical implications—*it must have.*

When talking about his work in the *da'wah* group the tone of his voice became more serious and he reflected more. The *da'wah* is all done on an ideal basis. Participants in the group do not earn money. There were, apparently, no plans to be more organized, yet at the same time that was not something rejected outright. At the time of our discussion, the *da'wah* group simply did not want to do that, he stated. It would, he noted, take time and they would need to be more structured. Working as they did at the time of our conversation, they had a lot of freedom and could cancel a lecture when they had too many outside matters to attend to.

The teacher was very engaging. His face showed a glowing enthusiasm when he talked about this work, and I had the impression that he held a curious interest in me as a researcher. While he looked at my website I briefly introduced my project. I told him how we teach about Islam and that the perspective of the history of religions is non-confessional. I made clear that we talk about Islams—in the plural. He told me he found that interesting, and I believed him. I presented my views on anonymity and about ethical research rules and informed him that he could read more about it on the website of the Swedish Research Council. This did not seem to bother him at all.[9] I told him that the results of my analysis

9.   I have attempted to be careful when reporting on the teaching promoted in the group, and to present longer citations and descriptions, to give the reader a possibility to see what derives from the group and what derives from me. The problem appears not in my description of the group, of *what* they say or do or

might not necessarily be to his liking, and that it might feel peculiar to be analyzed from an academic perspective. I made it clear that the research would ultimately be published and he seemed pleased with that idea. He asked if I intended to meet other groups of Muslims, and I was left with the feeling he would not like that. I reassured him that I had no plans to speak with another group, at least not in relation to the research I would conduct with him.

The teacher told me he had never been interviewed by a researcher before. He described the local group as transparent, stating that they had nothing to hide. He asked me directly why I wanted to study them, and I told him how I stumbled upon them while searching for groups that I could identify as Salafi in Sweden, and that I found this group very interesting, based on what I had uncovered in my initial research. I also informed him that I am not religious and that I had no interest in becoming a convert. He did not object to that, and he did not seem at all surprised.

The teacher was easy to talk to and very friendly. I could have stayed longer, but felt I should leave, knowing that he wanted to be with his family. For my part, I feel I am competent in my field. I know the sources, and I have read many of the books that I know the Salafi groups use. I know the names, concepts, and phrases they refer to. I have, I would say, a good working knowledge of Arabic. I can follow and understand a lecture delivered in Arabic and can work with the written texts. Of course, I could never pretend to be as skilled as the teacher, but as a researcher I believe I have at least the requisite knowledge to enable me to approach this field in a scholarly and fruitful way.

Main Activities and Views

The local group that is the focus of the present study has been active for several years. They began with small-scale lecturing with teachers, or 'students' as they call themselves, all of whom had been formally educated in Islamic institutions in the Arab world for many years, mainly specializing in *hadīth*. The activities have been more formalized during recent years, with recurring lectures being held in various suburban locations. One-off lessons and series of lessons are offered, with various

how they say or do it, but rather in my explanations. Hence, it is not the *what* or *how*, but the *why* that may cause trouble and signal that the group has a very different perception than an academic scholar. Yet, as a historian of religion, it is not my task merely to repeat what insiders say.

groups taking part. Often, the same small core group of individuals attends each time, while new faces come and go. The small cadre of regular attendees seems to grow over time. The group is maintained by volunteers and the teachers put a lot of effort into their lectures.

Lectures are always pre-prepared and the teachers usually read Qur'anic verses and *ahādīth* in Arabic, and this is often followed by a commentary which explains the meaning of the text that has been read. The readings are often related to the contemporary situation of the participants. The teachers inform the participants what it would mean in practice to realize the content of the presented text in their everyday lives. This means that the engagement with the text is not simply a recitation or reading; it includes, in my view, an element of something that approaches interpretation. In most cases, the teachers refer to other authorities, which they consider authoritative *'ulamā'*, seemingly in an effort to avoid making interpretations of their own. From the teachers' point of view, this method conforms to the Salafi norm of being true to revelation without adding meaning generated by individual preferences or desires.

With books and notes, they proceed to give those attending the lectures copious and detailed information about the topic. Towards the end of the lecture, there is a Q&A session. Men ask their questions directly; women write their questions on slips of paper and forward them to the teachers. Some women may simply be too shy or uncomfortable to speak in public, yet there is also an idea that women should not speak up in mixed groups. Some of the women I spoke to stated that they found writing down their questions an advantage, since it allowed them to ask whatever they wanted anonymously. They encouraged me to submit written questions, reassuring me that I should not feel nervous about it. The room is sometimes divided with a blanket, to separate men and women. Sometimes women are located in an anteroom, an audio speaker allowing them to listen to the lecture. The teachers are also keen on arranging lectures for women-only groups, for the purpose of educating them on various Islamic topics. It is important, the teachers argue, that women also learn about authentic Islam. Women are held to be an important part of Islam, and women choosing this particular version of Islam must accept many boundaries. Yet these boundaries are not fundamentally negative, and may be used as guidelines for becoming what they deem to be authentic Muslims.

The main dogmatic teachings are pretty straightforward and conform to what has been outlined above concerning Salafi theology. As such, I will not give too much space to this topic here. The *'aqīdah* is thoroughly presented at length in numerous lectures by the teachers as a pretty basic theological creed; there is nothing that would surprise anyone familiar with the contemporary Salafi discourse. The implications that the dogmatic teaching have in real life, not the theology per se, are the main focus of this study.[10]

The teachers often speak about the difference between what they consider true Islam and what Muslims do. One 'misunderstanding', as they call it, is that Islam oppresses women. As a response to this, they argue that women convert more frequently to Islam than men, and that this should be seen as a sign that Islam actually respects rather than oppresses women. Gender inequality is a prescribed norm and various strategies to persuade the participants about the Islamic authenticity motivating such a system are used. The argument in the group is of course that the Islamic system promotes equality: 'Muslims believe that the most pious is the best Muslim, regardless of gender'.[11] However, when viewed from the outside, gender inequality seems to be a recurring theme in lectures and established as a true Islamic norm. Not least, the physical organization of lectures reflects this—gender separation is practiced, and women are not heard, their voices silenced. The inaudibility of women is expressed most clearly by the need for them to write down their questions. This does not mean that women are passive, however. In some instances, as noted, it was considered by some women a benefit, since questions could be forwarded anonymously and even shy female participants could ask their questions. The teachers always consider questions from women. In one sense, the women are recognized and have a privileged position. They are encouraged to attend and their wishes are attended to. The fact that the group arranges a space for women during gender-mixed lectures is another sign of an inclusive attitude. There are also lectures that are not gender-mixed, for both men and women.

It could be said that the local group does not seek to awaken a spirit of political engagement, but is rather focused on the piety of the individual. This is evident in lectures concerning family life and gender roles, where

10. *'aqīdah* can be seen as a foundation for *manhaj*, the program of action. The elaboration of *manhaj* is not independent of *'aqīdah*, but not totally dependent on it either. In the group, a book used is al-Wahhab's *kitāb al-tawḥīd*, 'the book of monotheism', which presents his understanding of God's unity and what implications it has for behaviour, including the rejection and avoidance of all kinds of *shirk*, such as magic and saint worship, but also more 'mundane' aspects as well, such as ritual slaughter.

11. Lecture 4: Islam.

the teacher not only explains what the rules are but how they can be put into practice. Character traits beneficial to a marriage are expanded on and related to other kinds of relationships that people have. The teacher often reminds the participants that we humans are not perfect, in a way that seems to be meant to comfort those who may not live up to the standards that he advocates. Still, as mentioned, religion is not seen as a private matter only. One aim of the teaching seems to be to contribute to the growth of practicing Muslims in the local community, something which in turn can make society in general more open to religious practice and values. Thus, a religious polity, where the family is considered foundational for the preservation of Islam and the reform of society, is created. We cannot say that the teaching is completely apolitical and it is certainly not un-ideological: 'Preaching, as a medium of reaching the masses, is rarely bereft of ideology. There is so much talk about not just heaven and hell but women, poverty, morality, the West, and so on.'[12]

As we might expect, gender roles are often commented upon and the teachers also give lectures that explicitly concern the role, duties, and rights of women. The aim is to establish the family as the cornerstone of society. In a Swedish setting, this topic is particularly noteworthy, since—unlike Muslim majority societies—marriage is not considered particularly important; in Sweden the individual is the smallest and most important part of society, not the family. The teacher explores and expands on the need to have a happy family life and the contributions that it brings to individual salvation. Family life is described as being half of religion: 'An important subject, which all of us need, is how to gain family happiness. Some of us are married [...] and some of us think about getting married, which is an important part of our lives.'[13] In one lecture the teacher quoted Muhammad, who said that, if possible, people should get married and that a happy family life. Marriage and family life, ultimately, create a good society, and thus serve as important institutions that will benefit the growth of Islam. In a sense, marriage may be seen as a part of *da'wah* since, it is argued, it will change society for the better. In lectures outlining how to lead a good family life, (ideal) Islam is always contrasted with the practices of the Western world, and marriage is seen as a means of escaping the sins and strife surrounding Muslims in the Swedish society. Marriage is a safe haven that will help the participants to hold steadfast as good Muslims. In the following

12. Abu-Rabi' 2004, 18.
13. Lecture 5: Family.

citation, we also see how the teacher warns the participants that a person growing up without a good family may be drawn into criminal activity. He also repeats that humans are not perfect, and that there are differences between men and women. As such, we must expect disputes in marriage:

> It is an order [to get married]! If you can you should get married! And the Prophet *sas* said that the one who gets married has completed half of religion, so fear Allah for the other half. To get married is very important in Islam. Especially in these times of *fitnah*, of trials, [marriage helps you] to protect yourself from falling into *harām* [things forbidden]. We need to be married. And the family in Islam has a high position. The people of knowledge usually say that the society is built up on families. On individuals and families. So if families are good, the society will be good. [...] You know what the Swedes usually say, and in general *ya'nī* [meaning, I mean] non-Muslims, and there is a truth to this, that many criminals are people who grew up in unsafe environments, without a father, without a mother, in homes, in conflict areas, they had problems with the family sometimes. [...] There is no family without problems. Right? *Sahābah* [the righteous predecessors] also had problems with their wives. Disputes exist in all relationships. We are humans. We are not perfect. And men and women are different. So there will be disputes.[14]

Lectures are held every week and the teachers allow recordings. During the period of my research the number of lectures per week grew, as did the number of locations and participants. More teachers and guest lecturers arrived on the scene. It seems that the teachers are granted a position of authority due to their long education and their detailed knowledge about Islamic sources. They repeat what is written in the sources. They present several textual examples to prove their point. They try to avoid making their own interpretations and rely on other authorities. The stress on having proof (*dalīl*) for what is said is repeated and constantly demonstrated. But questions still come up that force them to expand on topics without relying solely on textual sources or other interpreters.

We can also note the specific language used, which is filled with key Islamic concepts in Arabic. These terms are even used by people who do not speak Arabic. While some participants are fluent Arabic speakers, some members appear to have no Arabic at all. The group's position is

14.　Lecture 5: Family. The word *ya'nī* is frequently used but I often omit it. It means 'I mean' or 'meaning', and is an expression often used in daily speech, even when the participants speak Swedish.

that it is recommended for non-Arabic speakers to learn the language. They call each other 'sister' and 'brother' when speaking to and about members of the group, and the use of Arabic concepts—*inshallah* (If God wants), *mashallah* (What God wants), etc.—is commonplace. Arabic appears to be a major source of religious self-esteem and seems to make others impressed and eager to learn more. At the same time, participants must not seek to impress others. The ideal is to be quiet, modest, and humble; bragging is to be avoided. The teachers know that many who attend the lectures cannot read Arabic and lament that there are no good Swedish translations of the Qur'an.[15] The languages used in lectures are Swedish and Arabic. Many participants know other languages as well. Some of the participants need assistance with the Arabic texts, so when guests lecture in Arabic somebody will typically prepare at least a brief summary in Swedish. However, participants are constantly encouraged to learn Arabic. One lecture specifically states that it is necessary in order to gain religious knowledge:

> To gain deeper knowledge of religion, you need to know Arabic! The language of Islam! We use it every day in prayer. Because of the status Arabic has in Islam, Allah has mentioned it many times in the Qur'an. [...] So how can we as Muslims let time pass without trying to learn Arabic!?[16]

Within the local group, the ideal for participants to model themselves on somebody else, principally in terms of behaviour, is apparent: how one prays, when and where, for example. This imitation also includes attitudes, ethical norms, and 'non-ritual' practice, such as dress codes and language usage, which in a sense can be described as 'ritualized' within the frames of the group. The importance of the local 'elite', the teachers, should not be underestimated in this respect. The male teachers are role models for male participants and many of the more 'initiated' female participants appear to be role models for the women attending lectures. Women teachers are not permitted, so there are no (living) female role models for the non-male participants to emulate. However, many lectures mention early Muslim women as sources of knowledge and authority, so there are female exemplars drawn upon from the 'golden past' that may offer inspiration. Muhammad is presented as the most important role model to be imitated, and the teachers highlight

15. Lecture 4: Islam.
16. Lecture 7: The Arabic Language. In all citations, I use 'Allah' instead of 'God'. This is due to the practice within the group to use 'Allah' regardless of the language spoken. Outside of citations, I use 'God'.

how nice he was to women, and that he helped out at home. None of the *sahābah*, they note, ever hit a woman, child, or servant, making them worthy of imitation:

> The one who reads his *sīrah* [Muhammad's biography] will be surprised, how kind he was to his women. 'Ā'ishah [Muhammad's wife] was asked what the Prophet did in the household and she said he used to help out. He mended his own clothes. Made his own shoes. He did not just sit around and give orders. He helped out. [...] The *sahābah never* hit a woman or a child or servant. That is a good character! You *don't* solve problems with violence or screaming or destroying things or slamming doors. That is *not* a part of the character of the Prophet! If you get really angry then just leave the house! Be quiet![17]

Though they would not express it that way, the male teachers may also be seen as 'objects of desire' to many women. The attraction is not necessarily of a sexual nature; rather, the teachers seem to embody a vision of a 'perfect man' and therefore become role models for what a good man, and a husband, should be like. A wish to appear as the 'perfect women' is apparent. This, it seems, will help them find a good husband in order to live their idea of perfection—living true Islam in real life. A good husband would be one of the teachers, and they therefore seem to function as role models to other men in this sense as well. In this way, it is not merely the texts of the Qur'an and Sunnah and the opinions of *'ulamā'* that have authoritative status, but also the teachers. These teachers, of course, have an authoritative status that is of a different nature—they function as *living* examples of Sunnah. This has also been noted by other scholars of Islam: 'Religious guidance, then, is not only laid down in a text of inviolable status. Muslims can look to living examples of proper thought and conduct, providing role models for Muslim men and women of all times and places.'[18]

It is notable that, in a visible sense, a gendered awareness is constantly present. Eyes are angled down, towards the floor, when moving in gender-mixed areas. A gendered code of ethics and behaviour is in place, guiding such things as dress, language, use of space, and body movement. It possible to speak about this as a strategy to create and embody a female and male Salafi persona. Female students seem to know what is expected from them and do not challenge male authority, even though some women are certainly very qualified. In exclusively female

17. Lecture 5: Family. See also Larsson 2014b for a discussion of beating, *daraba*.
18. Krämer and Schmidtke 2006, 4.

groups, meeting at somebody's home, a different hierarchy is apparent. On those occasions the women are supportive of each other and try to teach those present what good moral behaviour is and sometimes they comment on recent lectures or listen to recorded lessons together. Freer discussions are commonplace, and 'lecturing' is avoided. Dress code is not of such importance during women-only meetings.[19]

The women attending lectures seem to enjoy them. Should they become bored and start talking amongst themselves, the teacher will inform them that they should be quiet since there may in fact be people attending who wish to hear what he says. Some bring small children who run around playing, but nobody seems to object. The teacher did not seem to be bothered by it either. Bringing children may have been the only way for some of the women to attend at all. The lectures are sometimes more than one hour long, and it is hard to sit still, to be quiet, and to focus. Sometimes the women can be seen to whisper to each other, but it is not possible to say whether this is because of boredom or because they have heard something interesting they wish to discuss. Talking with a neighbour is, of course, much easier/less disruptive when the women are listening to the lecture in a separate room. Some seem to be especially 'provoked' by lectures concerning the place of women, and the rules and regulations about their behaviour and dress. They continue to discuss during breaks, after lectures, and at private meetings, but nobody questions the truth about what the teacher just said—at least, I never heard anything of that nature. The women's discussion seems to centre more on the difficulty of living up to the rules. At the same time, it should be noted that some, especially the younger women, express a feeling that some elements of the rules are simply too detailed and restrictive. There is a sense that they cannot understand why they are of such an importance to God, but this is

19. As will be seen below, the teachers say that a good way to reach out is to invite small groups into private homes, with a view to talking about Islam. These meetings are held to be a legitimate part of *da'wah*, 'calling others to Islam'. These meetings seem to be a way for female participants to meet and socialize at home, and, in greater privacy, talk about Islam and other things that are relevant to them. The topic of the discussion likely changes depending on who the participants are. I believe that the focus was more firmly on Islam when I and other 'newcomers' were invited, and that a 'plan' had been made beforehand that Islam would remain the primary the topic of discussion. Such meetings also left me with the impression that several women are indeed very skilled, possess a good command of the source and are well read on the authoritative *'ulamā'*.

never expressed aggressively. Rather, it is accepted, seen as a necessary 'sacrifice' considering the upcoming Judgment day, which is always somehow present. Such responses mainly relate to topics regarding female bodies and how to deal with clothing, body hair, and make-up. When the topics discussed concern ethical behaviour in general, applicable to both men and women, there seems to be a more straightforward acceptance that it is God's will that all Muslims should behave in certain ways.[20]

Knowledge and Authority

Gatherings of knowledge are gatherings of Paradise.[21]

Authority is stressed in the local group and the teachers spend a lot of time and energy on establishing what the sources of authority are, who the authoritative *'ulamā'*[22] are, and what the position of the teachers in the group is. Simultaneously, there is an ideal of education (*tarbiya*), to learn individually to master the sources, which is not restricted to an elite but open to everyone. This brings a certain kind of individual freedom, since individuals have potential access to an authoritative and scholarly position. This may be an empowering feeling and part of the explanation of the attraction to Salafism. However, what is considered correct knowledge is constrained by the opinions of authoritative scholars, including what they consider legitimate sources of knowledge. People in general are regarded as not competent enough to seek knowledge without proper guidance. A core acceptance of this view by the participants makes the authority of the teachers possible. The view on authority is returned to in several lectures.

> A student sticks to the people of knowledge! Refers to them! [...] A lot of the *fitnah* [upheaval] of today exists because people turned away from the people of knowledge. A lot would be corrected if people would return to the people of knowledge, the inheritors of the Prophet, that Allah has given us.[23]

20. I never encountered a male participant who was provoked by or commented on the lectures on gender. At the same time, however, I also never got acquainted with men and I never heard them talk about the lectures, so it does not necessarily mean that it was not discussed.
21. Lecture 14: Knowledge.
22. These are also called *shuyūkh* and people of knowledge within the group.
23. Lecture 13: *nawāsib*. In this lecture, as in many others, the authoritative scholars mentioned are Bin Baz, Fawzan, 'Uthaymin, al-Albani, and Muqbil.

All of the teachers I met had spent years abroad, studying in renowned Islamic centres of learning. This seems to be perceived as a kind of 'experience' from the lost past—travelling in search of learning, leading a simple life focussed on the pursuit of knowledge and the greater 'mission' of returning to and serving the local community that for various reasons must remain where they find themselves.[24] The 'sacrifice' of the teachers seems to be one aspect of the authority that the participants ascribe to them, an authority that they also use in order to legitimate their position. This view on learning and authority is also stressed by Fawzan, who is one of the main authorities used in the local group studied, and whose writings are often used to establish a specific view on authority. Fawzan too requires that knowledge is taken from the *'ulamā'*:

> Yes, the matters (of religion) have been explained. They however require research and seeking (for knowledge) whereby one learns and understands, acquiring knowledge from scholars. One should not depend on himself or ignorant people of his like or those who pretend to be learning from books. Rather he should acquire knowledge from its people (i.e. the scholars); because this knowledge should be acquired from scholars. Knowledge is acquired through learning (from scholars) and is not from books. This is because books are only instruments of research that are explained by the scholars. As for attaining the truth, it is taken from the people of knowledge; it is reported from them—generation after generation.[25]

The teachers in the local group agree to this position on knowledge and authority and behave as if they possess a kind of semi-authoritative status. They always take care to promote somebody from the established *'ulamā'*, who is regarded as authoritative and the foundation for what is being taught. The clear hierarchy of knowledge facilitates this establishment of authority. In the context of the local community, the teachers hold the highest position of authority, and are the local representatives of the *'ulamā'*, though with a lesser degree of authority. The continuous tropes used regarding authority and authenticity circle around the Qur'an as the literal word of God, though the textual authority includes the Sunnah as well. These are held to be the most

24. Among many Swedish Salafis, Medina is upheld to be the most important place for study. Some teachers have also studied in Yemen and other cities in Saudi Arabia, but then often in combination with Medina. It therefore seems to be the case that a specific Salafi tradition takes root in Sweden at large.
25. Fawzan 2012a, 56.

important sources for the purposes of gaining direct knowledge about the truth. However, textual authority is also extended to the selected *'ulamā'* that are referred to, since they are the ones explaining what the texts used in fact mean. Their *fatāwa* and treatises are also used by the teachers, and feature among the readings that are recommended to the participants. They are often connected to thematic series of lectures.

The question of authority must be understood in relation to the rejection of interpretation. Participants must accept the authority of people who have more knowledge in order to be 'worthy' members of the group. However, this should not lead us to think that the entire enterprise of the group is irrational. What we can observe, rather, is a *rationalization* of faith and of the program of action, one that is *always* textually bound to the Qur'an or Sunnah, or based on the opinions of the *'ulamā'*. Such grounding is considered to imbue authenticity and authoritativeness. Regarding reason, we can note in the following citation how the group refers to what is usually called the Islamization of science, which is a mode of interpretation that uses science to prove the divinity of the Qur'an. This is a 'modern' interpretative mode developed as a response to the 'demands' of a society promoting reason and science, creating a 'need' to state apologetically that Islam is compatible with science—often including polemical arguments that this is not the case with the Bible. However, during my period of observation the Islamization of science was mentioned only briefly and never elaborated upon in the group.[26] Moreover, the view that the Qur'an contains no contradictions, that it is a complete guidance for humanity, is stressed in the following citation. The Qur'an is held to include rules for humankind in its entirety, thus stressing universality. This citation also stresses that free will is given to us. This is presented as the reason why humans need guidance, to be able to tell right from wrong, and therefore revelation is needed:

> The Qur'an contains knowledge that proves that the Prophet Muhammad was a true prophet. It contains knowledge about things that you could not know at this time, except through revelation. For example how a fetus develops. [...] There are many scientific facts in the Qur'an. And also prophesies that happened. Another convincing thing is that there are no

26. Olsson 2012. In other groups, the strategy to emphasize scientific 'proofs' is more apparent. It seems that it is based on how *da'wah* is performed. Groups directing themselves more to a non-Muslim audience, or Swedes in general, are keener on speaking in terms of reason and science. See Stenberg 1996 for a thorough analysis of Islamization of science.

contradictions in Islam. Until today I have not seen a contradiction in Islam! Something that is wrong! In the Bible, there are facts going against science! Therefore many Christians have left religion! [...] The Qur'an contains narratives about earlier prophets. [...] The Qur'an also contains *harām* and *halāl*, permissions and forbiddance. It contains everything a person needs to know, which is another indication that this is the true religion! God, Allah, is perfect! His creation is perfect on earth, so why shouldn't His religion be perfect, complete!? That is logical, right? It has to be free from contradictions! [...] People, different from animals, have free will, so they need guidance in right and wrong! Islam contains everything from when you awake until you go asleep... From the person with the lowest position in society to the leader over a nation... All find guidance in Islam! How the man should be, how the woman should be, how children should be... Nothing is excluded![27]

There is a continuous 'positioning' of the teachers and the students. A notion that the teachers transmit authentic knowledge prevails and builds up the hierarchal structure or 'levels' of people. This view is the foundation of authority in the group. It seems that a common strategy among Salafis is the creation of 'local' authoritative leaders in this manner, so-called *istishyākh*.[28] Once accepted, participants are steered towards loyalty to local teachers, and with that the teachers' preferred textual sources and *'ulamā'*, as well as their definitions of what constitutes a 'proof' of truth (*dalīl*). In the citation above, the knowledge in the Qur'an is given the status as proof, or indeed fact. The question of proof is often returned to. Fawzan, who is used as an authoritative source, in this respect notes that:

> [W]hat is obligatory upon him [a person claiming to have proof] is to refer to the Book of Allah and the *Sunnah*; and he should not remain upon his assumption and what others tell him is the truth; for this does not form an excuse.[29]

This does not mean that Fawzan advocates debates or discussion; on the contrary:

> These matters, rhetoric, debate and arguments that took place between the sects, are all invented matters, and what caused them is following of vain desire. Anyone whose desire is subject to what the Messenger (*sas*)

27. Lecture 4: Islam.
28. See Poljarevic 2012.
29. Fawzan 2012a, 52–53.

came with, there will indeed be no doubt, dispute, debate or argument from him, because he is a Muslim who submits (to the Qur'an and the Sunnah).[30]

This too is agreed upon in the group.

Conflict of Sacred Authority

The importance of gaining knowledge from people of knowledge, *'ulamā'*, is stressed and related to the awareness of the multitude of existing interpreters and the conflict of sacred authority. This is an area in which the local group seemingly attempts to gain the upper hand. On one occasion I witnessed, the teacher took care to elaborate on the criticism of the many individuals who speak for Islam today. These latter are not regarded as a part of *'ulamā'*, and in that way their credibility is undermined. 'The *'ulamā'* turn people to Allah and their *athar*, effect, on society is great.'[31] As Judgment day approaches, it was explained, the *'ulamā'* will die and people will fall into sin because there is no one left to call them to Islam. 'If you turn away from *'ulamā'*, then people will get lost. We now live in *fitnah* [turmoil]. We speak without knowledge! If we turned to *'ulamā'*, Islam would be victorious!'[32] The teacher told those listening that at the end of time, when there are no longer any *'ulamā'*, then people will search knowledge from *ahl al-bid'ah*, the ignorant innovators without knowledge (*al-juhhāl*), and young people. He observed that this is the case today and, hence, we can assume that he means we now live in the end of times. Some people prefer to look to young TV-preachers than *'ulamā'*, he lamented. He questioned what they would do if they wanted a *fatwa*. Would they turn to a young person or somebody of age? With important questions, he counselled, participants must turn to *'ulamā'* and not *shaykh fulān*, meaning 'just anyone'. He further explained that the authoritativeness among *'ulamā'* must not depend on mere age, but rather on the knowledge possessed. Moreover, he told his listeners *never* to speak badly about *'ulamā'*. They are to be respected, since they are the inheritors of the Prophet.[33] The teacher also stressed

---

30. Fawzan 2012a, 107. Fawzan states that it is obligatory to submit to the Qur'an and Sunnah 'and refrain from argumentation and bringing doubt to the people because you have indeed been prohibited from that. Rather, it increases (you in) confusion.' Fawzan 2012a, 415.
31. Lecture 14: Knowledge.
32. Lecture 14: Knowledge.
33. Lecture 14: Knowledge.

the importance of understanding where knowledge comes from. Such an understanding would, he urged, help people avoid listening to those without 'true' knowledge:

> People who give *da'wah*, where does their knowledge come from? Did they study at home? Internet? From where did their knowledge come? [...] What did they do for people? What did they produce? What did their *da'wah* do for *islāh* [reform]? [...] How many of these YouTube shaykhs exist today? 'Oh, so nice...' and people spread information about it on Facebook and everywhere, 'he looks so nice', and *nashīd* is playing in the background. But who is he?! [...] Is he a source of knowledge!? Disaster! Disastrous utterances! They say that the people of *ahl al-kitāb* [people of the book] are not *kuffār* [non-believers] but Muslims, they are believers! If you ask them questions they will give whatever answer! Very dangerous! This is a sign of the Day of Judgment. [...] We don't need them! Put them aside! [...] *Hamdulillah!* We don't need these small ignorant people! It is important to turn to the *'ulamā'*.[34]

This citation shows a pressing awareness of the conflict between sacred authority and the increasing number of people who spread Islam in various ways, not least via social media.[35] In order to uphold the authority of the group, it seems to be necessary to speak clearly and often about the situation and to reject those who are not espousing authentic Islam. Repeated use of the names of the most important *'ulamā'*, who are held up as ones to be followed, appears to be instrumental to the argument for rejection. Those to be rejected are merely examples of *shaykh fulān*, 'just anyone'.[36]

34. Lecture 14: Knowledge. *Kāfir*, pl. *kuffār*, is used in the group to denote people who are non-Muslims, or non-believers, and sometimes in a more generalizing manner to include all people not belonging to their version of Islam. The translation often used, 'infidel' (Swe. avfälling), is not used in Swedish in the group, but rather 'unfaithful' or 'disbelievers' (Swe. otrogna), which is not as strong but nevertheless indicates that such a person is destined for Hell. Most often, the Arabic word is used even when speaking in Swedish.
35. See, for example, Eickelman and Anderson 2003 and Bunt 2009.
36. Lecture 14: Knowledge. One of those that he names critically is Yusuf Estes (b. 1944), an American convert to Islam. *Shaykh fulān* are not true callers, but may lead people to the fire of Hell. They do not call to the truth. Barbahari's *Sharh al-Sunnah*, commented upon by Fawzan, is often used as a legitimate source for this view, alluding to the historical time when different interpretations of Islam spread, comparing that to the contemporary era. The only straight path is to follow the Prophet and the pious predecessors. To have true knowledge is necessary, as is patience and steadfastness. Referring to Fawzan, this is held to

Fawzan too, who is used as an authority in discussions concerning knowledge and the search for knowledge, criticizes the fragmentation of voices and requires that people verify what they hear, to make sure it is in accordance with the Sunnah:

> Do not be in a haste with regards to what you hear from the people especially towards the end of time; as there are many who speak, issue religious rulings, raise (themselves) to (the status of having) knowledge and (possessing public audience) saying, especially (this time) when the media is modernized; and every one now talks in the name of knowledge and religion—so much so that even the people of misguidance and the strayed sects started talking in the name of religion on satellite television channels. The danger is very great![37]

Because of this situation, Fawzan demands that people verify what they hear. He compares the time of Barbahari, being close to Ahmad ibn Hanbal (780–855), to that of today: 'What about your own era; the era of desires and ignorance; the era of the intermingling world; part of it mixing up with the other till it becomes a massive wave of tribulations, evils and ideologies?'[38] He criticizes the increasing number of people speaking for Islam:

> Even nowadays—just as you know—because of these satellite television channels, speech and intellectual chaos, even the common people comment on knowledge-based issues, causing doubt therein and causing doubt in the rulings of the *Sharī'ah*. They cause the rulings of the *Imāms* to be doubted.[39]

be helpful in times of hardship. The teacher refers to Q 31:17: 'My son! Observe the prayer, and command right and forbid wrong. Bear patiently whatever smites you—surely that is one of the determining factors in (all) affairs.' Lecture 16: The 73, sect. 2.

37. Fawzan 2012a, 87, written in his commentary to *Sharh al-Sunnah* by Barbahari. Fawzan addresses this problem frequently: 'So many people claim to be inviting to Islam under this umbrella [of having the truth], but if you look at their methodology and conducts, you find them in complete opposition to Islam.' Fawzan 2012a, 460.

38. Fawzan 2012a, 89.

39. Fawzan 2012b, 10–11. In both volumes of Fawzan's commentary on *Sharh al-Sunnah*, he returns repeatedly to the refutation of Jahmiya. He claims that the Jahmiya is the origin of approaching the texts with desires leading the interpretation. 'This is the way of all the people of desires in every time; they would take from the proofs what agrees with their desires and abandon what disagrees with it!' Fawzan 2012b, 31.

Barbahari's treatise *Sharh al-Sunnah* is used to draw parallels to the contemporary era and the multitude of interpretations. On one occasion I observed, the teacher referred to the Qur'an in order to comment on the present situation, in which unity is broken: 'But they cut their affair (in two) between them (over the) scriptures, each faction gloating over what was with them' (Q 23:53). He explained that this means that the unity is broken and that various groups rejoice in their own views. Fawzan was once again referred to, specifically his criticism of the various groups today who, so he argues, proudly publish books about their own views. This is seen by Fawzan as a punishment from God. These people rejoice even though they have no 'true' knowledge and they, in his view, are therefore lost. While admitting that this may appear to be a scary description of the present situation, the teacher consoled the participants that the people with the truth will not be affected by this fragmentation. They are steadfast because they have knowledge, he argued.[40]

The teacher further highlighted the polarized status of groups who have different views on knowledge, rejecting those who reinterpret and 'twist' the meaning of the Qur'an:

> *Qiyās* [analogy] is ok to do in *fiqh* [jurisprudence], by the *'ulamā'*, but considering *'aqīdah*, there is no *qiyās*, and also not considering the divine attributes and so on. But people did this [when Muslims began to fragment] and based themselves on their views and their reason, and rejected that which did not fit their reason. [...] and people began to reinterpret, and twist the meaning of verses in the Qur'an.[41]

That reason is subjugated to a literal understanding of texts was clearly expressed: 'We know that considering the divine attributes, and [other] things that our intellects cannot apprehend, it is still impossible to try to use the intellect. We must go back to what the sources say, and what the Prophet and his *sahābah* said in these questions.' The teacher continued: 'How dangerous it is to put the intellect before the texts! We put the texts before our intellect! Even if you don't understand anything, you don't judge the texts based on your intellect!'[42]

---

40. Lecture 14: Knowledge.
41. Lecture: The 73, sect. 3.
42. Lecture: The 73, sect. 3. Fawzan, who is used as a source here, also rejects all comments on the essence of God as innovation (Fawzan 2012a, 110–124). He is also concerned with rejecting the view of the Qur'an as created (Fawzan 2012a, 125–135). He holds on to Barbahari's saying that disputing this is disbelief

Knowledge Is Action

In his commentary on Barbahari's *Sharh al-sunnah*, Fawzan underscores
what the Sunnah is, and that one must know it and act upon it:

> So this is the only way to unite the Muslims. If they are truthful, let them
> correct their *'aqīdah* and distance deviation and newly-invented things
> from it so that it can be as brought by Muḥammad (*sas*) in order for the
> Muslims to be united upon it. This is what the righteous predecessors
> (of this *Ummah*) like al-Barbahari and others intended by authoring
> these treatises and books explaining the sound Creed. So when trials,
> divisions and misguidance occurred, they wrote these (books on) *'aqīdah*,
> explaining through them the *Sunnah* which the Messenger of Allah (*sas*),
> his companions and the best generations were upon, whoever adheres to
> it is saved and whoever opposes it is destroyed.[43]

Fawzan explains that Barbahari's saying, 'Know [*a'lamū*], that Islam is
the Sunnah and the Sunnah is Islam. One of them cannot be established
except with the other', means that they should learn. Learning leads
to the knowledge that Islam is Sunnah.[44] He argues that a Muslim must
act upon the Sunnah. 'Whoever professes Islam without acting upon
the *Sunnah*, i.e. the way of the Messenger of Allah (*sas*) is not a Muslim.
And the one who knows the *Sunnah* without submitting to Allah is not a
Muslim although he knew the *Sunnah*. It is therefore a must to combine
them both.'[45] The importance of Sunnah is returned to in the discussion
of faith (*'īmān*), where Fawzan argues that faith must be in the heart,
speech, and deeds of a Muslim. He adds that it must follow the Sunnah.
Hence, others are not true believers.[46]

Fawzan states that a person may be a narrator, a transmitter, but this
does not mean that he is a scholar with understanding.[47]

> (*kufr*). The belief in seeing God on the Day of resurrection is to be literally
> understood (Fawzan 2012a, 136–144), as is the belief in a scale (*mīzān*) that will
> weigh good against evil deeds (Fawzan 2012a, 145–148). Many other subjects
> are presented which illustrate a literal reading. At the time of Barbahari, this
> was disputed, which explains why the themes are extensively addressed.
> Fawzan elaborates on the attributes of God and how to understand Him in
> Fawzan 2012a, 286–304.

43. Fawzan 2012a, 25.
44. Fawzan 2012a, 35.
45. Fawzan 2012a, 37.
46. Fawzan 2012a, 196–197.
47. Fawzan 2012a, 90–91.

I say: do not introduce religious verdicts, views, sayings and expressions that no one (among the Salaf) has preceded you regarding them. Take example from the righteous predecessors and from their sayings; were you to come up with something of which none has preceded you, it will be bizarreness; and its danger is more than its benefit.[48]

Moreover, in order to prevent others from being deceived by deviators, remaining silent is not an option. Fawzan's teaching is that there is a duty to warn others, and an obligation to refute and expose those espousing deviant views.[49] Fawzan refutes those who argue that there is freedom of speech, and argues that they are rather to explain the truth. Silence is not permissible. He notes that speaking up may cause others to argue that they are impulsive, but he claims that it 'will not discourage them [the people of knowledge], to speak up]!'[50] Fawzan states that the situation will change and that only that which is based on the Qur'an and Sunnah will remain. 'It is the sound methodology and the straight path.'[51] This, according to him, requires that people remain patient and steadfast; he reassures them that they have beneficial knowledge.

Fawzan states that knowledge is not the same as knowing a lot. This view was repeated by one of the teachers I interviewed: 'Knowledge is not abundance of information, acquaintance and books. Rather, knowledge is only through understanding, following and acting; even if the knowledge is little. [...] The goal is action. This is the meaning of knowledge.'[52] He continued, stating that 'knowledge is non-beneficial without action, and action benefits not except with knowledge. It is essential for knowledge and action to co-exist, and this is the way of those on whom Allah has bestowed His Grace.'[53]

In many of the lectures I attended, mention was made, in a positive sense, that Islam is the fastest-growing religion on earth and that there are now more than one billion Muslims. However, simultaneously, I heard lamentations that this does not mean that people have

48.   Fawzan 2012a, 91.
49.   Fawzan 2012a, 98–99.
50.   Fawzan 2012a, 100.
51.   Fawzan 2012a, 461.
52.   Fawzan 2012b, 51.
53.   Fawzan 2012b, 52. This is repeated in many ways in this book, and accompanies a presentation of what constitutes a scholar, concluding that 'the person who possesses a huge library but abandons action, or an innovator, such is like a donkey carrying books without benefitting from them!' Fawzan 2012b, 54.

knowledge about Islam, but that there are many misunderstandings and much ignorance—even among Muslims. This is the platform from which the Salafi teachers work. They try to remedy the problematic situation by spreading what they consider to be true knowledge, and by teaching others to distinguish between 'true Islam' and what Muslims do, between culture and religion. Importantly, what the truth is must be established on the basis of the sources. I frequently encountered polemics directed against the stereotyped media depictions of Islam. Such depictions, it seems, only served to illustrate the urgent need to find truth in the Islamic sources.

> So, this is an important question that we must ask ourself: What do I know about Islam? Not what you have heard in media, read in newspapers, but what do you *know* about Islam. Did you read the translation of the Qur'an? Have you read a book that explains what Islam is? There is a difference between what you hear in the media and what is written in texts. You have to go back to the facts, to the root. It is a big difference between thing and person. There is a difference between Muslims and Islam. A Muslim can do things un-Islamic. If a Muslim is a criminal, steals, that has nothing to do with Islam. If a Muslim follows culture and makes an honor killing or something, that has nothing to do with Islam. Islam is free from this. So, if you are sincere, you have to go back and check what Islam says about these things. Not what people do. And this is what a sincere person does, when he searches, is objective, does not only take the side of the media.[54]

The reason why knowledge is so often focused upon, having separate lectures dedicated to it, is that gaining knowledge is considered to be an obligation. The greatest gift from God is described as the guidance through revelation. The purpose of humans in this world is to worship God, who wants to be worshipped in a specific way. Hence, I heard the teacher ask, 'How can we know that if we don't have knowledge?'[55] He stressed the obligatory task to gain knowledge. 'It is a duty (*wājib*) to search for Islamic knowledge. You sin if you don't do it, to correct your worship, to worship Allah in the right way. To search for knowledge is obligatory (*wājib*) for each Muslim.'[56] The teacher drew attention to several verses from the Qur'an that praise those who seek knowledge, and told the participants that 'Allah gives the Prophet an order to ask Allah for more knowledge. [...] If Allah orders *him* that, the most knowledgeable

54. Lecture 4: Islam.
55. Lecture 14: Knowledge.
56. Lecture 14: Knowledge.

man, what then about us? If Muhammad needs knowledge, what do we then need?'[57] The teacher built up the theme by reading a verse from the Qur'an which states that those who fear God are those with knowledge. He added: 'The one who feared Allah the most was the Prophet Muhammad,'[58] thus making him the ideal person to imitate.

The teacher often addressed the importance of knowledge in relation to the Hereafter: 'The more *jāhil*, ignorant, of Allah a person is, the further away from Allah he is. [...] He will not long for Allah. Therefore, *kuffār* are not afraid of Allah. Nothing is there to prevent them from sinning.'[59] A *hadīth* from Tirmidhi and Abu Dawud was read, the stress being on the rewards for those seeking knowledge:

> It was narrated that Kathir bin Qais said: I was sitting with Abu Darda' in the mosque of Damascus when a man came to him and said: 'O Abu Darda', I have come to you from Al-Madinah, the city of the Messenger of Allah, for a *hadīth* which I have heard that you narrate from the Prophet.' He said: 'Did you not come for trade?' He said: 'No.' He said: 'Did you not come for anything else?' He said: 'No.' He said: 'I heard the Messenger of Allah say: "Whoever follows a path in the pursuit of knowledge, Allah will make easy for him a path to Paradise. The angels lower their wings in approval of the seeker of knowledge, and everyone in the heavens and on earth prays for forgiveness for the seeker of knowledge, even the fish in the sea. The superiority of the scholar over the worshipper is like the superiority of the moon above all other heavenly bodies. The scholars are the heirs of the Prophets, for the Prophets did not leave behind a dinar or dirham, rather they left behind knowledge, so whoever takes it has taken a great share.'"[60]

The teacher explained that this *hadīth* shows how searching for knowledge, which he equated to worship, brings rewards:

> To search knowledge is an *'ibādah* [worship], which is worship, which leads to Paradise. When you read a book on *hadīth*, you gain worship. [...] Knowledge will make your road to Paradise easier. When you practice what you learn [...] this worship will *inshallah* bring you to Paradise![61]

---

57. Lecture 14: Knowledge.
58. Lecture 14: Knowledge.
59. Lecture 14: Knowledge.
60. From sunnah.com with slight modifications. Sunan ibn Maja, *kitāb al-muqaddimah*, accessed February 10, 2014. It is also found in the collection of Abu Dawud and Tirmidhi.
61. Lecture 14: Knowledge.

Hence, we can note that the group stresses that seeking knowledge is considered part of worship, and that knowledge ought to be put into practice as well.

Stressing Rituals

> Human action and relationships of all sorts—religious and otherwise—are about a great deal more than maximizing rewards. The relationship between human and divine is sometimes oriented toward meaning, sometimes toward belonging, sometimes toward desired rewards, sometimes toward communion (or relationship), sometimes toward ecstasy, and sometimes toward moral guidance. Attempts to explain religious action that eliminate that human complexity may explain nothing at all.[62]

Belonging and loyalty can be regarded as founded in cognitive aspects such as beliefs, values, ideas, and morality, at the same time as it concerns physical aspects such as practices and things that concern the body (food, clothing, practice, rituals, movement). Both the cognitive and the physical aspects are a part of how a normative tradition is constructed and authorized. Considering this aspect, analyses of contemporary Islamic interpretations should address questions considering how they are authenticated as authoritative traditions, requiring loyalty, and how a particular identity is constructed and argued for. Issues of authenticity and loyalty are also connected to how Muslims conceive of themselves related to other Muslims and the surrounding society.

Scholars today observe the importance of the body in the study of religions. It is indeed right not to focus solely on cognitive aspects, since religion extends beyond internalized, intellectual processes. '[A]ny religion that speaks only to the cognitive aspects of adherents' experience (i.e. limited to their beliefs and thoughts) cannot address their emotional needs, their everyday experiences, or their whole persons.'[63] From what I observed, the local group puts a lot of emphasis on cognitive aspects. The notion of 'true' Islam and what it means is stressed and people are supposed to believe this. Islam is presented as a religion of peace and people must submit to God: 'The word Islam is from the word *salām*, peace. In this way, it means to submit to Allah! To capitulate! To submit to Allah! The only true God. And to only worship him! This is Islam!'[64] A clear definition of what constitutes a Muslim was

62. Ammerman 2007, 227.
63. McGuire 2008, 101.
64. Lecture 4: Islam.

given: 'Who is a Muslim? A Muslim accepts Islam! Submits to the will of God! Confesses the *shahādah* [confession of faith]!'[65] And yet, however, for all their emphasis on matters of cognition, the group simultaneously placed a lot of emphasis on practice, be that ritual practice or issues related to visible markers, such as clothing. The participant's entire life should conform to the teaching.

The teachers presented 'hard facts' about Islam and then made these relevant to the everyday lives of the participants. Strategies and necessary skills were presented and promoted as being truly Islamic. Several lectures dealt with how to perform religious rituals correctly, often in never-ending detail. This may perhaps be explained by the fact that many participants are not brought up as practicing Muslims in Sweden, and so lack detailed knowledge about such matters, thus making it relevant information. There was an opinion shared throughout the group that it is necessary to perform rituals *exactly* as they are prescribed in the religious sources, and even those who do pray may do so only out of habit, unaware of their mistakes. As such, the repeated, detailed discussion of correct ritual performance was justifiable.

The Hereafter is particularly important to Muslims. Given that the actions performed in life impact directly upon a Muslim's attainment of a place in Paradise, what is done in life is important, and needs to be done correctly. A prayer performed correctly, in terms of physical gesture, will not be accepted if the person prays half-heartedly and without full knowledge of what he or she is doing. According to the teachers, bodily movements performed without the right intention are void of meaning in the eyes of God. Religious duties must be understood in their 'religious' sense, and I observed the teachers making an effort to explain the motive behind rituals—*why* one should do them, and *how* one should do them *exactly*. Prostration out of mere habit was not regarded as a religious movement, but merely a bodily and mundane movement with no religious significance whatsoever. I saw religious ritual observance being held up as very important. The reasons given for this were that, first and foremost, God has proscribed this practice and human beings are to follow his will and submit to it, but also because rituals are upheld as strategic actions with great potential in this life. If Muslims submit and perform rituals, especially the five daily prayers, it is said to affect their lives in other respects as well. It can be seen as a ritual act that disciplines other aspects of life. It is something that helps Muslims cultivate a good Islamic personality that will spill over into their general

---

65. Lecture 4: Islam.

behaviour and attitude. I observed a continuous emphasis on ritual performance as obligatory. Ritual performance is seen as a sign of who is a true Muslim.[66]

The second pillar of Islam, the five daily prayers, is considered to be the most important ritual activity; it is described as an important foundation of Islam. Participants are advised that it is the first thing they will be asked about on Judgment day, and that it will affect how other actions are judged by God. In one lecture, the teacher clearly stated, echoing Fawzan, 'If you do not pray, you do *not* have religion!'[67]

Bodily practices (dress, rituals, and gestures, for example) have been analyzed as symbols used for political ends or as vehicles for expressing group interests. The bodily practices themselves may have political consequences—they are expressions of and shape cultural meaning. In her studies, Saba Mahmood promotes the idea of 'positive ethics'.[68] Among her informants, ethics 'is founded upon particular forms of discursive practice, instantiated through specific sets of procedures, techniques, and exercises, through which highly specific ethical-moral subjects come to be formed'.[69] This perspective, which builds on Michel Foucault, calls for the need to examine values in moral codes and also different ways people live or perform the codes. Mahmood is interested in how bodily technique influences the construction of specific conceptions of personhood:[70]

> the specific gestures, styles, and formal expressions that characterize one's relationship to a moral code are not a contingent but a necessary means to understanding the kind of relationship that is established between the self and structures of social authority, and between what one is, what one wants, and what kind of work one performs on oneself in order to realize a particular modality of being and personhood.[71]

Saba Mahmood's notion of the cultural construction of personhood is further elaborated in the insight that 'different configurations of personhood can cohabit the same cultural and historical space, with

66. A lot of the material used in the group reflects this opinion. Fawzan holds, based on Barbahari, that if a person does not pray, he is a disbeliever. Fawzan 2012a, 420–421.
67. Lecture 2: Meaning of Life.
68. Mahmood 2005, 27–29, 118–122.
69. Mahmood 2005, 120.
70. Mahmood 2005, 121 note 5. Here, Mahmood builds on Marcel Mauss' views on the cultural construction of personhood.
71. Mahmood 2005, 120.

each configuration the product of a specific discursive formation rather than of the culture at large'.[72] She suggests that different conceptions of self exist simultaneously, depending on the regimes of truth they consent to. There is thus not merely one conception corresponding to the discursive practices of a given culture.[73]

Saba Mahmood makes her point by focussing on her informants' views on prayer. Many of her informants did not observe the ritual obligation to pray five times a day. While acknowledging that they lacked the will to perform the prayers, many reported that they strived to cultivate the will to perform prayers in the midst of their daily life, 'until that desire became a part of their condition of being'.[74] The will to pray is something that must be disciplined and created, consciously and unconsciously. The desire to pray can be cultivated through various techniques, whereby the individual is recommended to reconsider each act in daily life and conform his or her behaviour to ethical norms in order to create or cultivate a pious desire to observe obligatory rituals and to become a pious self: 'ritual performances are understood to be disciplinary practices through which pious dispositions are formed, rather than symbolic acts that have no relationship to pragmatic or utilitarian activity'.[75]

The body is not merely a sign of the self; it is the means to its formation, a medium for the self.[76] One learns, acquires, and cultivates the pious self, which simultaneously is a provocation and a challenge to secular norms. This is actively cultivated since 'acting does not issue forth from natural feelings but *creates* them'.[77] Hence, Saba Mahmood's informants can be said to perceive the body as a tool, since they 'do not understand the body as a sign of the self's interiority but as a means of developing the self's potentiality'.[78] Hence, those who see expressions of piety as part of identity politics, a way of forming a visible sign of group-belonging, should note that from an analysis of insider perspectives, it rather appears to be an act of disciplining oneself in order to cultivate a moral and pious self. The motivation towards piety seems to be one stemming from a criticism of secularism, and this entire enterprise *is* a political project since the ideal image of society is something

72. Mahmood 2005, 120–121.
73. Mahmood 2005, 121 note 3.
74. Mahmood 2005, 124.
75. Mahmood 2005, 128.
76. Mahmood 2005, 116.
77. Mahmood 2005, 157.
78. Mahmood 2005, 166.

going against secular or liberal notions of freedom or a good life. The insider claim would rather indicate that the aim is not identity politics on a larger scale, but rather directed to the individual self, 'toward the *retraining* of ethical sensibilities so as to create a new social and moral order'.[79]

Considering the local group, there were an endless number of lectures concerning rituals. These had a typical structure. First, the teacher would inform the participants why they should do rituals and how to perform them. Next came an explanation of how to understand the rituals correctly. Last but not least came a clarification of why failure to perform rituals is so dangerous—Hell would be the final destiny. The main focus in this respect was the daily prayers. In numerous lectures, and in various ways, the teachers expounded the importance of correctly performing the daily prayers. As we might expect, the teachers hold that it is obligatory to perform prayers at the right time, with the correct bodily movements, and in a pure state with the right intentions. That the first question on Judgment day will be about prayer was frequently repeated. The teachers warned what happens to people if they approach prayer incorrectly. A reoccurring metaphor is that if the pillar of a house breaks, then the house will crumble. The participants were also warned that some people of knowledge equate a person who prays in an incorrect manner to a *kāfir*, an infidel: 'Some of the people of knowledge say that those who do not pray, they are not Muslims, he is a *kāfir*, he is like a Christian'.[80] The participants were repeatedly reminded that a *kāfir*'s destiny is Hell. Prayer was thus promoted in various ways. Prayer is held to offer protection and contribute to a good life. Warnings about being too aware of what friends and family say were frequent, and the teacher warned participants that the decision to pray was their own, and that the consequences would be eternal. Participants were counselled that should they place so-called friends before prayer, then they alone, i.e. the one who does not pray, will be punished. Thus, it is possible to see

---

79. Mahmood 2005, 193.
80. Lecture 15: *salah*. In this particular lecture, the teacher mentions that in Sweden people are allowed by law to pray at work and school. If they are forbidden to do so, they must leave that institution or report the matter. He stresses that praying at work is also a good way to do *da'wah*. He mentions that there is a *hadīth* indicating that the Prophet believed that the Earth had been made clean for him, and that the whole world is a mosque, meaning that one can pray anywhere, but that one must follow the detailed rules about how and when to pray.

a link between freedom of choice and individual responsibility. The teacher would state that a person who truly loves God prioritizes Him, accepting God and Muhammad as role models and taking full individual responsibility for all actions.[81] The teacher also spoke about prayer as a disciplining activity, in line with the results of Saba Mahmood's study: 'Prayer keeps people away from sin'.[82] In this way, prayer can be seen as a disciplining activity that will have effects on the participant's life as a whole, in this world and the next. Judgment day was, as always, alluded to: 'The punishments proscribed by Allah happen in this life and the next. So we know that we must fear Allah and keep away from sins.'[83]

Final Comments

From this presentation of the group's activities and outline of main teachings, we notice how Islam is addressed as a universal and holistic system. The main dogma is similar to what has already been described above in Chapter 3 on Salafi Islam. Islam is a fully developed lifestyle from which it is not possible to take a break, or to select preferred elements. Being Salafi means that the participant should conform to the teaching in every respect. The ideal version of Islam is the one that covers every conceivable detail, big or small. Salafi lectures can be incredibly detailed, yet I heard no complaints from the participants. Members of the group generally seemed happy to hear about minute aspects that they should apply in their own lives, regardless of the topic. This keen interest in—one might even say 'fetishism' for—detail appears to be a strategy for fully defining what it takes to be Salafi. Every step taken is either a Salafi one, or it is not. Each step leads towards the final, and eternal, destination, be that Heaven or Hell.[84]

Moreover, a 'true' Muslim is one who follows the authority of the *'ulamā'*. Local teachers function as their local representatives and there is a strict hierarchy of authority. However, the notion of authority in the group is open; it is possible, in principle, for anyone to climb the stairs of authority. Authority is dependent on the amount of 'authentic' knowledge a person gains, and the local group is there to serve the

---

81. Lecture 2: Meaning of Life.
82. Lectures: Jurisprudence. The idea of prayer as a tool for disciplining a moral self is of course not new. Augustine (d. 430), for example, clearly saw prayer as an aspect of discipline, a belief which has influenced the Catholic Church.
83. Lectures: Jurisprudence.
84. See also Moberg 2013 for a study on Swedish charismatic Christians which shows similar tendencies.

participants, teaching them about the truth, assisting them on their way towards eternity. Rituals are important, and of these prayer is of paramount importance. There is recognition that the performance of rituals will assist the participants in cultivating their piety. A person who does not pray, or does not pray in the correct way, is not considered to be a Muslim. In one sense the entire lives of 'good' Salafis can be regarded as ritualized, at least if all the teachings are put into practice.

The next chapter will focus on textual views and analyze the teachers' official stance on the juridical schools and hermeneutical principles. It will paint a clearer picture on their epistemological stance and fundamentalist attitude to texts and explicate how they relate to the juridical communities.

Jurisprudence and sources

This chapter will present the teachers' official stance on jurisprudence, sources and interpretation. Jurisprudence is ever present in lectures, regardless of the wider theme in focus. As we shall see, even though imitation of the juridical schools (*taqlīd*) is rejected, there are a lot of references to the founders of the juridical schools and the four Sunni schools in general. The aim of the present chapter is to attempt to nuance the relationship and to pinpoint what the relationship actually is.

This chapter is a reflection of the discussion above (Chapter 2) on 'orthodoxy', where it was shown that groups and individuals seemingly feel the need to distance themselves from the juridical tradition, regardless of whether or not they reject it, in order to establish what they consider to be true Islam. Below I offer an outline of the group's official view on jurisprudence, one based on the teaching delivered in the observed lectures. This will be particularly informative, allowing us to consider how Salafism differs from what is otherwise often regarded as normative Islam.[1] The stance taken on jurisprudence is significant in the overall framing of this study, since it also elucidates several of the main issues pertaining to authority and authenticity. The official view presented by the teachers on written sources, juridical methodology, and the historical development of the juridical communities is discussed in order to elucidate what their stance is and what makes Salafis different from those who accept the *taqlīd*ic norm. Following the discussion concerning the notion of the historical development into juridical schools, it should also become clearer why Salafi Islam cannot be equated with Wahhabi Islam.

---

1.   See for example Zaman 2002, 46.

My observations revealed that the teachers placed paramount importance on explaining the official stance on *sharīʿah* against the backdrop
of negative media portrayals of Islam and Muslims, which they argue is
primarily concerned with harsh physical punishments, such as stoning.
This is blamed on the 'unfaithful', who are considered to be against
Islam and Muslims. Nevertheless, such negative remarks are typically
accompanied by a hopeful counterpoint, namely that God has promised
the faithful that they will be victorious. In order to become victorious,
believers must have knowledge anchored in what are considered to
be authentic sources. These aspects lie beneath most of the lectures,
offering a glimpse of what underlies the definition of in- and out-group,
and helping to explain what the problem is, as they see it, and how the
problem should be remedied.[2]

> The unfaithful attempt to bring a faulty image of *sharīʿah*, but Allah
> has assured us that the Muslims will be victorious and Allah has given
> us guidance. We need knowledge to meet the doubts and accusations.
> Therefore we need to learn about religion and to practice it and to call
> others to this religion. Some people want to practice without knowledge,
> which brings chaos [...]. They don't know what *sharīʿah* means. [...] Do *not*
> act without knowing and take the knowledge from the right sources![3]

In lectures on jurisprudence, the negative media image of Islam is
frequently returned to and regarded as a cause to why the participants
need to learn about and practice 'true' religion. In the citation above,
we can also notice that the official stance is to reject people who are
not considered to have authentic knowledge, something which was also
noted in the previous chapter. Such people are called 'extremists', and
are presented as a contrasting example in order to develop the group's
view on what a true Muslim is and what constitutes authentic Islam.[4]

2. Lectures: Jurisprudence. This topic was dealt with in a long series of lectures,
    which I here collectively refer to as Lectures: Jurisprudence. The topic of in-
    and out-group is returned to more thoroughly in the following chapter.
3. Lectures: Jurisprudence. As we shall see, this polarization is repeated, with
    others being regarded as bringing chaos when acting upon a faulty under-
    standing of Islam. This perspective is influenced by Fawzan, who strongly
    condemns those Muslims who support bombers. He calls supporters of terror-
    ism 'people of *fitnah*', and argues that even if supporters do not actually carry
    weapons, they are still partners in sin. Fawzan 2012b, 115.
4. Lectures: Jurisprudence.

Humans are described in many lectures as fundamentally different from animals, owing to our God-given intellect, which we should use in order to take responsibility for all actions. In order to do that, individuals are recommended to reflect on a couple of key-issues that are frequently discussed: 'What is the meaning of life?' and 'Have I prepared for the Hereafter?' Once a person dies, the teachers make clear, it is too late for regrets; all that remains is for deceased to harvest the fruit according to what has been done, or not done, during their short life on earth. Apart from informing about the truth of this opinion, with the help of textual sources, the teachers also suggest actions that enable Muslims to change their lives in this world, here and now, in order to prepare for the next—which seems to be the sole purpose of all their activities.[5] Moreover, to determine what the meaning of life is has an important motivational function for the overall message: if people are unable to agree with the answer given to this question, everything else is pointless. The meaning of life is stated as the acknowledgment of having been created by God and submission to his will. God is described as considerate, and as giving us all that we need. This is said to be obvious if we look at his creation. Since God is all-knowing and merciful, he gave us his guidance to let us know for sure what the meaning of life is. Having the Qur'an, our intellect, and free will, so the teachers maintain, we have everything necessary to be able to make good choices. With the guidance given, it is argued, individuals are capable of distinguishing between right and wrong. Significantly, what is right is considered to be submission to the will of God.[6]

Universal and Holistic *sharīʿah*

As the introductory chapter showed, many contemporary interpretations of Islam make use of universalistic language; a rejection of 'culture' or 'ethnic' religious belonging is typically endorsed. Culture and religion are considered two different things, and Muslim practice is presented as distinct from Islam. This is an apparent interpretive strategy within this group as well. The image of Islam as a system that is holistic and complete, and therefore authentic, was stressed in several of the lectures I attended, and not only when the theme explicitly concerned jurisprudence. The teachers commonly spoke about Islam as a unique

5. See for example Lecture 2: Meaning of Life.
6. Lecture 2: Meaning of Life.

and universal religion for all of creation, with human beings being understood as the best of creations, on condition that they practice Islam:

> There is nothing good in this world apart from what Islam says is good. There is nothing bad in this world, if Allah did not warn us. This unique religion, that fits all people, all *jinn*, all times and places. This religion that calls people to develop into the highest and best of creations. Humans are, as you know, the best creation, but on condition that he practices Islam. So, we thank Allah *subhāna wa ta'āla* [Glorified and exalted be God] that has guided us to this religion.[7]

In one lecture the teacher stressed Islamic universality: 'There are so many proofs that Islam is the true religion. One example is that Islam suits all times and all places, and includes all aspects of our lives. No other religion does that!'[8] The emphasis here is on the miracle of the Qur'an, sent to the illiterate Muhammad, with a system that the teacher claims is also suitable today too. This is compared to human-made systems of law, which are regarded as defunct. The teacher explains that societies ruled by human-made systems are overrun with rapes and murders. A comparison is made with Saudi Arabia, which, so states the teacher, has less criminality than Sweden. The argument laid forth is that this is because Saudi Arabia follows an Islamic system, even though the country does not always implement it. The teacher laments on this, which he sees as illustrating a difference between Muslim practice and 'true' Islam: 'The system that works comes from the one who created us, who sent this system to us. That Muslims are not good at implementing it is another thing, but we will deal with that here [in this lecture]. This is a proof that this religion is from Allah.'[9] As another 'proof' of Islamic holism, the teacher mentions that *sharī'ah* covers people's spiritual needs, 'that which has to do with *rūh* [spirit]', while laws made by humans 'only concern bodily aspects'.[10] *Sharī'ah* is presented as nourishment for the human soul, brought to us from God through prophets, with the purpose of leading people to the worship of God. Studying God's will is held to bring more faith and an increase in piety, which is yet another motivation for studying:

7. Lecture 1: Steadfast.
8. Lectures: Jurisprudence.
9. Lectures: Jurisprudence.
10. Lectures: Jurisprudence.

The more you study Islam, the stronger your *īmān* will be. It is amazing!
This comes through studying and gaining knowledge. Islam is universal.
The last message is a message for the entire world, for all of humanity, for
all times and places, the most perfect and inclusive system. This is *sharī'ah!*[11]

As an expression of the universalist stance, jurisprudence, *fiqh*, is
discussed and presented as consisting of two main parts, namely (1)
rituals and related practices (*'ibādāt*), and (2) transactions between
people (*mu'amalāt*). In speaking about *mu'amalāt*, the teacher states that
there are rules about everything, and that these rules are highly detailed.
In his opinion, the detailed rules demonstrate that Islam is in accordance
with human nature and that it follows that it is important to adhere to
the will of God and not that of humans. In this respect, the teacher criticizes the rule against divorce in the Catholic Church as being against the
will of God: 'Allah knows better what is good for us than we know our
selves. When people start to decide things on their own, then it turns
out as it does... And we can see how bad it can become!'[12] The teacher
also refers to things he regards as positive in Islamic law, as compared
to 'the West'. Such differences include the esteemed role of Muslim
mothers, and how parents live with their children in Muslim countries.
Such things are directly contrasted with the 'Western' practice, thereby
elevating the position of the Islamic ideal.[13]

The teacher talks about differences between *'ibādāt* and *mu'amalāt*.
Considering *'ibādāt*, he argues that we must simply accept the rules.
The five daily prayers and the requisite bodily actions are held out as
an example. As the teacher states: 'We don't know why we should pray
exactly how we should. We should just do it!'[14] However, considering
mu'amalāt, he argues that we can understand the *reasons* behind the
rules, and he explains that the rules are reasonable based on justice:
'As for *mu'amalāt* it is understandable why the rules exist. Why we
should get married. Why interest is forbidden. Because it is unjust!'[15]
The teacher also argues that another difference between *'ibādāt* and
mu'amalāt can be found in the motivation laying behind deeds in these

11. Lectures: Jurisprudence.
12. Lectures: Jurisprudence. Marriage in Islam can be described as a social cono
    tract and divorce is allowed. Based on this view, he rejects the Catholic view
    on marriage as a sacrament.
13. Lectures: Jurisprudence.
14. Lectures: Jurisprudence.
15. Lectures: Jurisprudence.

two categories of action. When performing *'ibādāt*, the right intention (*niyyah*) is stressed, which is not really the case concerning *mu'amalāt*. Nevertheless, both actions are still important for an individual's relationship to God. 'Moreover, we need intention (*niyyah*) for rituals. But we don't need *niyyah* for trading, for example, but if you are honest [in *mu'amalāt*] you get closer to Allah. If you cheat in trading you get further away from him.'[16]

The teacher repeats that Islamic law is incumbent upon a Muslim. Acknowledging that not all people follow Islamic laws, which is particularly the case in non-Muslim countries, the teacher notes this is also the case in many Muslim-majority countries. He stresses that Muslims need to know the reasons behind this situation and to understand that following Islamic law is obligatory.[17]

> Muslims must follow Islam's law. What Allah revealed in the Qur'an and Sunnah. And we notice, when we live in a country like Sweden, that people don't follow the laws of Islam, but rather the jurisprudence that exists here, Swedish laws. [...] We can also note that even Muslim countries unfortunately follow laws taken from England and France for example. So, we as Muslims need to know *why* this is the case, what these laws are based on, and to know that the Islamic laws are better, more inclusive, and perfect, and that is what we Muslims should follow! And how we Muslims can regain Islamic rule to Muslim countries![18]

We should note that when the teacher speaks about the Islamic law, he does not equate it with the established rules in the juridical schools, but rather with revelation in the form of Qur'an and Sunnah. Moreover, in the above citation, we can see how he motivates the participants and confirms the superiority of Islamic law and how they through it can regain Islamic rule to Muslim countries, which seems to be an ultimate aim. Nevertheless, at present, the work is mainly done in the local group.

Human Laws vs. God's Laws

A distinction between religion and culture, or tradition, is also made regarding jurisprudence. Human-made laws are described as stemming from culture. According to the teacher in one lecture, '[T]his was the

16. Lectures: Jurisprudence.
17. Lectures: Jurisprudence.
18. Lectures: Jurisprudence. The attitude to Swedish laws is not explicitly commented upon in the material studied. Here we can note that the focus is on Muslim countries, not minority situations.

case in all times, that people followed the rules of the predecessors. [...] But they are not guided [by Allah].' The teacher refers to a verse: 'When it is said to them, "Follow what God has sent down", they say, "No! We shall follow what we found our fathers doing"—even though their fathers did not understand anything and were not (rightly) guided?' (Q 2:170). The teacher goes on to state: 'This is a big problem, that people follow their culture and traditions before Allah's revelation. This can be observed among non-Muslims but also among Muslims, unfortunately.'[19]

> Concerning what Allah has revealed, how to worship, things that concern *mu'amalāt*, then we follow what Allah has ordained! Not the tradition of a country! Only in some cases is that permissible, when it does not contradict Islam. [...] As Muslims, we should prioritize our love for Allah and his Prophet before everything else![20]

This citation shows that human-made laws are only acceptable when not in contradiction to the will of God. This is not elaborated upon further. Apart from such generalized comments, I encountered no detailed explanations of how participants should relate to Swedish laws.

Islamic law was compared with human-made laws, seemingly in order to prove that Islam is superior and to stress that human intellect and knowledge is limited.

> Why should we understand that *sharī'ah* is better to implement? Because it comes from Allah! [...] He is the only one with the right to create rules. People follow their lusts and political views. [...] Human intellect is flawed and people don't have the knowledge like Allah, the All-Knowing. [...] *Sharī'ah* promotes the good and forbids the bad. Human-made rules only think about this life, while *sharī'ah* also considers eternity. *Sharī'ah* has been steady and stable during a thousand years. *Sharī'ah* tells us how we should behave (*akhlāq*). It is more inclusive.[21]

Good *akhlāq*, it is maintained, *prevents* crime. Indeed, Islamic laws are considered to be preventive, proactive: 'Human-made laws allow things that lead to crime, for example alcohol. [...] Islam forbids those things that lead to crime.'[22] Moreover, Islamic rules 'raise people to fear Allah,

19. Lectures: Jurisprudence.
20. Lectures: Jurisprudence.
21. Lectures: Jurisprudence.
22. Lectures: Jurisprudence.

which leads you to take responsibility, even when other people don't see. Here, for example, you see people who cheat as soon as they get the chance.'[23]

The rejection of laws based on non-Islamic sources is frequently repeated. The teacher acknowledges that while many human-made rules may be based on Jewish or Christian sources, they also include rules that are faulty and non-Islamic. Seemingly a bit surprised, during one lecture the teacher explains:

> Even Muslim countries follow this, even though we have something much better! [...] This leads to chaos! A lot of disasters follow in countries with human-made laws! They *don't* lead to safety for its people! [... Even] when Muslims have a chance to follow the divine rules that will give them safety, they nevertheless choose different laws![24]

The teacher then repeats the rule that Muslims must follow the will of God and that Muslims shall neither enjoin in innovation on an individual level nor on a state level. 'We Muslims need to know that it is not allowed for us to rule with anything that is not revealed by Allah! This does not only concern how to rule a country, but how we behave and relate to each other! [...] It is not allowed to make our own laws, or make things up!'[25]

The teacher speaks about the great scientific achievements of the early community and how things then began to deteriorate successively. The reason given is that innovations began to spread among the early adherents of the religion—they did not practice the Sunnah, and instead sought guidance elsewhere. He explains that the Prophet said in each *khutbah* (preaching on Friday) that the most truthful speech is the Qur'an and that guidance is to be found in his Sunnah; each innovation is misguidance. Nevertheless, innovation occurred, he laments, and as a result the Muslims fragmented and hated each other. The *ummah* deteriorated:

> The *ummah* began to deteriorate and did no longer develop. They did not create new things that could benefit them. The *ummah* began to deteriorate step by step. [...] The Crusaders took over al-Andalus, which at this time was highly developed. [...] Another centre of knowledge and development was Baghdad that was taken by the Tatars who burnt the books [...]

---

23. Lectures: Jurisprudence.
24. Lectures: Jurisprudence.
25. Lectures: Jurisprudence.

and the *ummah* deteriorated even more, and those who helped them were Muslims [...] who hated *ahl al-sunnah*. [...] This led countries to colonize the Muslim *ummah*. [...] The Prophet said that this would happen in the future![26]

This is a description of what has caused the present situation, which the group attempts to remedy with its program of action. In this respect, the teacher explains what the authoritative sources are and what methods should be used to find out about God's will. The Qur'an and Sunnah serve as the foundation for people with knowledge to find out about God's will. Related to this, he also speaks about 'general rules' (he is likely intending *qiyās*) that may apply to things not explicitly mentioned in revelation. As a 'general rule', he argues that everything that is bad for people is forbidden, even if not explicitly mentioned in the sources, such as smoking. Here, the notions of 'general rules' or 'general proofs' are used to legitimate this opinion.

Smoking did not exist at the time of the Prophet. However, it is forbidden because it is bad for us. Even though it is not mentioned [in any textual source]. There are general proofs that show that it is forbidden. [...] The people of knowledge can tell if something is allowed or forbidden, even if it is not mentioned in the sources.[27]

In line with the view on authority, the opinions of the '*ulamā*' on what constitutes 'general proofs' are presented as authoritative. The thoughts of Muslims in general, and even the local teachers, are not important.

The official interpretation of Islam in the group can be described as 'traditionalist', based on the group's adherence to the view that 'true' knowledge can be derived only from revelation and consensus (*ijmā'*), not reason. The rejection of reason does not in practice mean that reason is completely refused; instead, this line of argumentation may be a part of the teachers' rhetoric. Reason, it should be noted, is not given any advantage over the sacred texts, which constitute the starting point and *the* sources and proofs of truth. The texts function as the basis of what the intellect may obtain.[28] In Binyamin Abrahamov's words, tradi-

---

26. Lecture 10: *ummah*. This refers to the Mongol invasion of Baghdad 1258, which was the end of the 'Abbasid Caliphate and often described as the end of the Islamic golden age. The Mongols destroyed libraries and sacked the city of Baghdad.
27. Lectures: Jurisprudence.
28. See also Abrahamov 1998, ix–x, 1.

tionalists 'do not altogether annul the function of reason in religion, but assign to it a secondary function, namely, to prove what has been revealed or transmitted, or to know how to perform the precepts.'[29]

A recurring framing motivation for change is the explanation of why the situation is so bad in many Muslim countries applying secular laws. With decreasing knowledge, adherence to and imitation of the jurisprudential schools (*taqlīd*), and, finally, the colonial era, divine rules were replaced with secular ones.[30]

> New things happen all the time and they need new rules. And the people who know can apply them according to the general rules, based on the Qur'an and Sunnah, so that it is just, and based on the spirit that they [the Qur'an and Sunnah] forward. We note that in many Muslim countries they do not rule according to this. What have Muslims done wrong to have caused this situation? We as Muslims are not happy with this situation. That they rule with foreign laws. This is what is called secularism, *al-'almāniyah*, to have other laws than the divine. This happened in Muslim countries until a lack of knowledge spread among Muslims and they could not deal with the new situations. This is called *taqlīd*. They stuck to old rules and regulations and could not apply the rules on the new situation. In this way, during colonialism, the Muslims began to apply other [secular] rules, so that bit by bit the divine laws were exchanged.[31]

Through such a view on history and explanation of the problematic situation today, the teacher asks rhetorically how the Muslims can change this situation. He rejects other groups, without giving examples, that claim that they want to rule in accordance with *sharī'ah*. This is, he argues, because they do not have knowledge, which he uses as an explanation for 'terrorism'. Thus, according to the teacher, it is not only secular (or human-made) laws that are to be rejected, but also faulty understandings of Islam, which may also lead to disastrous results. In the following citation, we also see that the teacher elevates the people of knowledge from what he calls *ahl al-sunnah*. As authoritative interpreters, they are to reject terrorism:

29.   Abrahamov 1998, 13.
30.   Lectures: Jurisprudence. This refers to the creation of nation-states and the implementation of secular laws, often based on, for example, the French constitution. These were often called *qanūn*, and subsequently *sharī'ah* was influential mainly in family laws.
31.   Lectures: Jurisprudence.

This leads them to do things based on what they themselves think and believe and this leads them to terrorism, to kill Muslims and non-Muslims, and this leads to chaos and leads Muslims further away from the divine rules. All this goes back to their unfathomable lack of knowledge, and that they do not have any contact with the people of knowledge from *ahl al-sunnah* and instead create their own groups with their own rulings and methods.[32]

The teacher rejects such groups, arguing that they only cause harm and lead people away from Islam. He also speaks of them as not being real Muslims; instead, they merely 'claim' to be:

They did not bring anything good to the Muslims. [...] We see the problems that are caused when people claim to be Muslims and practicing Muslims, when they begin to commit terrorist actions they scare people away from Islam and from being practicing Muslims, which leads to incredible problems.[33]

Thus, the teacher rejects the claims of the 'terrorists' to know the truth. He argues that their actions actually serve to scare people away from Islam, bringing about negative effects. Based on the teachers' pronouncement, the effects of an interpretation or action seem to be important. This follows the view on *manhaj*, where the *manhaj* seemingly must conform to the situation that Muslims are in.[34] The view on 'terrorism' will be returned to in Chapter 7, 'Constructing In-Group and Out-Group'.

Jurisprudence: Sources and Methods

The development of the juridical communities is thoroughly presented by the teacher in order to show that God completed religion with revelation and that what followed is the creation of jurists. Because of this view, the teacher criticizes those he calls the 'Orientalists' (without

32. Lectures: Jurisprudence.
33. Lectures: Jurisprudence.
34. Considering the developments in Egypt following the revolution in 2011, we can note how previous puritan Salafi groups activated themselves in the political process and the political party al-Nour was established. With this, Salafis turned into what Wictorowicz calls 'Politicos'. This development was due to the changing historical situation, one in which political participation suddenly became a possibility. See also de Koning 2012.

being more specific), who, he argues, claim that *fiqh* has developed throughout history, and states instead that the divine law was completed during the time of the Prophet.[35] What happened later is described as the work of the people of knowledge using 'general rules' or analogies:[36]

> We Muslims say that Allah completed his religion and what came there-after is what the people of knowledge have brought out through the means of general rules, or making analogies, *qiyās*. But the basis of it all was completed during the time of the Prophet. We don't have to remove something or add something, because the *sharī'ah* is totally perfect. Before the Prophet came to humanity, the humans were in a total darkness of polytheism and without faith, and they oppressed each other and humans committed all sorts of crimes [...]. We can compare to the Viking age here in Sweden [8th–12th century], a bit later than the Prophet's time, what a disgusting and horrible life they led! They attacked others in order to steal their money and they were unclean, oppressed each other and in this way the entire world lived! Barbarism! When the Prophet came with the light of Allah he spread the message from Allah [...] and oppression disap-peared. Crimes [too]. People learned how to be clean and behave towards others and everything else that came with Islam. And this led humanity to develop with discoveries, and Islam and Muslims laid the grounds for the European Renaissance that even the unfaithful acknowledges.[37]

We may note here that those speaking about *fiqh* refer to the devel-opment of jurisprudence, while the teacher intends the will of God. The teacher wishes to highlight that the will of God was revealed and that all that followed is human work. This can be compared to the rejection of human-made laws. The description of the development offers critical insight into why things went wrong, in his opinion.

The teacher speaks about how the advent of Islam made the world a better place: 'Before the Prophet came, only seven to ten people could read in Mecca. With the Prophet, Islam spread and caused people to leave *kufr* and *shirk* [...] with [the help of] the Qur'an and the Sunnah.'[38] The teacher goes on to speak about the historical context of revelation and shows a detailed knowledge of differences between verses from Mecca and Medina, and comparisons are made to earlier revelations in order to conclude that the Qur'an has not changed. The Qur'an is also

---

35. No names of Orientalists are presented.
36. Lectures: Jurisprudence.
37. Lectures: Jurisprudence.
38. Lectures: Jurisprudence.

compared to the Bible, and the fact that different versions of the Bible are used among Christian congregations.[39]

> The Qur'an that we hold today in our hands has not been changed even with a dot since the time of the Prophet and what Jibril [the angel Gabriel] brought down to him, as different from the Bible, where we can note the different groups which have different versions that differ from the original version and we cannot trust what is written therein. [...] We Muslims know that in the Qur'an and in the Sunnah everything is true![40]

The teacher also explains why the rulings from God came step-by-step, in the Qur'an *and* Sunnah. He gives the example of the increase in the number of daily prayers, the establishment of the various prostrations in prayer, as well as the ruling on alcohol. 'Because people at this time loved their alcohol, just like Swedes today, so it could be difficult for them to immediately leave alcohol'.[41] The explanation for this, then, is that God inserted rules successively in order to avoid making the human transition too difficult.[42]

The teacher speaks about the Sunnah as a revelation and explains how it differs from the Qur'an. He confirms the obligation to follow the teachings of both:

> The Sunnah is also a revelation and everything that the Prophet said is revelation in the same way as the Qur'an, but the difference is that the Qur'an is the word of Allah and the Sunnah is [the word] of the Prophet. And the difference is that reading the Qur'an gives '*ajr* [reward] for each letter you read to the reader, and you can read it in your prayers. But both are revelations from Allah and you must follow both. It is not the case as some say that what is in the Qur'an is obligatory and what is in the Sunnah is not. [...] One example is that in the Sunnah, when the Prophet said that the martyr will be forgiven for all his sins, and the person who heard that then asked Muhammad about it and he then said that it does not include debts, which Gabriel had just explained to him. This shows that the Sunnah is part of revelation as well.[43]

39. Lectures: Jurisprudence.
40. Lectures: Jurisprudence.
41. Lectures: Jurisprudence.
42. Lectures: Jurisprudence.
43. Lectures: Jurisprudence. This is also addressed by Fawzan, who claims that God forgives all sins except debt. 'This is because debt is a right of humans; and the right of a human being cannot be cancelled except by paying him or that he pardons it.' Fawzan 2012a, 347.

Considering proofs (*dalīl*), Fawzan's comments on *Sharh al-sunnah* are used. Fawzan refers to the three foundations of evidencing, as described by Barbahari. It is established that Muslims must comply with the *ahādīth*, since it is the second revelation after the Qur'an. The fundamentals of proof are described as (1) the Qur'an, (2) Sunnah and (3) the consensus of the scholars (*ijmā'*). 'These are the proofs.'[44] Fawzan differentiates between the Qur'an as the word of God and the Sunnah as the word of Muhammad, but states that its meaning is from God. The Sunnah is described as essential to the Qur'an, as it explains it and clarifies it.[45] Moreover, Fawzan repeatedly states that the Qur'an is more in need of the Sunnah than the Sunnah of the Qur'an. This, he claims, is because the Sunnah 'is the clarifier and interpreter of the Qur'an'.[46] However, the Sunnah and the Qur'an do not have exactly the same status as written word, since all *ahādīth* are not regarded as authentic, which the teacher elaborates upon:

> The Qur'an was preserved in memorization and written down and it is the same with Sunnah. The difference is that in Sunnah there are some weak *ahādīth*, because the chain of narrators is not strong. Some are authentic and the people of knowledge have explained this. But in the Qur'an everything is authentic. This was during the time of the Prophet. Then it was no problems because they could ask the Prophet so they did not have to disagree. After the Prophet died the *sahābah* lived and they were the ones to turn to with questions, because they had met the Prophet and learnt from him.[47]

This citation shows that the group regards the role of the *sahābah* as important and authoritative following the death of Muhammad.

Fawzan's views are also used when commenting on reason and having opinions. Fawzan rejects the use of opinion (*ra'ī*). 'The religion is not based on opinion. The religion is nothing but following (*ittibā'*). It is not based on opinion and analogy. [...] Rather, it is based on the revelation, revealed to the sent Prophet. This is the religion.'[48] He also explains *taqlīd*, which is of two forms, in his view. The one that is correct is held to be

---

44. Fawzan 2012a, 359.
45. Fawzan 2012a, 361.
46. Fawzan 2012a, 368. Fawzan gives the example that the Qur'an enjoins prayer, but that it is explained in the Sunnah, through the example of Muhammad.
47. Lectures: Jurisprudence.
48. Fawzan 2012b, 55. The word *ittibā'* has the same root as *tābi'ūn*, the 'followers' of the first generation. In Wehr, *ittibā'* is defined as 'following; pursuit (e.g., of a policy); adherence (to), compliance (with), observance (of)'.

taqlīd in the sense of 'following' or 'imitating' (*al-ittibā'*) and emulating the people of knowledge who follow the Sunnah. However, he rejects *taqlīd* in the sense of blind following (*taqlīd al-a'mā*), which is devoid of proof, in his opinion. People should stick with the 'saved group', those who follow the Sunnah, he argues.[49] This comment by Fawzan reveals his stance toward the juridical schools. Fawzan can be seen to accept 'following', or imitation (*al-ittibā'*), but not the blind imitation of the jurisprudential schools. People are encouraged to stick with the 'saved group' that follows the Sunnah. This is also the promoted opinion of the local group.

The Position of *sahābah* and *tābi'ūn*

The teacher refers to the straight path, *sirāt al-mustaqīm*, on which they ask to be guided each day (i.e. when reciting the opening chapter of the Qur'an), asking the participants what this path is, answering the question himself directly that it is what the Prophet said, namely to follow his Sunnah and the *sahābah*. 'This religion is one straight road! So, search for it! And follow it! May Allah make us become people who follow this road, and practice it!'[50] Following and practicing the straight path is explained as the means of obtaining stability and peace of mind. Those following the straight path will understand why there are such problems as war and death, and will know what the remedy is. True happiness and peace of mind can *only* be reached by means of a relationship with the creator, the teacher states.[51]

Regarding the *sahābah*, the teacher elaborates on their elevated position, and simultaneously rejects the Shi'ites as non-Muslims. This rejection is based on differences in the views on some of the early Muslims. As noted, the stress on the so-called pious forbearers is foundational in this group, and there is no acceptance of any other view, which is the reason to this attitude and the rejection of Shi'ites.

> The *sahābah* has a great position in the hearts of the *ahl al-sunnah*. They collected the Qur'an, they compiled it. So people such as the Shi'ites who speak badly about the *sahābah* and claim they were non-Muslims are very dangerous. It is very dangerous what they [Shi'ites] do because they speak badly about the people who brought us the Qur'an and Sunnah. If you do

49. Fawzan 2012b, 256–258. The notion of the saved group is returned to in the following chapter.
50. Lecture: 73 Sects: 3.
51. Lecture 2: Meaning of Life.

not trust the *sahābah*, you cannot trust the Qur'an and Sunnah and then the Muslim has no religion. As Abu Zura al-Razi said: the one who speaks badly about the followers of the Prophet is a *zindiq* [heretic], like a *munafiq* [hypocrite]. Because the Qur'an and Sunnah came through the *sahābah*.[52]

The *sahābah* are elevated since they met Muhammad in person. They are often presented as having had the same *'aqīdah*, which is brought up as an explanation of why opinions did not differ among them. This is often contrasted with the later juridical schools, where more differences can be observed. Having heard the Qur'an directly from Muhammad, and having seen how he acted, the *sahābah* have a unique status. However, differences among them *are* acknowledged, and the teacher puts effort into explaining the reasons for this, offering a line of thought that is also important for understanding the group's view on jurisprudence and the development of the juridical schools. Regarding disagreements among the *sahābah*, the teacher says:

> [Muhammad] was the best teacher and he was the teacher of the *sahābah*. Therefore there were not many disagreements among them in questions concerning *fiqh*. The differences were in, for example, if one should war against those who did not pay *zakāt* [obligatory taxes], as during the time of [the caliph] Abu Bakr. Some questions on inheritance. The reason behind the differences of opinions is that not all of them had heard all of the *ahādīth*. At the end, it was more than one hundred thousand *sahābah* and all of them did not hear everything. He [Muhammad] gave lessons, but some of them [*sahābah*] worked, went out on *jihād* et cetera, so they were not with the Prophet all of the time. Because of this, some *sahābah* knew more than others and it was easier for them to understand. Another reason is that they spread out to different regions that came under Islamic rule.[53]

During my time observing the group, I sensed that the teacher was aware that some participants either had not followed his line of argument, or were not fully convinced by it. Accordingly, he explained that he discussed the topic because he wanted the group members to understand the importance of agreement. His rationale was that when Muslims have the same *'aqīdah* and *manhaj*, and follow scripture and consensus, few disagreements arise. The teacher elaborated on how to avoid disagreements and mentioned that of the 130 or so *sahābah* who

52. Lectures: Jurisprudence. Al-Razi was a scholar of *ahādīth* from present-day Iran (ca 200/815–264/878).
53. Lectures: Jurisprudence.

issued *fatāwa*, seven from Medina stand out as *fuqahā'* (jurists) more skilled than the rest, having more knowledge. 'The reasons why we mention this is that when there are disagreements today, we should note that utterances from these seven people have an importance because they were among the most knowledgeable about *fiqh* and issued many *fatāwa*.'[54] The *sahābah* spread out geographically. There were also *tābi'ūn*, 'followers'—in the sense of being born after the death of the Prophet Muhammad—who were contemporary with the *sahābah* and their students. These followers also have an important position today in Salafi circles. One of the most important among them is Hasan al-Basri (642–728), who is said to have met more than 500 *sahābah*. During the time of the *tābi'ūn*, *ra'ī*, 'opinion', developed as a method. Importantly, *ra'ī* is rejected by the teacher. The teacher confirms the status of the *tābi'ūn* when mentioning that they continued to use analogies and consensus as method, yet he entirely rejects the method of *ra'ī*. In the following citation we can note his view that one either follows the 'truth', or belongs to a sect:[55]

> There is only '*qāla Allāh*' [God said] or '*qāla al-rasūl*' [the Prophet said]! So don't bring up this 'I think' or 'in my opinion'! This was how *tābi'ūn* argued, at the time when opinions grew. The *tābi'ūn* also saw different sects appear. In their time it was the Khawārij and the Shī'ah. Peoples' *'aqīdah* and *manhaj* began to scatter. Those who followed the Prophet are the *ahl al-sunnah wa al-jamā'ah*, they are the *sunnī* Muslims and then it was those who followed sects.[56]

The teacher mentions that some *sahābah* had memorized parts of Sunnah and then established themselves in a particular region or city and influenced its people on the basis of their knowledge. However, he informs the group that not all of *sahābah* knew the entirety of the *ahādīth*. This is explained as a reason for differences developing among the followers of the *sahābah*.[57]

54. Lectures: Jurisprudence. He also mentions 13 other very important *sahābah* who also produced many *fatāwa*, though not as many or as frequently as the seven. The first four caliphs are among these. I will not go into detail here or mention these people by name, but in the lectures the names of all of them were mentioned. Fawzan, in his commentary to *Sharh al-sunnah*, presents several of the names that were also mentioned in various lectures given by the group. See Fawzan 2012, 199–219.
55. Lectures: Jurisprudence.
56. Lectures: Jurisprudence.
57. Lectures: Jurisprudence.

During the time of the *tābi'ūn* the juridical schools began to divide in two. One was the *ahl al-hadīth*, the people who follow *ahādīth* strictly and keep away from opinions. They were in Medina. And then it was those who followed opinions, in Iraq. The four schools of law today must be understood from this background. That the Hanafi school follows opinions and differs from the other schools stems from the time of the *tābi'ūn* [...]. Those in Medina held strictly to *ahādīth*. In Kufa they accepted opinions more. More *sahābah* stayed in Medina and they had lessons in *ahādīth* and based their views on that. To Iraq, people came who lied about the Prophet and made up *ahādīth*. [...] Because of this, the people in Iraq did not know *ahādīth* as much as the people in Medina. [...] In Medina it was a huge amount of knowledgeable people. Some were famous and well-known. Especially *fuqahā' al-madina al-sab'a* [the seven jurists of Medina]. They are still the most important. When they agree upon something, it is considered strong opinion. They studied with *sahābah* in Medina.[58]

Following this, the teacher speaks about how collections of *ahādīth* were gathered, and how the caliph 'Umar (r. 634–644) ordered the writing down of *ahādīth*. The most authentic collection is said to be Bukhari's. The teacher compares Bukhari with a computer, in that he knew so many *ahādīth* by heart, as many others also did. The teacher adds:

Allah gave them this capability. They had a lot of *taqwā* [fear of God] so Allah made their hearts open to collect the *ahādīth* and not forget. This indicates that this religion is something that Allah has preserved. The *ahl al-hadīth* preserved this religion so that it could never be twisted. If a person in the East thought about doing it, the rest of the world could correct him because of this preservation. Compare this to Christians and their texts which they don't know if they are authentic. They don't even know who the people were that wrote the *injīl* [the Gospel]. This differs from Islam, because we know a lot about the people who collected the texts. When we read Bukhari it is like hearing the Prophet himself. He [Bukhari] also showed that 7563 *ahādīth* are authentic. There are some repetitions, but around 4000 are individual authentic *ahādīth*.[59]

58. Lectures: Jurisprudence. 'The seven jurists of Madinah' designates seven influ‌ential *hadīth*-transmitters in Madinah who also produced many *fatāwa*. A full consensus about the names has not been reached, but what is known is that they all lived during the second-century *hijrah* and were active in Madinah.

59. Lectures: Jurisprudence. The term denotes piety and dutifulness. See Lewisohn 2015.

It is within this historical situation that the juridical schools developed. In these, teachers in various locations gained in influence and specific schools gradually developed:

> Now we know that *ahādīth* collections were written down. At the same time the people of knowledge gave lessons. We know for example that al-Albani lectured in Jordan. Shaykh Muqbil in Yemen. Shaykh 'Uthaymin in Saudi Arabia. They all had students who took from their sayings. So, as in the old time there were also people of knowledge with students who wrote down their sayings and then juridical schools developed. [...] Their sayings were collected and schools developed.[60]

The teacher offers an outline of the historical situation of the juridical schools that seeks to equate 'true' Islam with the following of the *ahādīth*. He outlines two main strands regarding epistemology, wherein the main issue is the scope of reason. Medina is portrayed positively, based on the argument that the people there followed more *ahādīth* than others. They are therefore called *ahl al-hadīth*, which is also a concept used within the group I observed when referring to themselves. In the teacher's reasoning, Medina is compared with Iraq, where fewer *ahādīth* were known and no effort was made to add to their number. The teacher explains that the scholars in Iraq accepted more analogies and opinions, assigning them to the *ahl al-ra'ī*. The teacher mentions that they even spoke about things related to the future, something which he finds *totally* unnecessary, and he argues that this is a reason why the people of Iraq began to differ in opinions. As a comparison, he stresses that the *manhaj* of *ahl al-hadīth* was to follow the Qur'an and the Sunnah. If they did not find an answer in Scripture, he holds that they would look at the sayings of *sahābah* or *tābi'ūn,* and only after this make analogies, *qiyās*.[61] The teacher accuses the *ahl al-ra'ī* of making many mistakes because of their faulty view on proof. The teacher defines a proof as something that is written in revelation, or a saying of the *sahābah* or *tābi'ūn*. He states critically that in Iraq the *ahl al-ra'ī* argued that they needed opinions because there were not enough proofs. This is something the teacher is keen to discredit: 'Even though there are so many! Thousands of *ahādīth* exist! They also went against proofs with their opinions and argued and discussed the text of the Sunnah.'[62] This is again compared to the *ahl*

---

60. Lectures: Jurisprudence.
61. Lectures: Jurisprudence.
62. Lectures: Jurisprudence.

al-hadīth, who followed the example of the Prophet. Moreover, he refers to the Qur'an as proof of the authenticity of his opinion that people should accept what is written and avoid speculation:

> It is not for a believing man or a believing woman, when God and His messenger have decided a matter, to have the choice in their matter. Whoever disobeys God and His messenger has very clearly gone astray. (Q 33:36)[63]

The teacher mentions the group known as the Dhahiriya,[64] who followed the Qur'an literally as a response to the *ahl al-ra'ī*. Yet, the teacher argues, it was difficult for them since they did not use analogies. Interestingly, it is in his criticism of Dhahiriya that the teacher's view on how to understand revealed text appears: '[the Dhahiriya] thought that the rules in the Qur'an do not hold a specific wisdom behind them. We from *ahl al-sunnah* believe that there is wisdom behind everything that Allah has ruled. [...] Either we know this wisdom or not. Allah is *al-hakīm*, the All-Knowing.' The teacher apparently holds that this kind of literal stance of accepting the Qur'an alone is not only inefficient but also wrong, and it shows the need for analogies in some cases. He mentions, for example, that we should not, according to the Qur'an, say 'Uff!' to our parents. While the Dhahiriya understood this 'proof' as referring to juvenile insolence, the teacher explains that the *meaning* of the verse must be expanded, and understood to mean that general mistreatment of one's parents is not acceptable. Between these 'extremes' there is a 'middle way', he argues, which is the Islam that he promotes, that of the people of Sunnah: '*Ahl al-sunnah* is a way in the middle! This is the correct way!'[65]

The Founders of the Juridical Communities

As the introductory chapter showed, there are many who comment upon and make use of the juridical schools. Some reject the authority of the schools, while still devoting considerable time and effort to

---

63. Lectures: Jurisprudence.
64. The jurist Dawud ibn Khalaf al-Dhahiri (d. 883) is usually regarded to be the founder. The main idea is that that which is manifest or apparent (*dhāhir*) in the texts of the Qur'an and the Sunnah is the only thing that is important and constitutes all that is necessary. All speculation should therefore be avoided. Thus, they reject metaphorical reading and methods such as analogy, *qiyās*.
65. Lectures: Jurisprudence.

explaining why this is so. Despite the rejection of the juridical schools, it is often the case that highly respectful tones are used when speaking about the founders. This was the case within the local group I observed. While the teacher comments on the differences between the four Sunni juridical schools, it is notable—though, considering the group's opinion of Shi'ites, not surprising—that the teacher never mentions the Shi'ite school.[66] He asks a rhetorical question: 'Why do they [i.e. the schools] differ when the Qur'an is one and the Sunnah is one?'[67] He repeats some historical information of the multitude of schools developing and only these four remaining. The teacher introduces those scholars who are seen as 'founders' of the four Sunni juridical schools, which is interesting since it sheds clear light on the opinion of this particular group concerning sources and jurisprudence. He begins with Abu Hanifa (80–150AH) from Baghdad. While Abu Hanifa lived during the time of many *sahābah*, the fact that he never met them means that he is counted as coming after the *tābi'ūn*. Abu Hanifa had many students, among the most famous being Abu Yusuf (d. 798) and Muhammad ibn Hassan al-Shaybani (d. 805), who collected Abu Hanifa's views on *fiqh*. The teacher gives the example that Abu Yusuf did not think Muslims should lift their hands after prayer as Muhammad did, since Abu Hanifa did not do that. The teacher states that this is very dangerous reasoning and argues that it most likely stems from their lack of knowledge of authentic *ahādīth* concerning this topic. The authentic *ahādīth* should be imitated, not an imam, he states. 'We shall follow the authentic and not what somebody else says!'[68] To prove his point, he again refers to the Q 33:36 (see above) and Q 4:65, referring to the importance of Muhammad: 'But no! By your Lord! They will not believe until they make you judge concerning their disputes. Then they would have no difficulty with what you decided, and would submit (in full) submission.' In his rejection of imitation (*taqlīd*), the teacher argues: 'It is not up to us to follow a specific imam, if he differs from what the Prophet has said'.[69] He speaks positively about the founders, but states that we shall follow the Sunnah.

66. They do not spare their words when speaking about Shi'ites, calling them all sorts of things, such as 'creeps', as the next chapter will illustrate further.
67. Lectures: Jurisprudence.
68. Lectures: Jurisprudence.
69. Lectures: Jurisprudence.

> So, we can without doubt gain a lot and learn a lot from the imams, but
> if something contradicts the Sunnah we shall not follow them. All imams
> said that if this happens, they should follow the Sunnah. If we know about
> a confirmed *hadīth*, this is what we shall follow.[70]

Although Abu Hanifa is praised and his school viewed positively for
following the Qur'an and Sunnah, including the sayings of the *sahābah*—
practices that the teacher promotes to the group I observed—he is
nevertheless critical of how the school today is somewhat selective in its
use of the Sunnah. He notes, in particular, that in relation to the *ahādīth*,
the school refuses to follow the *ahād hadīth*,[71] choosing instead to rely
on their own opinion or analogy as method. He also claims that perhaps
many *sahābah* knew the *hadīth*, which is now considered to be *ahād*, but
did not report it. This juridical school is widespread even today, the
teacher tells the participants, due to Abu Yusuf, who was an 'Abbasid
judge who required that other judges were Hanafites as well.[72]

Malik ibn Anas (95–179AH) is also discussed by the teacher. He was
related to the Prophet and came from a family of knowledge. Malik
was the teacher of al-Shafi'i (150–204AH/767–820) and Ahmad ibn
Hanbal, and many of his students collected *ahādīth*. These students also
preserved Malik's own book, *al-Muwatta'*. Malik followed the Qur'an, the
Sunnah, and the *sahābah*. However, the teacher criticizes him for also
using the *'amal ahl al-Madīnah*, the practice of the people of Medina.
This, according to the teacher, caused him to make faulty rulings. He
remarks critically that Malik's view was that the people of Medina must
have possessed the most knowledge about the Prophet, and he therefore
followed them even when a *hadīth* said something different. If the
people there agreed, Malik considered it to be the consensus (*ijmā'*). The
problem, according to the teacher, is that some *sahābah* who travelled to
distant places had memorized *ahādīth* that the people in Medina did not
know, which makes this method wrong.

The Shafi'i school stems from al-Shafi'i, who is described positively.
He is known to have been very clever, with a brilliant memory. The
teacher mentions that al-Shafi'i had memorized *al-Muwatta'* when he

---

70. Lectures: Jurisprudence.
71. An *ahād hadīth* is not *mutawātir*. A *mutawātir*, 'successive', *hadīth* refers to a
    hadīth with numerous narrators, which renders it authentic. Concerning *ahād*
    hadīth this is not the case. The number of narrators is not considered sufficient
    to define it as *mutawātir*.
72. This follows Fawzan, who criticizes this in Fawzan 2012b, 106–107.

was just 10 years old, and that by the age of 15 he had begun to give his own *fatāwa*. The teacher criticizes the fragmentation of interpretations when he tells the participants that some young people today misunderstand the example set by al-Shafi'i and other young and respected teachers, such as ibn Taymiyah (1263–1328), who pronounced his first *fatāwa* at 17. Modern-day youngsters, the teacher warns, should not equate on-line browsing with the learned scholarship of the Qur'an and Sunnah. Such individuals are surely misguided in their belief that they rank among the *'ulamā'*, and they should desist in trying to issue their own *fatāwa*. The teacher, in a rather patronizing tone of voice, says that he has had many discussions with such youths. Noting that these youngsters typically know no Arabic—only how to use Google—the teacher suggests that perhaps they should slow down, since they have *totally* misunderstood things.[73]

After praising Shafi'i's skills and knowledge and informing about his life and travels, the teacher tells the participants that it is his later work that is correct, not his early work. He explains that Shafi'i's early work was written in Baghdad, at a time when he possessed somewhat less knowledge. Fuller knowledge, the teacher opines, was gained later, in Egypt, where he learnt new *ahādīth*. This increased knowledge led to Shafi'i changing his mind on certain subjects. Shafi'i's book on law, *al-Risālah*, is praised, as is his following of the Qur'an and Sunnah and his limited use of analogies. 'Different from Abu Hanifa he did not often use analogy, only in cases of emergency. It is like eating rotten meat. It is only allowed in times of emergency.'[74]

Ahmad ibn Hanbal (164–241AH) from Baghdad is, based on the teacher's pronouncements, held in high esteem and is clearly the most respected of the founders. The teacher informs the participants that ibn Hanbal, just like Bukhari, was raised by his mother. In the teacher's view, mothers clearly have an important and formative role in the raising of children. Should mothers shirk their responsibilities, the teacher warns, their children are likely to hang around street corners, destined to become involved in criminality. Ibn Hanbal, who is often referred to as Imam Ahmad, is also called *imām ahl al-sunnah*, the leader of the people of Sunnah. The teacher informs the participants that ibn Hanbal not only memorized a huge amount of *ahādīth*, but also practiced them, which is clearly an ideal the teacher wants to promote. The teacher

---

73. Lectures: Jurisprudence.
74. Lectures: Jurisprudence.

talks about how the inquisition (*mihnah*) spread during the time of ibn Hanbal. The *mihnah*, and its official dogma of the created Qur'an, are considered by the teacher to be an expression of idolatry.[75]

> Different sects developed. For example that the Qur'an is created. This is *kufr*, as the people of knowledge have explained. The caliph al-Ma'mun loved Greek philosophy, and opened *dar al-hikmah* to translate books.[76] He was influenced by philosophy and did not follow the Sunnah. And he was influenced by sects such as this one. Mu'tazilah and Jahmiya. He forced people to say that the Qur'an was created. [...] Imam Ahmad refused to obey and was punished. [...] [The caliph] Mutawakkil believed Imam Ahmad and allowed him to go and removed this obligation to conform to the dogma [of the created Qur'an].[77]

Ibn Hanbal is described as giving victory to Islam at a time when Muslims were weak. The teacher stresses that his school followed the Qur'an, Sunnah, and the sayings of the *sahabah* and that ibn Hanbal refrained from personal opinions. In the event that the *sahabah* espoused different opinions, the teacher says that ibn Hanbal would choose the one closest to the Qur'an and Sunnah.[78] Moreover, the teacher mentions that although ibn Hanbal disapproved of people writing his opinions down, they were nevertheless gathered in *al-Jami'* after his death. Seemingly with admiration, the teacher says that, today, this school is, in terms of geography, the least spread out. The teacher makes clear that is down to the fact that ibn Hanbal's students refused to be judges—they did not 'sell out'. This view can be contrasted to the comment, noted above, about the Hanafi School being the most widely dispersed.

75. The *mihnah* is often translated 'inquisition' since it refers to a period in which the 'Abbasid caliph al-Ma'mun (r. 813–833) persecuted those who did not agree to the Mu'tazili doctrine regarding the created Qur'an. The *mihnah* took place from 833 and was abolished during the reign of the caliph al-Mutawakkil (r. 847–861).

76. This refers to the medieval *bayt al-hikmah*, 'house of wisdom', established in 'Abbasid Baghdad, an institute of translation and knowledge influenced by Hellenistic ideas.

77. Lectures: Jurisprudence. The term Jahmiya is used pejoratively, referring to theological ideas attributed to Jahm bin Safwan (d. 746), which in many respects were similar to that of Mu'tazilite ideas concerning the attributes of God and the createdness of the Qur'an.

78. *Al-athar* usually refers to a narration attributed to a *sahabah*.

The teacher refers positively to Ibn 'Abd al-Wahhab (1703–1792) and his *da'wah* (mission) in Najd, which led to the development of what we now call Wahhabism.[79] The teacher mentions that this mission led to a revival of the Hanbali School and with that the spread of books written by famous Hanbalis, such as Ibn Taymiyah and his student ibn al-Qayyim al-Jawziya (1292–1350). The teacher mentions that many recent *'ulamā'* began their studies in the Hanbali School, for example bin Baz (1910–1999) and 'Uthaymin (1925–2001)—figures who are also considered authorities within the group I observed. It is also the case that the teachers of the Swedish group have studied, or continue to study, in Hanbali institutions.

Final Comments

Following this presentation, we can state that the group seeks to distance itself from the juridical schools. This follows the rejection of human-made laws and the weight laid on adherence to the will of God. The will of God is seen as bringing about a holistic, perfect, and universal system. Nevertheless, it is not spread among humans, for various reasons—such as people being materialistic, and too occupied with 'this world' (*dunya*) instead of the Hereafter. The imitation of the *madhāhib* (*taqlīd*) is rejected because one should not seek to imitate a person, that is, to seek to equal innovation. One should only imitate Muhammad and the early generations, based on revelation. Simultaneously, we can note that the founders of the juridical schools are not spoken badly of. The development of jurisprudence into schools is explained through a historical contextualization whereby the teachers show the participants the reasons behind the development of the faulty doctrine of *taqlīd* and disagreements among the founders. The group does not advocate *ijtihād* in the sense of individual reasoning. Rather, they require reform through a return to the revelatory sources, the Qur'an and Sunnah, and a literal understanding—and practice—of the texts, based on the authority of the selected *'ulamā'*. Moreover, they wish to limit the use of analogy, though, as the above discussion has hopefully shown, it is regarded as necessary in some cases. This was illustrated by the prohibition against smoking, even though smoking is not mentioned in any of the sources. As we noted, the smoking prohibition, like others, is based

---

79. The term Wahhabism is an outsider term. The term *muwahhidūn*, 'unitarians', is often used by adherents, stressing the faith in one God. See for example al-Fahad 2004, 487 note 6.

on what are called 'general proofs'.[80] The teacher argues that smoking is bad for us and, as a general rule, we must avoid what is bad for us. Hence, the group rejects imitation of the juridical schools (*taqlīd*), but retains what is considered good in them. Imitation is advocated, but only that of the Sunnah of Muhammad and the pious predecessors (*ittibāʿ*). This thus represents an important difference from the Wahhabi stance, where the Hanbali School is considered normative. The call for a strict adherence to Sunnah makes the teachers repeat the importance of being part of *ahl al-sunnah*. This comes with a rejection of the use of opinion (*raʾī*). As a conclusion, we can note that the group does not reject the juridical schools categorically, but rather refutes them, or questions them, with respect, and retains that which is considered good and in line with the Sunnah, as they understand it. No explicit comments are made concerning obligations to follow national laws, but it becomes clear that they hold that *sharīʿah* should be followed.

Moving now from a theoretical understanding pertaining to sources and interpretations, in the following chapter we will focus more on action, related to *manhaj* and the call to Islam, *daʿwah*.

---

80. That smoking is prohibited is commonly agreed upon among Salafis. There are a number of scholars who have written *fatāwa* to legitimate the opinion that it is forbidden, for example Bin Baz. See for example a *fatwa* entitled 'Ruling on smoking and using hookah' by Bin Baz.

Da'wah—The Call to Islam

Contemporary Islamic piety movements often organize as *da'wah* groups. Several Muslim groups and individuals argue that their activities are a part of *da'wah*, in the sense of spreading information about Islam. The local group I observed ranks among these. Activities are directed to the Muslim in-group in many cases, but there are also more public displays of activism noticeable nowadays. The activities can be directed to all kinds of people, Muslims and non-Muslims alike. A well-known international *da'wah* group is, for example, the Tablighi movement, which is active internationally.[1] The word *tablīgh* means 'increase' and is used here in the sense of increasing the amount of people with Islamic faith and strengthening a Muslim identity. Professor of History Barbara D. Metcalf's research on the Tablighi in America and Europe shows how the group creates a Muslim space in a Diaspora setting:

> Tabligh can be seen as one response, that of drawing boundaries and reasserting absolute truth, in the context of the pluralism engendered by our increasingly integrated global society and ever more intrusive modern states. [...] Tabligh ideology gives participants in the diaspora a powerful script unlike those the dominant society offers—they are reliving Medina and they are concretely blessed. In embracing that picture, the space they inhabit becomes their own.[2]

Individuals also reach out and engage in public space, trying to attract new converts. In Germany, for example, an ex-boxer convert to Islam, Pierre Vogel, advocates street *da'wah* and draws large crowds—and, of course, media coverage. On his eponymous website, Vogel states that

---

1. Sikand 1988. The Tablighis are rejected by the local group. See further the discussion on in-group and out-group in the following chapter. See also Fawzan 2012b, 241–242 for his rejection of Tablighi, used in the group.
2. Metcalf 1996, 124.

neither mosque nor organization is needed for participation in street *da'wah*. Instead, Vogel advocates spontaneously outreach to the worst parts of one's city and the distribution of *da'wah* material.[3]

Internationally, *da'wah*-groups are becoming more vocal, inspiring others to perform similar activities. Engagement in *da'wah* is becoming more commonplace in both Muslim congregations and in less well-organized and informal groups. Individuals are also increasingly active in *da'wah*. The activities range from the dissemination of information in the form of booklets, websites and lectures, as well as giving active street *da'wah*.

This chapter will initially discuss the term *da'wah* and various understandings of it, and then proceed to outline what it entails in the local group.

Views on *da'wah*

It is certainly not the case that all who seek to spread Islam by means of *da'wah* activities are Islamic scholars, *'ulamā'*. Indeed, many of those engaged in *da'wah* lack an Islamic education. In the contemporary setting, anyone can function as a *dā'ī*, a caller, and there are no explicit, agreed-upon rules that can be used to decide who is legitimate or not. The title *dā'ī* is in most cases a self-designation, and often a means of circumventing criticism when talking about Islam without having the 'right' position or education. That is, a *dā'ī* may be a person who is not claiming to be a part of the *'ulamā'*, but one merely seeking to spread information about Islam.[4] A *dā'ī* designates a person calling or inviting people to Islam, and high moral standards are usually explicitly required.[5]

---

3.   'Du kannst völlig selbstständig und spontan in die schlimmsten Viertel deiner Stadt gehen um die Menschen mit verschiedenen Dawah Materialien zu beschenken.' See his website http: //www.pierrevogel.de/ for more information, accessed November 5, 2012.

4.   Olsson 2015a.

5.   Many things have traditionally been demanded of the *du'āt*: (1) virtue of sincerity, *ikhlās*; (2) knowledge of the topic discussed (Q 12:108); (3) imitation of the behaviour of Muhammad, i.e. following his example (Sunnah), which includes characteristics such as patience and tolerance, referring to the Qur'ān (Q 3:159; 16:125; 20:44). Moreover, they should also practice what they teach. See van Doorn-Harder 2006, 221. The called for character traits of *du'āt* appear on most websites; see for example the above-mentioned website of Pierre Vogel, where such an outline is presented.

The term *da'wah* literally means 'call' or 'invitation' to Islam, and among Muslims the translation 'mission' is often avoided. The increase of *da'wah* activities is connected with societal changes at large. The secularization of Muslim societies has provided fertile ground for *da'wah* work, and Muslims living as minorities perform *da'wah* in order to inform the non-Muslim surrounding society about Islam as well as to gather those already identifying themselves as Muslim, returning them to what is perceived as the straight path. *Da'wah* is a multifaceted word, the meaning of which can be somewhat fluid. In spite of the general tendency, just noted, to avoid rendering the word as 'mission', such a translation certainly seems permissible, considering how various groups explain what it means in practice, where targeting non-Muslims for conversion is often an explicit goal.[6]

Groups engaged in *da'wah* may be considered to form part of a larger, unorganized piety movement. While they are most often not explicitly political, the activities of the groups may nevertheless have political effects. There may be a focus on the conception of the self and *moral agency*. While it is possible to analyze the actions of such groups as the result of a deliberate decision to opt for some kind of subordination, seen from the inside it is rather regarded as an expression of autonomy of the subject, where the individuals strive to realize religious piety in their everyday lives. From one analytical angle, this may be seen as an expression of resistance to the surrounding society, or of things 'Western'. *Da'wah* 'has increasingly become a space for the articulation of a contestatory Islamic discourse on state and society',[7] argues anthropologist Charles Hirschkind. *Da'wah* often unfolds as an individual practice aimed at improving the morality of the wider community in which the individual lives, and such moral reform is connected to public activism. *Da'wah* can entail social and educational services and organizations that attempt to spread information about Islam. The spreading of information can take place in the streets, in lectures, as well as online. The aim, typically, is to perfect society as a whole and gain more converts to Islam. As illustrated above, similar strategies appear among European groups and individuals who advocate *da'wah*.

Muslims are spread around the globe, with many living within minority groups. There are many who regard this global situation as an opportunity to renew Islam and gain converts in new areas. Muslims live and teach Islam in various ways and address the past from different

6.   Olsson 2012.
7.   Hirschkind 2005, 32.

perspectives, creating new strategies for coping with new situations. Often, the Islamic past and Islamic sources are used to legitimize new attitudes and practices. And, as Talal Asad stresses, rituals are produced in new circumstances—they are not mere repetitions of past forms.[8]

The use of the term *da'wah* to legitimize proselytizing practices makes it possible for the in-group to view the various activities as authentic Islamic practice. Connecting verses from the Qur'ān and *hadīth*-material recording the practices of Muhammad adds legitimacy to the callers and their activities; the callers can claim to represent and perform authentic Islam.

Da'wah activities often transgress the boundaries between public and private, boundaries which become more visible within secular surroundings where Muslims are a minority. *Da'wah* is not confined to mosques and appears in public spaces in various ways—for example, actively in street *da'wah*, or merely passively by dressing in what is regarded as correct Sunni style. Those who give *da'wah* in a sense re-politicize private issues, making them public, as a consequence of their wish to Islamize society or to create a society permitting Islamic virtues to be practiced. Charles Hirschkind, who studied *da'wah* movements in Egypt, regards such groups as constituting a counter-public element, as something standing apart from civil society.

> While in practice *da'wa* may entail an oppositional stance regarding the state [...], this type of public does not in its present form play a mediatory role between *state* and *society*. In other words, the practice of *da'wa* does not take place within, nor does it serve to uphold, that domain of associational life referred to as civil society. While the nation inhabits the *da'iya's* [caller's] discourse as a necessary object of reflexive self-identification, it is as an object embedded in (and subordinate to) the broader moral project of an Islamic *umma*. As performatively enacted within *da'wa* discourse, the nation's claims on loyalty and identity are relativized in light of the demands of this moral project, one understood to be irreducible to the concepts of territory, ethnicity, and collective historical experience upon which the nation is founded.[9]

Many groups present an Islam that in several respects is set apart from other religious traditions prevalent in contemporary Sweden. The groups must overcome common accusations and Islamophobic rhetoric

---

8.   See Roy 2004; Martin and Barzegar 2010, 185, 194; Asad 1986, 15.
9.   Hirschkind 2005, 43.

against Islam and Muslims, views that are ever more widespread in the media and among growing right-wing political movements. Such attacks are mainly related to the perceived connection between Islam, violence, and the oppression of women.

The *da'wah* activities seek to show Muslims as profoundly moral, as individuals guided by a Sunni-oriented interpretation. Among other things, the *da'wah* activities present Islam as an inherently non-violent religion. Moreover, individuals are often invited to find out things for themselves, free from the influence of Islamic authorities or the media image of Islam and Muslims. As regards moral behaviour, Muhammad is cast as the main role model. Islam is presented as something more than mere inner faith, since faith should be expressed in the very actions of Muslims. Importantly, these actions are guided by the example of Muhammad himself.[10]

Discussed already in Chapter 3, it is helpful here to recall the observations made by Jocelyne Cesari regarding Salafi Islam. As Cesari notes, many groups can be seen to show similarities to Salafism. Further, as the Salafi discourse gains influence in Europe and serves to affect minority Muslim communities—in particular the opinion about what it means to be a 'good Muslim'—this in turn affects groups engaging in *da'wah* activities.[11] Importantly, the influence of Salafism does not necessarily include a stance against the juridical schools, nor a clearly defined Salafi approach to the sources or methods of interpretation. In some sense, the influence of Salafi Islam may be considered subtle, nuanced, and perhaps even adaptive to local contexts. This may explain how a gender-conservative ideology can easily combine with a view of Islam as logical, as having been proven to be divine by science, a view that is observable in some groups. That different interpretative stances are held on a given topic must not necessarily be a problem to those advocating them, but may indicate that we need to be more careful in our application of typologies and terminology. In the history of religions, the identification of contradictions within a religious interpretation is nothing new. Neverthless, it never ceases to awaken the curiosity of scholars.[12]

---

10.   Olsson 2015a.
11.   See Cesari 2005.
12.   See Olsson 2012. With this, I do not wish to claim that some groups are 'more Salafi' than others. I merely wish to illustrate the differences between groups, and that in some groups there is a clearer demand to follow the sources strictly. This was as outlined in Chapter 3, on Salafi Islam.

Becoming Steadfast

Let there be (one) community of you, calling (people) to good, and commanding right and forbidding wrong. Those—they are the ones who prosper. (Q 3:104)

Returning to the participants of the group that is the focus of this study, it can be said that they seem to view their particular historical situation in Sweden as a problem. Notably, they appear concerned by the lack of authentic knowledge of Islam and the failure of some Muslims to engage in authentic practice. Due to this, the group is engaged in the development of a program of action aimed at showing clearly how to live an authentic Muslim life, and how to influence society at large in order to move it in the direction of the straight path. This is seen as a critically important intervention in today's world in general, and one that is particularly needed in what is perceived to be an immoral Sweden. One of the main strategies is the perfomance of *da'wah*, which is understood as valuable action that serves to improve society, transforming it into a more virtuous one. The significance of the term *da'wah* is illustrated in several lectures, many of which include recommendations of how individuals constantly can perform *da'wah* in their daily lives. Significantly, the group I observed make use of Fawzan's ideas concerning *da'wah*, who uses the expression 'commanding good and forbidding wrong' as a call to motivation. According to Fawzan, *da'wah* should be done with the hands if possible (i.e. be visible in physical actions), or else be expressed in words. Lastly, it should be found in the heart. This last aspect seems to legitimate segregation: 'So forbid it with your heart, withdraw from the gatherings of evil and its people; do not sit with them in order to save yourself'.[13]

The foundational aspect of *da'wah*, as it is promoted in the group, is for members to begin striving for it within themselves, in order to become steadfast Muslims. A person can give proper *da'wah* only when he or she is being steadfast. For this reason, being steadfast is a theme that is constantly brought up, a reminder of the importance of always following the rules and behaving according to the Sunnah. In several lectures, the teacher repeatedly states that we have to leave our bad company behind in order to change our lives and to be steadfast in Islam. Those wishing to be good Muslims cannot 'hang around' with bad people. Bad people are described as those who take drugs, go to discos, waste time in the city centre, and people who drink alcohol. The teacher recommends a change of friends, notably with a reference to a *hadīth*.[14]

13. Fawzan 2012b, 170.
14. Lecture 2: Meaning of Life.

You must change your friends! That is a fact. You have to take this step. If you have bad friends, I am sorry... *Hamdulillah*, there are many nice brothers that you can be with instead. And sisters. Change your friends! As the Prophet *sas* said: a person is like the religion of his friend. [...] *al-ṣāhib sāhib*. A friend pulls. As the Prophet *sas* said: A good friend is like the perfume seller. Either you will buy perfume or he will offer you some. At least, you will smell good. You will be affected by good people. The bad company is like the smith. He will either burn your clothes, since sparks will jump around, or you will get the smoke on you and smell disgusting.[15]

This is also reflected in Fawzan's commentary on *Sharh al-sunnah*, which includes several headings of the 'Warning against sitting with the people of...' variety. The importance of choosing the right company is returned to in the group in discussions on marriage, where the teacher stresses the need to choose a partner based on religion and character, a person needs to have 'good *dīn* and good *khuluq*', religion and character. This teaching applies to both men and women and, importantly, is based on Muhammad's example.[16]

The teacher tells members of the group that when Muslims came to new areas in early history they did not have to force people to convert to Islam. Simply by watching the Muslims, the *sahābah* and the *tābi'ūn*, people came to accept Islam. It is hard not to see such teachings as directly targeted, as a strategy intended to inspire a local group that finds itself living in a minority situation. By means of a rhetorical question, the teacher asks the participants how Muslims could come so far in so short a time, presenting their actions as a remedy to the present situation:

15. Lecture 2: Meaning of Life. This particular *hadīth* was retold in several lectures. It was also mentioned by Fawzan 2012b, 125 (referring to Bukhari 2/741, 1995 and Muslim 4/2026, 2628), and related to the advice of not sitting with people of theological rhetoric. Fawzan also demands that people should sit only with scholars. 'If you sit with them, then you are like then. So one should beware of sitting with evil people and scholars of misguidance. He should stick to sitting with the people of knowledge, people of sound *'aqīdah* and correct *Manhaj*. He should sit with them and benefit from them.' Fawzan 2012b, 128. Fawzan also rejects Sufis who, in his explanation of Barbahari's saying, 'Beware of sitting with those who invite to desires and (lustful) love', are defined as Sufis, who are also accused of committing homosexuality, *zinā'*, and gazing at unlawful things. Fawzan 2012b, 131–135. In this citation, an emphatic letter is added in order to differentiate between the words in transcription, which would otherwise look identical.
16. Lecture 5: Family.

The *sahābah* and their students stuck to what the Prophet said. They implemented it in their lives and lived and died for his message. They managed to build this amazing society with knowledge about *tafsīr* [Qur'an commentary] and the Sunnah. [...] They were ready to sacrifice and do what they could to implement his message in their own lives and they then got success. They did not only correct their religion, they also corrected their *dunya*, their worldly lives.[17]

The teacher further emphasizes the future success of Islam, referring to the Sunnah where Muhammad said that God showed him East and West and that his *ummah* would own all of it.[18] To emphasize even further, the teacher refers to a *hadīth* where Muhammad said that Islam will reach every place that night and day have reached since God will not leave a single house without bringing Islam into it.[19] Such narratives seem to be used to bring hope to those listening, and to motivate members of the group to adapt their lives according to the teachings. To underline the future success of Islam, the teacher informs the participants that Islam is the most rapidly growing religion today. However, the contemporary world is described as being in a state of *fitnah* (upheaval) and *ghurbah* (separation), where religion is considered as something strange and where temptation is ever present. This, the teacher argues, means that we must care about the things that make us strong in faith and obey God, and keep away from sins.[20] To do this, the teacher highlights the importance of the scriptures and the biographies of the Prophet and the pious predecessors: 'The sources that will make us steadfast in Islam is the book of Allah, the *sunnah* of his Prophet, and his *sīrah* [biography], *sas*, and the *sīrah* of the *salaf al-sālih*, their lives. The stories about their lives.'[21]

An important aspect is the acceptance of the righteous predecessors as role models. This appears to have an important function as a strategy helping to delineate the in-group and define *da'wah*. This is reflected in the insistence on the choosing of good friends and the withdrawal from others: 'And to spend time with *al-sālihīn*, the righteous people who care about Islam. *Al-sālihīn* are described as people who give good advice (*nasīhah*) and follow the Sunnah of the Prophet.'[22] The teacher admonishes the participants that they should stay away not only from

17. Lecture 10: *ummah*.
18. Lecture 1: Steadfast.
19. Lecture 1: Steadfast.
20. Lecture 1: Steadfast.
21. Lecture 1: Steadfast.
22. Lecture 1: Steadfast.

non-Muslims, but also non-practicing Muslims.[23] The argument is that members will be affected by their friends no matter how strong they think they are. Prophetic narratives are brought up as evidence, notably the example of Muhammad saying that there are people who possess the keys to good, and who close off the roads to evil, while there are others who have the keys to evil, and who close off the road to good.[24] All teachers present such polarized and dichotomous images of people— they are either good or they are bad. According to the teachers, members should always strive to be good and to be among the good. Importantly, not only is the non-Muslim Swedish context mentioned, but also that of Muslims who do not belong to the 'true path'—the influence of both will lead members astray. Various Muslim positions are rejected, for the benefit of the people of the Sunnah and consensus:

> Another thing that helps [you to be steadfast in religion] is to keep away from *ahl al-bid'ah* [people of innovation], *al-hizbiyūn* [those who belong to a group or party], and to stick to the *ahl al-sunnah wa al-jamā'ah*. Because they are people that keep you away from and guides you away from the right understanding of Islam, and that may lead to you straying away from the religion altogether.[25]

A main aspect of *da'wah* for the various groups that perform it seems to be the encouragement of Muslims to become better and more fully emerged in the practice of it. This is not least the case in the local group, where how to be a better, more steadfast, Muslim in this life is seen as an important part of *da'wah*. The teachers place great emphasis on explaining that the participants need to understand what 'true' Islam is, and that they need to practice it in order to be steadfast Muslims.[26] It seems that this is considered particularly relevant in the Swedish context, where Muslims are a minority and where many are not practicing.

In one lecture, the teacher argues that there are not many *practicing* Muslims today, and that the people belonging to the local group should thank God for guiding them, for choosing them. He says that 'Allah states in the Qur'an that He protects us and brings us to light. He is our

23. Lecture 1: Steadfast.
24. Lecture 1: Steadfast.
25. Lecture 1: Steadfast.
26. What being 'steadfast' includes in the local group will be outlined below, where it will be shown that it is connected to good moral behaviour, through which one may function as a role model, which is one central aspect of what *da'wah* is understood to be in the local group.

friend. He gave us the light of *īmān* and knowledge.'[27] He refers to Q 2:257, which reads: 'God is the ally of those who believe. He brings them out of the darkness into the light. But those who disbelieve—their allies are al-Ṭāghūt, who bring them out of the darkness into the light. Those are the companions of the Fire. There they will remain.'[28] The teacher then explains that God 'gave us a real life after having been like the dead' and that God says in the Qur'an, chapter 6, that the *kāfir* was like a dead person, but that God gave him light:[29]

> We must thank Allah who has given us this happiness. Those who live righteous, regardless if it is a man or a woman, a *mu'min* [a believer] will be given a good life and be rewarded [in the Hereafter]. 'Whosoever doeth right, whether male or female, and is a believer, him verily we shall quicken with good life, and We shall pay them a recompense in proportion to the best of what they used to do' [16:97]. Allah has given us the *halawāt al-'īmān* [sweetness of faith]. Three things are necessary to achieve this: to love Allah and his Prophet more than anything else. To love another person only for the sake of Allah. To hate falling back to *kufr* [unbelief] after Allah has guided you to Islam. You must hate that as much as hating to be thrown in fire. As Muslim and Bukhari reports, Muhammad said that Allah forgives everything that you did before [you became a true believer]. Islam is the religion that brings you to Paradise with the will of Allah. Allah has completed his religion in Islam. 'Today I have perfected your religion for you, and I have completed My blessing on you, and I have approved Islam for you as a religion'. (Q 5:3)[30]

Several comments in this lecture emphasize the gift of faith as the highest gift, and that the aim of creation is to worship God: 'Without the guidance of Allah we would not have found this path'; 'The gift of *īmān* is the best gift that anyone can get on this earth'; 'He guided us to what we were created for; to worship Him, *subhāna wa ta'āla*'.[31] The

---

27. Lecture 1: Steadfast.
28. The word al-Ṭāghūt is explained by Droge as 'perhaps "(other) gods" or "idols" (cf. Q16.36; 39.17), but sometimes taken as a proper name (see Q4.60, 76, where it appears to be another name for Satan). It may be related to the word for "gods" in Ethiop. (*ṭā'ōt*).' The following is Pickthalls' translation: 'Allah is the Protecting Guardian of those who believe. He bringeth them out of darkness into light. As for those who disbelieve, their patrons are false deities. They bring them out of light into darkness. Such are rightful owners of the Fire. They will abide therein.'
29. Lecture 1: Steadfast.
30. Lecture 1: Steadfast.
31. Lecture 1: Steadfast.

teacher also argues that Islam must be defended, and that God will help Muslims to be victorious. He mentions a verse from the Qur'an: 'You who believe! If you help God, He will help you, and make firm your feet' (Q 47:7).[32] He does not explain what 'defend' means here. Another strategy mentioned is to make *du'ā'* (voluntary prayer, supplication) to God and this is motivated with Muhammad always making *du'ā'*, praying to God to turn his heart to religion. The teacher informs the participants that a good *du'ā'* is something that people should know by heart.[33]

Forgiveness is also constantly referred to as a strategy involved in becoming steadfast. Members must constantly repent (*tawbah*), asking God to forgive them. They should guard against thinking they are something special. The narrative of Abraham building the Ka'ba in the Qur'an (chapter 14) is used as an example of how even he feared committing *shirk*, and how he asked God to protect him from worshipping statues. Even such a person, a *hanīf* (a person of monotheistic faith), the teacher emphasizes, feared that he would commit *shirk*. Members of the group should similarly realize that they need to pray for guidance.[34] Regarding guidance, the teacher refers to Q 16:102: 'Say: "The holy spirit has brought it down from your Lord in truth, to make firm those who believe, and as a guidance and good news for those who submit"'. The teacher mentions that Jibril came with the Qur'an, with the truth in order to strengthen faith, as guidance and a glad message to the Muslims. This, according to the teacher, further protects members of the group from the attacks of *kuffār*, making them steadfast.

> The Qur'an is the greatest reason to be steadfast in this religion. The Qur'an is the tight rope of Allah. His bright light. The one that sticks to the Qur'an will find guidance and find the straight path. It strengthens our *'īmān*. It cleanses our souls. And it teaches us to know our Lord. It makes us feel peaceful as human beings. It answers the evil and false accusations from *kuffār*, regardless if they are atheists, Christian, Jews, polytheists, we will find that Allah *subhānu wa ta'āla* in the Qur'an answers their *shubuhāt* [doubts].[35]

32. Lecture 1: Steadfast.
33. Lecture 1: Steadfast. He mentions Q 3:8, 'Our Lord, do not cause our hearts to turn aside after You have guided us', as an example of a good *du'ā'* to learn by heart.
34. Lecture 1: Steadfast.
35. Lecture 1: Steadfast. The 'rope of God' refers to Q 3:103, which in Pickthall's translation is rendered as 'cable': 'And hold fast, all of you together, to the cable of Allah, and do not separate'. Droge translates: 'And hold fast to the rope of God'.

Searching for knowledge is also pointed out as something that will make people steadfast in Islam, as will remembering Allah (*dhikr*), which the teacher explains will make people feel calm in their hearts and at peace in their bodies. He explains that each morning and each night, a Muslim shall do *dhikr*. Moreover, to read *ayat al-kursī* after each prayer will protect Muslims from going astray.[36] The emphasis of continuously performing *dhikr* and *du'ā'* seems to be a strategy aimed at constantly reminding members of their religion, of living a life 'absorbed' in Islam. This is reflected in the obligation to pray and to remember God (*dhikr*) during daily life. The *continuous* remembering of God and the imitation of the Sunnah, regardless of the time and place, is promoted as the best means of avoiding potential pitfalls. This constant calling of God to mind through *dhikr* is attested by the fact that many participants listen to the Qur'an while travelling on public transport or while moving around in 'unfaithful' settings. This, it seems, is considered as a way to keep the outside world at a distance. Remembering God is also held to be beneficial for the creation of a good family life:

> To fill your house with *dhikr Allāh*. Remembrance of Allah. To read the Qur'an. To remember Him when you come home. When you eat. Before you go to the toilet. When you sleep. All such things fill your house with happiness. The angels of *rahmah*, mercy, enter the house and the devils flee it. As different from many other people today who play music in their homes that draw the devils there and scare the angels away. They don't mention Allah in these things and do not get the mercy and the angels won't come and the house is filled with devils. And if your house is filled with devils, how on earth can you have a peaceful family? [...] Allah said in the Qur'an that the heart finds peace in remembering Allah. This is one of the gains of always remembering Allah. The heart will find peace. You will feel comfortable. Happy inside. The same with your home. If you remember Allah he will fill your house with happiness and peace. So you should read a lot from the Qur'an in your home.[37]

36. Lecture 1: Steadfast. *Ayat al-kursī*, the 'Throne verse': 'God—(there is) no God but Him, the Living, the Everlasting. Slumber does not overtake Him, nor sleep. To Him (belongs) whatever is in the heavens and whatever is on the earth. Who is the one who will intercede with Him, except by His permission? He knows whatever is before them and whatever is behind them, but they cannot encompass any of His knowledge, except whatever He pleases. His throne comprehends the heavens and the earth. Watching over both of them does not weary him. He is the Most High, the Almighty' (Q 2:255).
37. Lecture 5: Family. The verse in the Qur'an referred to is most likely Q 13:28.

In this citation, we see how important *dhikr* is held to be. It is an action that constantly brings God to mind, regardless of what menial task is being performed. Here, the notion of evil *jinn* who try to seduce people and lead them astray appears, and the teacher recommends behaviour that will bring about a happy family life. Thus, *dhikr* and reading or listening to the Qur'an function as remedies against the evil whispering of *jinn*.[38]

Being a steadfast Muslim appears to be a requisite for giving *da'wah*. The teacher lists several strategic actions that will make a person steadfast in Islam: to spend money for the sake of God, to hate and love for the sake of God, to invite to truth (*al-haqq*) and forbid evil, to do anything that protects from Shaytān, to know what is evil and bad, and stay away from that. Constantly thinking about the Judgment day and the Hereafter is also a strategy which functions as a motivation to live a proper Islamic life: 'A motivation in this world is to continuously think about Paradise and the reward. You think about the Fire. Then you will stay away from sin. Think about Judgment day. Then you will

38.   The topic of *jinn* was discussed in separate lectures. In these, teachers outlined what *jinn* are, how humans should relate to them, and how to protect oneself from evil *jinn*. In these lectures, ibn Taymiya's writings on *jinn* are used. These lectures present *jinn* as real beings that may affect the existence of humans. I believe that a reason why the topic of *jinn* was addressed in detail was to warn group members against the use of magic and the influence of visiting magicians not qualified in Islamic sciences. Only a 'knowledgeable' person should be turned to in the case of problems with *jinn*, such as possession. In such instances the person affected is to have the Qur'an read to them. In the lectures, the teacher also turns against Sufis, who, he argues, may be in contact with *jinn*. The teacher criticizes such practices as leaving gifts by graves or circumambulation around a grave. Such things are referred to as *shirk*. The belief in *jinn* affects daily life. For example, if food is dropped on the floor it should be picked up and eaten; otherwise it will be eaten by *jinn*. Moreover, sitting in sun and shade at the same time should also be avoided, since this is a place where *shayatīn* like to be. The topic of *jinn* is important since it is connected to *wiswās*, the whispering of *jinn*, or *shayatīn*, who try to make people leave the way of God. The best protection from such things, the teacher makes clear, is reading the Qur'an and remembering God (*dhikr*). The teachers repeatedly say that knowledge, especially concerning *'aqīdah*, is a way of protection. The danger of *wiswās* is returned to in several lectures, even when the 'official' topic was something different. The preoccupation with *jinn* seems to be increasing in Sweden at the moment, in several groups, which may be an explanation why the topic is being addressed so frequently. See for example Marlow 2013.

become steadfast in religion.'[39] The teacher mentions that Muhammad passed some of the oppressed people of Mecca and encouraged them to have *sabr* (patience) because that would bring them to Paradise, and he states that: 'a person who knows what awaits him in the next life, will be stronger in this life. He will stick to religion more firmly. Why? Because if you know that something big and good awaits you it becomes easier to do good now.'[40]

Correction

> Few Muslims say that they do *not* follow the Sunnah! What makes us different? That we have the *manhaj* and follow the pious predecessors![41]

All teachers strive to present Islam as a worldview, a way of life that should be made relevant for *everything* a person does in life. Religion is *not* merely a private matter to be performed at home. It is constantly practiced, or not. In their lectures teachers present norms for evaluating individual practice, both obligatory rituals and other practices that are more 'mundane', for example how you treat other people, and how you behave at work or school. What a person does is either Islamic or non-Islamic, an action that will affect the person's life in eternity. Eternity is always around the corner, influencing the content of lectures. One aim of the teachers seems to be to warn people constantly about Judgment day and the Hereafter, making this life merely a 'transit station' on the way to eternal bliss or fire:

> Allah will let all people resurrect to be rewarded and go to Paradise. Non-believers will go to Hell. Each person will get what he deserves. There is no escape. You cannot lie or excuse yourself. Allah knows what is in your heart. Be honest in this life so that you don't have to try to escape on Judgment day. It will not be easy to stand in front of God to try to explain why you did not become Muslim. And then you are thrown in the fire. [...] It is a real fire. 69 times hotter than fire here on earth! People will burn in eternity! Not one year! ALL eternity! You cannot escape! There is no second chance! Take the chance now! Think about the meaning of life... You can be objective! Study Islam! Ask the people of knowledge about Islam before it is too late! Do not delay it! You never know when death arrives! Many healthy people have died suddenly![42]

39. Lecture 1: Steadfast.
40. Lecture 1: Steadfast.
41. Lecture 9: *ahl al-sunnah*.
42. Lecture 4: Islam.

This is elaborated in several lectures and the teachers try to make the participants accept that the Hereafter is of primary importance, not this world. The Hereafter can only be reached by following the 'straight path'. The criticism of materialism is returned to here, since, the group's teachers argue, some people may wish that this life is all there is. The teachers stress that anyone not knowing the truth possesses a void that must be filled. They argue that some fill it by chasing after money, status, respect, and so on. All of this, however, is meaningless—to feel good and to be truly happy in this life, submission to Islam and a remembrance that this life is not the final destination is paramount. The important thing is what follows after physical death:[43]

> If we follow our lusts and needs, or if we follow an ideology created by humans, or live the life that the big companies want us to live, those who want to make money out of us, then we will lose. Those who have chosen to be Muslims must reflect on several issues. Do you live as a true Muslim? Do you follow authentic Islam or do you only do what suits you? Do you really love Allah and his Prophet? You must realize that Islam is submitting to the will of Allah. He has decided that we shall follow his book and the example of the Prophet and the first generations. It is not enough to carry a Muslim name.[44]

The teacher is explicit in that it is not enough for participants to follow the traditions of their home country, since these are human-made customs that have nothing to do with 'true' Islam. The teacher repeatedly states that there is an inescapable obligation on all to learn what true Islam means and to follow God's will. He states that members should constantly ask themselves what they know about God, the Prophet and his companions. Such reflection, it is argued, will result in the realization that nothing is known about how the pious predecessors lived. The teacher laments that this contrasts with the modern world, wherein someone interested in football may know such inane details as the shoe size worn by a famous player. This is compared to the lack of knowledge of religion, and serves as a call for Muslims to wake up and set their priorities straight. Non-Muslims too should dedicate themselves to learning about *al-islām*. Nothing is to be lost in finding out about such information, the teacher stresses:[45]

43. Lecture 2: Meaning of Life.
44. Lecture 2: Meaning of Life.
45. Lecture 2: Meaning of Life.

> Those who are *mukhlasīn* [sincere], who follow the straight path, must constantly struggle to stay on it. Life is a constant struggle between good and bad. People must have patience, obey Allah and keep away from sins. But even if we try our utmost, we will sin. Nobody is free from sin. However, the best sinners are those who ask Allah for his forgiveness (*tawbah*). Allah likes to forgive and even if a person feels stupid and dirty, they should never stop to truly ask Allah for forgiveness. Allah loves the *mutatahharīn*, those who cleanse themselves from sins, but he also loves those who repeatedly sin and then honestly ask for forgiveness. 'Those who avoid al-Ṭāghūt—for fear that they serve it—and turn to God (in repentance)—for them (there is) good news. So give good news to My servants.' (Q 39:17)[46]

The teacher says that this Qur'anic verse includes everyone. If someone sins, it is not God who is hurt but the sinner. God does not need people. People need him. Those who drink alcohol or take drugs will hurt themselves, not God. The teacher comforts the participants, telling them not to despair, since God is merciful and forgiving. He tells them that God even forgives *shirk* (associating something with God), *kufr* (infidelity, unbelief), and *zīnā'* (extramarital relations) as long as true *tawbah* (repentance) is made. All these things mentioned are regarded as horrific sins within the group. The teacher warns that when a person dies it is too late to repent, that as soon as the angel takes out the soul nothing more can be done—the deceased can do nothing more than lay in the grave, waiting for individual judgment without any chance of changing the eternal future.[47]

Having explained why there is a problem today and having defined what the in-group is, the teacher tells the participants how to solve the problem. He emphasizes that the individuals must be strengthened in order for God to make them victorious, thus stressing the importance of being steadfast. 'If Allah gives you victory, nobody can win over you! If Allah abandons you, you will never make it! Those who believe, if you give victory to God and his religion, then God will give you victory.'[48] The teacher refers to the Qur'an as proof (*dalīl*) of this:

> Surely the hypocrites will be in the lowest level of the Fire, and you will not find for them any helper, except those who turn (in repentance), and set (things) right, and hold fast to God, and devote their religion to God. Those are with the believers, and God will give the believers a great reward. (Q 4:145-146)

46. Lecture 2: Meaning of Life.
47. Lecture 2: Meaning of Life.
48. Lecture 10: *ummah*.

Another verse is brought up from the Qur'an in order to show how God gives sovereignty to whom he wills:

> Say: 'God! Master of the kingdom, You give the kingdom to whomever You please and You take away the kingdom from whomever You please. You exalt whomever You please and You humble whomever You please. In Your hand is the good. Surely You are powerful over everything. (Q 3:26)

A *hadīth* from Abu Dawud's collection is presented concerning people dealing with usury (*al-'īnah*) and focusing on worldly things (*dunya*), refraining from striving (*jihād*). The teacher explains that such people will be humiliated by God until they return to religion. 'What is then this religion to which Muslims should return? They must return to and establish the religion!'[49] He reads a verse from the Qur'an as an answer: 'Today I have perfected your religion for you, and I have completed My blessing on you, and I have approved Islam for you as a religion' (Q 5:3). The teacher then explains what this religion is that they must return to and establish: 'In worship, the pure Islam that Muhammad brought, that is the Islam that we shall return to in order to be victorious'.[50] In referring to the last sermon by Muhammad, the teacher institutes what they should follow, based on the Prophet mentioning that he leaves them two things: the Qur'an and his example, the Sunnah. The teacher mentions that the problem is clearly that Muslims have left the true way, the way of the *ahl al-sunnah*.[51]

It is noticeable how the teacher puts pressure on the need for members to change themselves first, before seeking to change anything or anybody else.[52] Islam must be 'established' in a person. He refers to the so-called *hadīth* of the strangers, *hadīth al-ghurabā'*, where Muhammad said that Islam began as something strange and will return as something strange, concluding that Paradise is for the strangers. The teacher also mentions the tree in Paradise that will give them shade. Those who will be shaded are those who correct the corrupt, and he adds that the strangers, *al-ghurabā'*, are those who stick to Sunnah and who correct society when it is corrupt. Moreover, emphasis is repeatedly placed on *doing* throughout the lectures. Guidance on how people should behave in

---

49. Lecture 10: *ummah*.
50. Lecture 10: *ummah*.
51. This is repeated in Fawzan 2012a, 79.
52. The verse 'Surely God does not change what is in a people, until they change what is in themselves' (Q 13:11) is referred to in the group. See below for a discussion.

a general sense is often given, explaining how group members are to live up to the expected character traits and function as good role models: 'To *say* something is easy! But where are we? We have to search ourselves and make a step! [...] Actions are what counts! *Actions* are what counts!'[53]

The teacher gives concrete examples of what members can do to aid the *ummah*. He tells them how the *'ulamā'* in Saudi Arabia, for example Bin Baz, began to work to correct peoples' Islam. The *'ulamā'* established a university in Medina to teach people about Islam. The teacher mentions that the idea was to bring students from all over the world and then have them go back and spread the knowledge to their people. He mentions that in the first instance not many students came, but that in time the numbers grew steadily and that the university in Medina has had a great effect on the Muslims around the world. The teacher also mentions Albani and Muqbil, who devoted their lives to spreading knowledge of the Sunnah. The point of telling the participants this is that it took a long time to reach the goal and therefore they need patience to give *da'wah*.

Correction, as it is understood in the group, is to gain knowledge, follow the Sunnah, and function as a good role model. The idea is that society will eventually change as a result. Teachers do not call for members to enter public space or political life, to offer moral chastisements directed towards others. Instead, there is a repeated emphasis on the fact that small steps are needed, that members should start by looking at their own conduct. Violence is to be avoided:

> In order to speed the process up, just look at the TV to be reminded about the hard life Muslims live, there are things we can do to change it. Many wish to change everything at once. But they forget about themselves, their family, and the society around them. So they waste their time and forget what they have power to change; themselves. So, the first thing is to correct yourself. Learn knowledge. Learn about Allah's religion. *'aqīdah*. Implement it in your life. Worship Allah. Implement Islamic *ahklāq* in your own life. Be a real Muslim. Begin with yourself. Do not be a bad Muslim and say you will change the world yourself! That does not work! The Muslim *ummah* today consist of various individuals. If they correct themselves, then the *ummah* will be corrected. And also, we shall correct our family, our surroundings, to build an Islamic family. Marry a righteous Muslim and build an Islamic family. Raise your children as Muslims. Make them motivated to study. Children that can lead to development of the *ummah*. Not another child that will hang around and be yet another part of what the Prophet said, the foam of the sea that is of no use to the Muslims. To

---

53. Lecture 9: *ahl al-sunnah*.

raise practicing children that can benefit the *ummah*. If the Muslims can do this, it will lead to good things. One of the biggest problems today in the *ummah* is that children are not raised with Islam. We shall *not* fall into this trap![54]

Barbahari, who is encountered through the comments of Fawzan, was a charismatic leader who conducted a pietistic struggle to impose his view of a moral vision on society. He held that the correction of others, in the sense of ordinary people who did not abide to his views on morality, should be conducted with the hands, which led him into great difficulties.[55] However, the local group I studied apparently rejects hands-on correction and prefers to withdraw and act as good role models, which can be understood as a strategy of 'correction' suitable for the Swedish context. It is, perhaps, a way of avoiding problems. Having established the need for members to focus on themselves first, then their immediate surroundings, emphasis is placed on the group seeking knowledge. If possible, members are to travel in order to gain this knowledge, in order to return later and help the local community. This, it seems, is precisely the route taken by the teachers of the local group.

> The best thing you can do to correct the *ummah* is to search for knowledge. The Prophetic knowledge! The Prophet said that the people of knowledge are the inheritors of the Prophets. The Prophet gave them knowledge, not money. So, if we have this knowledge and spread it... That is the foundation to correct the Muslim *ummah*. There are many who wish to correct the *ummah*, but they don't do it based on knowledge. There is a beautiful saying by a pious predecessor. He said that there are people who wish to correct things, but they don't do it based on knowledge which led them to revolt against the Muslim *ummah*. But if they had had knowledge that would have prevented them from this! Many wish to make the reform fast, in one day [...], but the *ummah* has degenerated over a long time so it will take a long time to revive it. The best way to gain knowledge is to travel and become a *tālib al-'ilm*, a real student of knowledge, and then to return to spread this knowledge. This is mentioned in the end of *sūrat al-tawba*: 'And the believers should not all go out to fight. Of every troop of them, a party only should go forth, that they (who are left behind) may gain sound knowledge in religion, and that they may warn their folk when they return to them, so that they may beware [9:122].' Allah encourages you to travel to search for knowledge, [and then] to return and correct your people.[56]

54. Lecture 10: *ummah*. The expression 'foam of the sea' is also commented on in Chapter 7, Constructing In-Group and Out-Group.
55. See for example Cook 2003, 33, 103.
56. Lecture 10: *ummah*.

The teacher is also concerned explicitly with the situation in Sweden, which he sees to be a bad one. Apparently he sees some improvement and suggests how the participants can help to recover the Swedish part of the *ummah*. For this, he emphasizes the need for more teachers.

> The situation for the Muslims in Sweden is bad in many ways. But *hamdulillah* we also see a lot of light among sisters and brothers who practice. But to correct this, the best way is to study and then bring the knowledge back and call others to Islam through lectures, preaching, write books, articles, and so on. This is the foundation to lead people back to Islam, to give victory to Islam. So, the Muslims in Sweden are in need of hundreds of *shuyūk*, of *'ulamā'* [Islamic scholars], that can strengthen their situation. To be one of them is one of the best things to do to help out. Some cannot do this. Some cannot travel. It takes years. But the Muslims are in need of people of knowledge that can teach the local community.[57]

Emphasis is placed on the fact that a person from a specific area knows best how to speak to and engage with the people there. The teacher also mentions that people who cannot travel should try to strengthen the place where they live and to make it more Islamic. He tells members about another group that he considers very successful. Participants are advised that they can assist children doing homework, since many people originally from Muslim countries lag behind in Sweden. 'Sisters' can educate themselves to become pedagogues. That can be done by taking a distance course that allows them to study from home. They can then open Muslim nurseries. Participants can assist Muslim criminals and drug addicts, open Islamic shops, and engage themselves in any activity that may strengthen the *ummah*. Importance is placed on becoming engaged, in whatever way possible; being passive and expecting others to perform this requirement is not acceptable. 'The small things lead to something big!' the teacher says, before warning them: 'Don't expect others to do everything! Engage yourself! Correct the *ummah*! Make Muslims return to their religion!'[58]

We can see from this how criticism is directed to those who want to speed things up. For example, those who go abroad to participate in fighting, or who launch attacks like those seen on 11 September, 2001, the bombings in London 2005 and Madrid 2004, are rejected. 'This is something that does *not* build the *ummah* up in any way! It does *not* bring

57.　Lecture 10: *ummah*.
58.　Lecture 10: *ummah*.

khayr [good]! It is forbidden in Islam! It only leads to problems!'[59] Such things are criticized because they serve only to make it more difficult to spread Islam to others. The teacher stresses that it is better to do nothing than to participate in such actions.

> If you cannot participate to build up the *ummah*! Then do at least not be a part of ruining the *ummah*! Don't do these things that lead to ruin and hardship! I hope that this will be a reminder that we shall struggle and do what we can to build up, correct, improve the *ummah*. Not be a part of ruining, oppressing, and making things worse![60]

Hence, the recommended program of action is that each individual starts with him or herself and then successively tries to influence others in the local community. This is presented as an individual responsibility, with each person able to do something to revive the *ummah*.

The next section will outline in more detail how the *da'wah* should be conducted in practice.

Motivating *Da'wah*

All the teachers I observed seem to be concerned with the secularization of the surrounding society, as well as the fact that many Muslims do not practice Islam, but rather show an interest in worldly things, becoming Westernized and materialistic. A desire to re-Islamize non-practicing Muslims, and the wider society, is always present. This fact is perceived as a problem and the teachers wish to change the situation. Some participants voice their concern and then practically try to do something about it, while others seem to join more passively, seeking to change only their own lives, hoping that it eventually will bring about a change in larger society. The lack of 'authentic' knowledge about Islam is often presented as a problem, and the teachers do their best to remedy this. Teaching others about Islam and encouraging others to spread the word further, as well as bringing friends and family to lectures, is said to be a part of *da'wah*. While *da'wah* is described as a religious duty that has great relevance for this world in general, for the individual giving *da'wah* it is also carries considerable potential rewards in the Hereafter. Calling others to Islam, awakening a greater spirituality and religious practice, would potentially change this world, making it a better place. *Da'wah* has

59. Lecture 10: *ummah*.
60. Lecture 10: *ummah*.

the potential to bring more people to the straight path, thus offering more people the chance to spend eternity in Paradise. It is understood to be the will of God, and human beings are to submit to it—if they are true Muslims.[61]

Da'wah is often connected to the phrase *al-'amr bī al-ma'rūf wa al-nahy 'an al-munkar*, to command the good and forbid the evil. In Saba Mahmood's study on the Egyptian piety movement, she notes that the terms are interrelated and used in three different ways. Sometimes they are used synonymously. *Da'wah* is sometimes understood as a vocation while *al-'amr bī al-ma'rūf wa al-nahy 'an al-munkar* is understood as a duty which Muslims undertake generally in their lives. The third way is to regard both as ways of enjoining in piety, but where *al-'amr bī al-ma'rūf wa al-nahy 'an al-munkar* extends acts of encouragement to the use of force in order to prohibit certain actions. Mahmood claims that: 'Thus, we find that 'amr bil ma'rūf is more likely to be used to legitimate the use of physical force than is da'wa; the latter remains primarily an instrument of moral exhortation and reform.'[62]

Considering the local group, the issue of who can perform *da'wah* or *al-'amr bī al-ma'rūf wa al-nahy 'an al-munkar* is addressed in the lectures. Since the participants are in Sweden, where Islam is not the religion of state and where there is no Islamic organization that upholds interpretative authority, the topic is negotiated within the individual Islamic groups. Within the local group I observed, the identity of those held responsible for the moral reform of Muslims is clearly stated: it is the task of every individual (virtuous) Muslim. However, depending on the level of knowledge possessed, there are seemingly different obligations and opportunities, ones corresponding to the hierarchy of authority upheld within the group.

Development within contemporary Salafi groups has led to an active stance against imitation of *taqlīd*. This is certainly the case in the local group I observed. Opposition to *taqlīd* may be seen as an attempt to criticize religion as a specialized field of knowledge that has no relevance outside of the religious establishment. However, this does not mean that there is no such thing as religious authority. While there is a recognition within the local group of certain *'ulamā'* holding a specific authority relevant to the understanding of the religious sources, those regarded as belonging to the religious elite are different from those we would find within the frames of the normative discourse we call *taqlīd*. Participation

61.   Lecture 3: *da'wah*; Lecture 4: Islam.
62.   Mahmood 2005, 60.

in *da'wah* activities is not necessarily connected to a person's knowledge of doctrinal issues. It is, at least in the group studied, rather concerned with a person's moral behaviour and knowledge about the practical performance of rituals. Both men and women can participate in the performing of *da'wah*, though there are different recommendations on what they can do in this mission. Moreover, we can observe how the group attempts to morally reconstruct individuals, and by extension the surrounding society, without explicitly aiming for a direct or immediate transformation of the state or public space.

One objective held by the group is to actively work to spread information about Islam based on the idea of Islam as a universal religion. In one lecture, the teacher explains that God did not send different religions to humanity. That would not have been logical, he argues. He describes God's religion as a singular expression—always Islam, in the sense of submission to the will of God. This is described as the message of all prophets. In articulating this view, the teacher argues that true religion must be universal, which makes it easy to distinguish true religion from others. Being universal also implies a missionary zeal, he argues.

> Just check some other things, such as Allahs' religion must be universal, [it is] for everyone, not only one people. [...] Check Judaism, you cannot become Jewish. Some say you can today, but Orthodox Jews says no. It is a religion that is not missionary, they do not call people to their religion. The same with other religions. But Allah's religion must be universal. It must be for everyone. [...] What is the final message? Allah says in the Qur'an that he sent a messenger to each nation [...] and Muhammad came to all of humanity [...] and it is open to everyone. Everyone is welcome to the religion! It is not so that you must be born to the religion! Everyone is welcome![63]

The notion of Islam being from God and other religions being created by humans is also used as an argument supporting Islam's authenticity and divine origin. The logic echoes the discussion on human-made laws versus divine legislation presented above. The teacher states: 'This religion Islam, as different from other religions, comes from the

---

63. Lecture 4: Islam. No reflections were made, to my knowledge, about what would happen if people accepted their teaching in large numbers. As we have noted, a lot of effort is put into creating and enhancing the notion of 'in-group'. One aspect of this seems to be to emphasize the groups marginalized position.

Creator. And who knows the creation better than the Creator? *Nobody!*
Other religions are made up by people!'[64] The Qur'an is presented as a
book that is universal in scope and which functions as guidance for all
people, in all times and places and containing answers to all existential
questions people may have. In the following citation, the teacher
elaborates on the relationship between the Qur'an and Sunnah, the
preserved writings, which, in his opinion, make Islam, as a universal
religion, stand out among religions. Moreover, this citation shows
how contextualized reading of the Qur'an is regarded as wrong, since
revelation is considered to be universal. In addition, the citation shows
that the Sunnah, preserved by God, explains the meaning of the Qur'an.

> It is a book that some people think is suited to the situations of old times,
> but we follow it because it is the word of God. It is guidance and light to all
> of humanity. In it there is guidance. It answers the questions people need
> to have answered: What is the meaning of life? What happens after death?
> Why does evil exist? All these questions are answered in the Qur'an. The
> Qur'an suits all times and places and people. It is not for one particular
> people, but for all. In the same way that Islam suits all times, places, and
> people. The Qur'an is also unchanged, as different from other books.
> [...] Allah has preserved the scripture and the same Arabic. [...] He also
> preserved the Sunnah. The Prophet's speech which explains the meaning
> of the Qur'an. All this is preserved. As different from other religions.[65]

Having established this 'unicity' and universality of Islam, the group
uses it as a 'theoretical' proof (*dalīl*) that *da'wah* is required.

Merits of Da'wah

Da'wah is a recurring topic in lectures, and the entire enterprise of the
group can be said to be about *da'wah*, which includes teaching directed
to other Muslims. The group strives to validate this claim and argues for
the merits of *da'wah*. For example, one lecture is specifically concerned
with the merits of conducting *da'wah* and how to perform it.[66] The
lecture is introduced with a comparison of what contemporary Muslims
who conduct *da'wah* (should) do with the mission of the prophets. God
loves all who perform *da'wah*, the teacher says, referring to a saying
of Muhammad, who said that those calling others to do good will be

64. Lecture 4: Islam.
65. Lecture 4: Islam.
66. Lecture 3: *da'wah*.

rewarded. As an example, the teacher says that each time the name of Muhammad is mentioned, a Muslim should read the *salāt wa salām* over him.[67] If the believer reads it once, the teacher states, then God will read it over the believer ten times as a reward. It is the same thing, the teacher says, if the believer teaches someone to read *al-fātihah*, the opening chapter of the Qur'an. When this person reads it in the future, the believer too will get a reward each time. So, the teacher asks rhetorically in support of *da'wah*, what would happen if the believer teaches another person about *tawhīd*, divine unity, and authentic *'aqīdah*, worship?[68]

The teacher encourages the participants to give *da'wah* in promoting the benefits and the gains for the caller. He takes care to state that it is God who leads other individuals to Islam *through* the caller. A *hadīth* is brought up that states that when a person dies, only three things can continue to influence his or her future: if the person has given *sadaqah* (charity) that continues to have effects, for example that he or she has supported the building of a mosque where people pray; if the person has a righteous child who makes *du'ā'* (supplication) for him or her after the person's death; and if the person has given others knowledge about Islam, for example taught someone *al-fātihah*. This will be of benefit to the believer on Judgment day. Hence, to give *sadaqah* every day in this life is important. *Da'wah* is the recommended action, and it may turn the scales in the right direction, the teacher argues,[69] on Judgment day.

Indicating that true believers conduct *da'wah*, the teacher says that *if* a person is a true believer, he or she *will* feel the obligation to spread the message of Islam. The teacher simultaneously stresses the importance of having knowledge and avoiding talking about things of which one knows nothing. The participants are to avoid giving their own explanations of things. The strict hierarchy of authority, outlined in Chapter 4, is further expressed when the teacher expands on his view that *da'wah* can be performed on three levels. One level is that of the *'ulamā'*, who have enough knowledge to write books and issue *fatāwa*.

---

67. This means to say *salla Allāh 'alayhi wa sallam*, abbreviated *sas*, each time Muhammad's name or 'the Prophet' is mentioned. This is abbreviated as *sas* in many citations in this study, but several *sas* are omitted for the sake of readability. It should be noted, however, that the teachers are notorious in remembering this phrase, and many others.
68. Lecture 3: *da'wah*.
69. Lecture 3: *da'wah*.

They can debate with others and answer questions. Underneath them are the 'students', here called the teachers, who have what the teacher calls 'basic knowledge' of Islam after spending years studying at Islamic institutions. These students can give lectures and spread information, for example via the internet. The teacher informs the group, referencing to a shaykh from Medina, that a basic knowledge of Islam was needed in order to open a website or to give lectures, thus limiting the actual behaviour of what people can do as a part of *da'wah*. Below these two levels there are the ordinary Muslims, those without a formal religious education. The majority of participants in the local group belong to this third level.[70]

When the teacher advises the participants on how to conduct *da'wah* in their lives, he offers two overarching possibilities: individually, or collectively, with others. Doing *da'wah* in a group is most beneficial, the teacher argues, since larger projects can be carried out, for example giving lectures or organizing conferences. He underlines that the leaders of such projects must have knowledge in order to make sure that all situations dealt with are managed in accordance with 'true' Islam. Someone who has studied with *'ulamā'* should therefore be the leader, and he in his turn should refer to the *'ulamā'* on matters about which he is not certain.[71] Thus, larger projects should be led by those belonging to the first or second level of authority. To validate this, the teacher gives the example of the Swedish TV documentary, mentioned in the introduction of this study, in which women in *niqāb* with a hidden camera asked imams for advice on whether to report an abusive husband to the police. He comments that it can be difficult to know as a *da'wah*-organization how to behave in such circumstances—whether one should remain silent or engage in debates. To answer this, he argues that participants should turn to *'ulamā'* for guidance,[72] again acknowledging

70. Lecture 3: *da'wah*.
71. Lecture 3: *da'wah*.
72. Lecture 3: *da'wah*. I have been asked by several participants, not the teachers, to refrain from giving any detailed comments on the group's views related to the TV documentary, and I have chosen to respect that. I believe many felt that it would stigmatize them and bring about a misleading representation of the group's teachers and teaching. The documentary was commented upon by the teachers and taken as an example of the risks that they potentially may meet when 'ending up' in the 'public eye'. This was used as a way of further legitimating the hierarchy of authority, and the need to speak only about things and do things that they know conform to the truth, and to stay among their own people.

their authority. This can be contrasted with the counter-public element that Charles Hirschkind studied in Egypt, one that encouraged debate and argumentation.[73]

The teacher also spends a lot of time talking about the merits of individually engaging in da'wah. Discussions with individuals may be more effective than speaking to large crowds, he argues. The teacher supports this by observing that Sweden is an individualistic country, one in which people like to engage in discussion.[74] The teacher outlines important things for those performing da'wah to consider, and it is here that we see a succinct summation of the main priorities of the group: participants are to have the right intention, to follow the Sunnah and to avoid innovations. The teacher underlines that da'wah must be done for the sake of God, and he warns the participants that all actions are judged depending on the intentions that underlie them. Hence, if a person calls people to God, he or she should do it for God's sake, since it is God who will be pleased with the da'wah. He adds, importantly, that da'wah should not be done in an attempt to appear 'cool', or in an effort to impress others—which may be a comment directed at other groups in Sweden in which da'wah seems to be much about style and appearance. (This comment might also be directed towards newcomers to the local group, in order to inform and proactively guide them.) This line of reasoning is in agreement with the observation made by Jocelyn Cesari that 'Salafism' to a large extent seems to be about style.[75]

The teacher stresses that members must always follow the Sunnah of Muhammad and that they must avoid inventing their own ways— something that he says some people do today, for example when they do da'wah through theatre or songs.[76] That is not prescribed, he states.

73. He notes that this did not entail a move towards liberalism. Hirschkind 2005, 48.
74. Lecture 3: da'wah.
75. Olsson 2012; Cesari 2005.
76. He does not mention any specific group that gives da'wah in such a way, neither in Sweden nor elsewhere. In informal conversations, I got the impression that singing and dancing as a part of da'wah was seen as something associated with Sufism. Moreover, in these conversations, reference was made to an audio link published at a Swedish website, Darulhadith.com, where Fawzan issues a fatwa against hymns (anāshīd), acting, theatre and cinema. He states that such things are taken over from non-Muslims (ghayr al-muslimīn), and are only meant to entertain and will not benefit Islam or the Muslims. http://www.darulhadith. com/v2/anashid-och-skadespel-i-islam/ (in Arabic with Swedish subtitles).

The use of modern transmission techniques is permissible for the spreading of information, but the creation of genres of teaching has no foundation in Islam.[77] The teacher returns to the requirement that the participants must give *da'wah* with knowledge. He stresses that people have different levels of knowledge, underlining the levels of authority. Moreover, he stresses that members should *never* try to explain things according to their own intellect or faith and must have knowledge about what they are called to. Furthermore, the caller must have knowledge about the person he or she is calling to Islam. For example, if the person is a Christian, or even an atheist, the caller needs to adapt his or her language and method in order to best present the intended message.[78] Another important thing is that callers must pay attention to their language. Callers should speak softly, like Muhammad. The teacher also speaks about the importance of having patience, something which Muhammad possessed in abundance, because it takes time to convince people. He also stresses that when giving *da'wah* members must be good role models, living according to what they teach. They must be steadfast, which, as we saw above, is a prerequisite for and integral part of *da'wah*. This, he explains, means that members must have good *akhlāq*, character traits, and always behave in accordance with the Sunnah. As mentioned, ethics and good behaviour are stressed in many lectures. To be a good role model also means, according to the teacher, to be prepared to sacrifice both time and money.[79] He again stresses that group members must know that all guidance is in the hands of God and that they can only do their best. The last point requires that participants should do sincere *du'a* (supplication) for the person they are calling to Islam, and to wish wholeheartedly that God will open his or her heart to Islam.[80]

77. Lecture 3: *da'wah*. The participants and the teachers seem to have no objections to technological developments and gadgets. The question is more about what they are used for.
78. It seems to me that the group in fact did not actively attempt to reach out to non-Muslims, even though they allowed such people to attend lectures, asking only that they adhere to the normative gender segregation. To my knowledge, they never conducted street *da'wah*, for example.
79. As far as I know, the teachers active in lecturing all had full-time jobs, doing the teaching on a voluntary basis. Based on the number of lectures delivered by each teacher, one can assume that preparation also takes up a lot of their spare time, making this vocation to spread Islam a very time-consuming mission.
80. Lecture 3: *da'wah*.

Following this more theoretical presentation, which in the lecture was filled with references to the Qur'an and Sunnah, the teacher turns to more practical comments on how, actually, *da'wah* is to be given. Since most of the people present are of a Muslim background, he mentions various places where they can do it and how. He tells the group members that their families may already be Muslim, but that their practices may differ and that they may even have elements of innovation, *bid'ah*, in their practice. He therefore recommends that the participants acquire a small library of Islamic books and try to encourage members of the family to read them. He advises them to bring flyers about Islam into their homes, to listen to lectures and to encourage the rest of the family to participate. The teacher speaks positively about participants explaining to family members what he has learnt (during lectures) and about talking generally about Islam (so that not all of that is discussed at home is about *dunya*, worldly matters). Group members should talk about *'īmān* and *'aqīdah*. To listen to Qur'an recitation is said to have a tremendous effect on people, including reaching parents who are not practicing. Group members should also try to bring friends and family to the group's activities as well, since they too may be guided through the lectures.[81]

The teacher mentions that members can also invite small groups of people home—for example, those who wish to convert, those who have already converted, and those who are Muslim but not practicing—in order to show them what Islam really is and how generous Muslims are.[82] He urges group members to come to lessons, telling them that new people are often in attendance. The group members, he says, should make sure to talk to new attendees after the lecture, giving them printed information if possible.[83] The teacher also says that 'sisters' have a specific responsibility at home, since they bring the children up. They are to teach their children to love Islam. Reflecting the discussion above on *al-'amr bī al-ma'rūf wa al-nahy 'an al-munkar*, the teacher says that members should not 'enjoin the good and forbid the evil'. They should avoid being overly stern, but rather seek to create a nice environment in which all that has to do with Islam is liked by children, making them happy.[84]

81. Lecture 3: *da'wah*.
82. Lecture 3: *da'wah*.
83. Lecture 3: *da'wah*.
84. Lecture 3: *da'wah*.

Belonging to the third level of authority, members of the group are also advised to conduct *da'wah* in their local mosque. The teacher says that it may belong to *ahl al-bid'ah*, people of innovation, but that most people praying there are common Muslims that are open to influence. He tells the participants that they must behave well in such settings and show respect to the elders. The worshippers may practice in a way that is wrong, he says, because they have always done things that way; members of the group should avoid criticism and correction. Furthermore, maintaining good relationships with the people in charge of the mosque is always beneficial, as this may facilitate the distribution of flyers, posters, and other information about lectures, and allow invitations to be extended to new students (i.e. those called teachers in this study, belonging to level 2 of authority) to give a lecture (*dars*) or sermon (*khutbah*). The teacher returns to the importance of books and suggests that the group members can also buy books and donate them to a mosque. He laments that there are few libraries in Swedish mosques and notes that reward is to be gained if someone reads a book that a member has donated. The teacher tells members that prayer rooms are a common feature of work or school settings in Sweden, and he encourages them to ask people to join in prayer and to place books and flyers in these locations—if they obtain permission, he adds. He stresses that, in the case of students (whether at university or at school), members must serve as good role models; they must do their homework and not be late. The teacher stresses that if a members behaves badly in this world (*dunya*), nobody will listen when he or she speaks about religion (*dīn*), stressing the importance of being steadfast as a part of *da'wah*.[85]

The teacher admonishes each individual in the audience to take responsibility. It is not possible simply to blame others, such as the non-Muslims, or to claim that the leaders are bad, since each individual is responsible and must take action:

> Each Muslim has the responsibility to improve the situation! Don't blame others! You should start with practicing. Learn about Islam, teach your family, and then the Muslim society where you live. Don't do more than you can deal with. Do what you can, according to the wisdom given to us from the people of knowledge.[86]

---

85.   Lecture 3: *da'wah*.
86.   Lectures: Jurisprudence.

This citation shows how each individual is personally responsible, and how he or she should perform *da'wah*, calling others to Islam, according to his or her abilities. The first step is to practice and learn about Islam oneself, and then to spread knowledge within an expanding circle. This is in line with the views held by the local group on *da'wah*. At least for now, *da'wah* does not include proselytizing in public space; it is, rather, restricted to relatives and friends.

Several creative and technical ways of giving *da'wah* are recommended. Members can create an e-mail list or SMS group, which can be used to distribute lectures. The teacher also mentions Facebook. While admitting that Facebook may be problematic, he nevertheless sees it as a useful way of reaching out. The teacher stresses that debates should be avoided.[87] He observes that while there is a lot of *da'wah* being performed in Sweden's large cities, little is done in the countryside—this seemingly being a call to group members to become active there. The teacher tells participants that it is up to each and every one of them to take responsibility. A problem today, he argues, is that Muslims expect somebody else to step up and assume the role. But, he stresses, they should think about the merits of *da'wah* and remember Judgment day. The good (*khayr*) shall be spread, and he adds that those who lecture, the teachers of this group, cannot do everything. Therefore, others (i.e. people of the third level of authority) can help to disseminate information about the lectures. He adds that if they want to help out, they can inform the 'brothers', in this case the local teachers.[88]

Final Comments

The handling of this kind of constantly required religiosity does not appear to be easy. Is it possible to be a proper 'Salafi' role model at all times and in all spaces—when going to work or school, riding a bus or shopping for groceries, or when surrounded by *kuffār* in this immoral society? How can this dilemma be solved? The teachers attempt to answer such issues and legitimate their stance on how to behave. It is considered a dilemma, it is hard, a test from God. However, that it is hard should not stop members from doing a 'Salafi-walk' through life. In a sense, it is a constant claiming of space, even when the ideal is to stay away from wider society. The way one walks, what one looks like,

---

87. This follows Fawzan, who, in his comments on Barbahari, stresses that they should avoid debates, because it may lead you stray. Fawzan 2012b, 271–283.
88. Lecture 3: *da'wah*.

what one looks at, and how one looks at it—all of this functions as an element of *da'wah*. Being oneself is, in effect, to be a *dā'ī*, a caller—even when one is only trying to learn about true Islam and how to practice it, belonging to the third level of authority. The ideal of non-integration is certainly there, but some members of the group have to move outside of the confined Salafi place into the public space, and it seems that a way to legitimate this move into 'immoral space' is to rationalize it as an act of *da'wah*. This is naturally easier for men than women, who are more restricted in terms of their movements; and yet, despite the restrictions, women do successfully perform *da'wah*. Women are considered important tools for the survival of authentic Islam. Simply by wearing the clothes they wear, women are seen as performing *da'wah*. Performing *da'wah*, even if merely on the level of dress code and behaviour, will bring reward on Judgment day. Such actions will assist in the group's mission to transform the grassroots community, and by extension the wider society. This attitude of striving to create moral selves can also be seen as a form of protection—a protection from the *kuffār* surrounding the group. Dressing, walking, and thinking in an Islamic way is a means of maintaining separation, even when members are in other ways 'forced' to 'integrate', or obliged to move around in the *kāfir*-society for some reason. To do *dhikr*, to focus on God, to listen to the Qur'an, and to attempt not to observe the immorality in the surrounding world seems to be a strategy. It can be seen as a way to 'sanctify' place and space, and a means of conducting a silent *da'wah*. To constantly remind oneself of God, through *dhikr* and *du'ā'*—according to what is defined as authentic teaching and method—is something that can 'save' the situation that group members find themselves in.[89]

The presentation in this chapter has shown how the ideology of the local group is put into practice in terms of *da'wah*. The group's teaching activities are considered to be a part of this mission, even though the group does not actively engage in public outreach. At present, *da'wah* seems to be restricted to the participants of the group, and there is no encouragement for group members to actively go out in public to spread information about Islam. Rather, members are to conduct small-scale *da'wah* missions among friends and family, or merely to strive to be steadfast Muslims themselves, which is the first practical *da'wah* step.

89. See Dogan 2012 for a presentation of similar methods among Swedish Salafis. See also Karlsson Minganti 2007.

The next chapter will focus on how the group legitimizes its view of itself as representing the authoritative voice of Islam. The strategies used to define in-group and out-group are also addressed. In addition, a discussion of how the group views *kuffār*, and how *kuffār* should be treated, is offered. The chapter will also address how this minority Muslim group views itself within the wider Swedish context. Understanding this better may help us to understand why there is a current focus on performing *da'wah* that is directed only towards the in-group.

Constructing In-Group and Out-Group

In this chapter, we shall probe into the construction of in-group and out-group. This is a very important issue in the group, and one that is addressed in various ways in almost every lecture, including those concerning creed and rituals, which are not focused upon in the present study. The empirical chapters above addressed how the group distances itself from the notion of imitating the juridical schools, in distinguishing what they consider the true method of understanding God's will, and the activity of giving *da'wah* as a main strategy to spread Islam. As we have seen, *da'wah* includes striving to be a steadfast Muslim, which is the most basic requirement. This chapter will show how the group elaborates on 'othering' in order to prove that the in-group is the righteous group. Here, dichotomies such as Islam versus the West and Muslim versus non-Muslim and other Muslims are established and used. When presenting the views on 'othering', the group also comments on the situation in Sweden, pertaining to views on segregation and emigration, which is also of relevance to this chapter.

Speaking in general, Salafi Purists mainly concern themselves with the purification of Islam (*tazkiya*) including spreading their creed (*da'wah*) to eliminate deviant practices through education (*tarbiya*).[1] Political activities, such as engaging in party politics, are regarded with suspicion since they are taken to lead to corruption. Salafi teachers draw an analogy with the Meccan period and the beginning of the Islamic mission, when the early Muslims used propagation and advice as methods, not rebellion. Purists thus interpret *jihād* as a peaceful struggle. Purist Salafis regard 'the West' as an eternal enemy polluting Islam. The struggle

---

1.   See Chapter 3, under the heading 'The Appeal of Salafism' (p. 65), for a presentation of the terms Purists, Politicos and Jihadis.

against the enemies involves the application of concepts and methods used by the pious predecessors, regarding everything else as innovation (*bid'ah*). Purists also regard Politicos and Jihadi Salafis as threats. As such, they usually boycott (*hajr*) their rival Salafis in order to avoid becoming polluted.[2] This is a reason why Puritan Salafis are not involved in inter- or intrafaith dialogue. Muslims in Europe are encouraged to leave, and Puritan Salafis in Europe often form enclave societies. Attitudes to other Muslims have caused a differentiation between creed (*'aqīdah*) and method (*manhaj*), and Purists argue that both must follow the example of the Prophet and his companions. This leads them to reject active engagement in politics through mass protests, for example. Engagement in political parties is seen as a Western innovation and Muslims engaged in such parties are accused of committing *irjā'*, in the sense of separating belief from action.[3] Purists accuse such people of following human desires and of having a rationalist strategy, one where religious sources do not set the agenda but are rather used to support the strategies. Purists can be described as seeking gradual change. More activist Salafis seek rapid success, sometimes through violent means.[4] The terminology used among Salafis can function as the foundations for political activism of various sorts, even though the ideal appears to be quietist, rejecting *takfīr* as part of *manhaj*. Roel Meijer argues that 'Political *takfīr* is a monster that mainstream Salafism desperately tries to keep in its cage while other currents within the movement have done their best to let it escape'.[5]

Westernization and Materialism

Jacques Waardenburg has reflected on insider views in a discussion concerning the problem of defining 'Islam' and 'the West', and he argues that attitudes to others change due to context, as do definitions. He holds that the antagonism between the two, 'the West' and 'Islam',

2. Wiktorowicz 2006, 217–221.
3. *Irjā'* refers to the opinion that a person was to be considered a Muslim as long as he or she had faith, i.e. confession of faith, and that acts were excluded as a means to judge whether a person was Muslim or not. It is an opinion associated with the group Murji'ah that reacted against the Kharijis who turned against 'Ali in early Islam, holding him to be a sinner. According to the ideology of Murji'ah, a person could not be excluded from the *ummah* due to sinful acts. If one confessed the faith (*shahadah*) one was regarded a Muslim.
4. Wiktorowicz 2005b, 215.
5. Meijer 2009, 19.

is understandable from a Muslim (insider) viewpoint based on the colonial past, which created a strong need for defence of the 'Muslim self' against the dominating West.[6] Such a perspective can also explain the ubiquitous criticism of Westernization. Ibrahim Abu-Rabi' shows that 'the West' has been regarded in different ways by Muslims. In some cases, the West has been seen as a source of inspiration and of salvation from the problems in society and an identification between the 'Self' and the 'Other' has then been made. Another position is represented by the Arab Left, which takes the approach of analyzing the genesis and development of capitalism in the centre (the West) and its impact on the periphery and the process of globalization. The West has also been apprehended as a political/cultural project aimed at the colonization of the Arab and Muslim world, which indicates that the 'Self' is identified in opposition to the 'Other'.[7] In the case of the group in focus, it can be said that it demonstrates the latter category of thought, whereby the West and Islam are constructed as opposites. The West is often represented as being equal to materialism, which is thoroughly rejected, as an aspect of the mundane (*dunya*).

As the introductory chapter illustrated, we find among many Muslims a meta-narrative binary which underlies the interpretation of Islam, where the West is associated with negative aspects and Islam becomes the positive pole of identification. This has already been shown in the empirical material presented above. However, in several lectures, this is expressed more explicitly than above. The teachers criticize the West, or Westernization and materialism, in various ways, and the participants are told what true happiness is and how avoiding Westernization *should* affect their lives. The teacher explains that people have different opinions about happiness and frequently make mistakes based on a misunderstanding of what true happiness is. To gain money, material stuff, and engage in forbidden actions are false ways to reach happiness. The only way to find true happiness is to follow the scriptures, the teacher argues. In the following citation, the polarization against materialism is apparent and the way to have a happy life based on scripture appears. Moreover, there is no excuse given to those who are employed and work with things that are defined as forbidden, *harām*, showing the serious effects adhering to the teaching would entail if put into practice.

6.   Waardenburg 2003, 495.
7.   Abu-Rabi' 2004, 55.

All people strive to get a happy family. Nobody wants to live in an unhappy relationship. Right? But people have different ways to have a happy family. Some people think that it is to collect a lot of cash, money. The husband works day and night and neglects his family. The children hardly see him. When he is at home he is tired and has no time for the kids. And if you tell him to take care of the family he will say that he works in order for them to have a good life. That is the usual argument. Right? Some have one job, two jobs. And some *'audhubillāh* [I seek refuge in Allah] has a *harām*-job [that includes forbidden things, for example selling pork]. They take a *harām*-job because they say they must support the family. This is wrong! Then you have gone to extremes, which Islam did not order. Others believe happiness is to have a big family. That you get happy when you have many kids. Ten kids. Fifteen kids. But this is also not the truth. It is good to have many kids, *mashallah*, in Islam, but it is also good to take care of them and give them an Islamic upbringing. Others think that happiness is to buy larger apparatuses, a larger TV, and then everyone will be happy. Everyone gets their own TV. More x-boxes, play-stations, games, and our kids will be happy. More films. More Internet. Faster Internet. Everyone will be happy. But is this the way to happiness? No! It may rather be the way to unhappiness. Right? So, there are different understandings of how to get a happy family and today, *inshallah*, we will mention some things from the Qur'an and Sunnah concerning how people can have a happy family. A happy life.[8]

The teacher follows up with the next significant teaching about how to achieve true happiness, which he defines as building one's life on faith and good deeds and to fill one's life with subordination to God, which will lead to a reward in this life and the next.

The two most important things in happiness are to complete *'īmān* [faith], and this also requires to gain knowledge of religion, and to do good deeds. What is the definition of a good deed in Islam? A good deed is the one who is conducted for the sake of Allah and in accordance with the Sunnah of the Prophet *sas*. These people will be given happiness. And Allah *swt* says that He will reward them for the best things that they have done. This is for the next life. In this life happiness and in the next reward for good deeds. A total, *ya'nī*, eternal happiness in Paradise that Allah *swt* says is an eternal reward. Gift. People will get what they wish in *Jannah* [Paradise] in eternity. This is the largest reward for those who obey Allah *swt*. So you shall fill your home with faith, *'īmān*, and obedience to Allah *swt*. Then *inshallah* your home will be happy.[9]

8.   Lecture 5: Family.
9.   Lecture 5: Family. *Swt* is the abbreviation of *subhāna wa ta'āla*, Exhalted and Glorified be He.

This is said in a lecture centred on family life, one in which marriage is described as cooperation in good: 'To cooperate in good. The husband reminds his wife to do good deeds. And the wife reminds her husband to do good deeds.'[10] The teacher ends this particular lecture repeating the weakness of human beings, and comments that, especially in societies such as the one in which they live, there is a need for someone to remind them and help them to be steadfast in religion to gain reward, and here marriage is held to be very important:

> Humans are weak and forgetful. And especially in this society, you will need someone to remind you and therefore the Prophet mentioned that one of the best things in this life for a man is a woman who reminds him to obey Allah, who helps him to enter Paradise. This is the biggest gift you can get in this life. Of course after Islam and Sunnah *ya'nī.* [...] And the same for a woman. That she gets a husband that helps her to become a better woman so that they together, *inshallah,* may go Paradise.[11]

This next citation concerning women further illustrates the idea that there is a conflict or contradiction between Islam and the West. Once again, ideal is compared to practice, just as culture is distinct from and compared to religion.

> The woman in Islam is not a sex-object, as she is in the West. She is a kind of thing used for ads to sell cars or something. Beautiful women. Scantily clad women. A woman is more than that. That which matters is what is within her. Her faith. Her character. And the woman wears the dress that Allah ordered her, not as some say that it is [because of] culture. It says in the Qur'an that women should cover. And that is not culture, but religion. [...] The Muslim woman is respected. You don't whistle after her. You don't flirt with her. She is respected, right? [...] And people may think it is right or wrong, but it is a fact and will always be. Men are weak for women and if she dresses in a provocative way, she will be treated differently. It is simply like that and it cannot be changed. The woman in Islam got, 1400 years ago, many rights that the woman in the West recently got. A few hundred years ago or something there was a conference in Europe on the topic whether the woman is a human being or not. What is that? In Islam it was always the case. She is created from Adam. They are human beings. And the best of them are the most pious. She got rights of inheritance 1400 years ago. Look at the many societies where women today don't have that. [...] In Islam she has the right to inherit. She also has the right to be

10.   Lecture 5: Family.
11.   Lecture 5: Family.

financially supported. The husband must support his wife in Islam. It is an obligation. He must pay the rent, buy food and clothes. [..] These clothes are comfortable. We don't have to think about what we look like. I wake up in my pajama, put the *abāyah* on and go out. Nobody looks at me. But what happens in Sweden? A woman stands in front of the mirror perhaps one hour before she goes out, before she dares to open the door. Two hours for some. [...] And that people treat women bad maybe has to do with culture. Some un-Islamic cultures that unfortunately exist. That people may have taken from other religions or the country where they live that has nothing to do with Islam. There is no honorary killing in Islam! Forbidden! So you have to differ between thing and person! In Islam you respect women! You shall be kind and soft to your woman![12]

One topic often presented in relation to Westernization is the preoccupation with this world instead of the next (*al-ākhirah*). *Zuhud*, renouncing worldly pleasures, is explained as working for the next life and avoiding being preoccupied with this world (*dunya*). The teacher stresses that members need 'to have the *dunya* in the hand, not the heart!'[13] He explains that participants should adopt the role of a stranger or a traveler in this life. 'This life is like a market where you should invest, in good deeds. Or, we are like farmers, who plant good deeds like seed that give good plants.'[14] The teacher informs about how Satan distracts people, giving false promises and leading them astray. '*Dunya wa Shaytan*' are the two things that must be avoided.[15] He exclaims that 'this life is nothing in comparison [to Paradise]! It is worthless!'[16] He is very critical and demands sacrifice. 'Who is ready to change their work in order to be allowed to pray [at work]?' He mentions other things that Muslims do in order to be 'a part of this world', like shaving their beards. He simply says: 'This is wrong!' He equates this to giving priority to *dunya*. But this does not mean that all responsibility to this world should be given up, and that this life should be dedicated exclusively to prayer. The teacher rejects such forms of ascetic behaviour. A Muslim, he states, shall marry, get a family, and provide for the family. Moreover, he says that a Muslim should have a good education, a good job, and make money. With this the Muslim can help the *ummah*. Yet most important of all is Islamic education. He complains that there are no *'ulamā'* in

---

12. Lecture 4: Islam.
13. Lecture 12: *Zuhud*.
14. Lecture 12: *Zuhud*.
15. Lecture 12: *Zuhud*.
16. Lecture 12: *Zuhud*.

Sweden or Europe and that an increase and spread of Islamic knowledge is needed. 'This is the best investment (*tijārah*) that you can do today! To spread knowledge about and to strengthen Islam!'[17] In this sense, a fundamentalist community like the one I observed may be viewed by group members as a rescue vessel, one offering protection and escape while living in an environment considered impure and materialistic. As part of the group, they are called to avoid giving priority to worldly matters, focussing instead on Islam.[18]

Limiting *Takfīr* within the Group

Salafism is, as we have seen, multivocal and decentralized. Salafis create an 'imagined community', one which bypasses loyalty to states and blood relations, and one which spreads certain values through networks of like-minded individuals.[19] Salafi interpretations diagnose the problem as Islam being threatened. The threat comes from people or states having contact with unbelievers (*kuffār*). The proposed remedy is to avoid such contacts, and the action required depends on what political stance the interpreter has. Some call for a rather passive separation, a segregation; others call for *takfir*, accusing others of being infidels; others call for violent *jihād*.[20] The view of *jihād* has divided the Salafis into two groups—those who believe that it is permissible, and those who believe that it is not. The groups accuse each other of ignorance. Purists argue that others have deviated and call them, for example, Qutubis or modern Kharijites, whereas Jihadis accuse other Salafis of being 'shaykhs of authority', insinuating that they are bought by the regimes.[21]  Here we can also note that there seems to be a difference that is related to whether the interpreters frame the problem in terms of either a religious or a political threat.

17. Lecture 12: *Zuhud*.
18. This strategy is of course not unique to Islamic groups. See for example Wilsson 1992.
19. The notion of 'imagined community' is from Benedict Anderson in his discussion on nation. Here, the 'imagined community' of Salafis shares the notions he presents, not least the idea of community conceived as a deep and horizontal connection of fraternity. Anderson 2006, first published 1983.
20. See also Wagemakers 2008.
21. Wiktorowicz 2005b, 215–216. Using the word Qutubis is a way to portray a group or individuals negatively as partisans. It refers to Sayyid Qutb (1906–1966), an important ideologue for the Muslim Brotherhood.

As Salafis act to promote a network of shared meaning, there is profound disagreement over interpretations of tactics and jihad. This disagreement— and the resulting fragmentation—is exacerbated by the decentralized nature of network-based activism, since there is no coordinated authority capable of imposing interpretations or standards. [...] As a result, the community speaks with multiple voices, especially when it comes to violence.[22]

Da'wah can be seen as a striving (*jihād*). The possibility, or the allowance, to proselytize (or not) is a major issue for how to approach the non-Muslim environment.[23] The others, the non-Muslims, may be regarded as potential Muslims.[24] Regarding Purists in general, it can be stated that they argue that certain conditions must be fulfilled before *jihād* can be performed. Purists hold that Muslims must first purify themselves (*tafsiya*) and be educated (*tarbiya*). Through a transformation of individuals, society is expected to change. 'Jihad is thus viewed as the final stage of development that can be reached only after the Muslim community is unified and strong, certainly not the conditions that prevail today.'[25] The group that is in focus in this study corresponds to such a puritan view, and as such polarizes against other views on *jihād*.

As already mentioned, an important aspect of the discussions on jurisprudence within the local group is the insistence on a holistic law, one including both rituals and transactions on a more mundane level. This aspect is brought up apologetically against those who hold that Islam is important only in relation to ritual practice. This, the teacher argues, actually leads holders of this view away from Islam. Simultaneously, he argues that those who advocate violence against such people are non-Muslims.[26]

22. Wiktorowicz 2005b, 216.
23. March 2009a, 72–73. March refers to, for example, Mahmud Shaltut (1983), *al-Qur'ān wa al-qit'āl* (Beirut: Dar al-Fath); Muhammad Abu Zahra (1964), *al-'alaqāt al-duwaliya fī al-islām* (Cairo: al-Qawmiya). March also mentions Shaltut as an example of a modernist who strongly enforces the right to proselytize, which marks an activist stance.
24. March 2009a, 75–76. A discussion unfolding as critique of this view of 'da'wah-as-expansion' is found in March 2009a, 76–91. Here, he rather elaborates the contemporary view of striving for *da'wah* as a doctrine of recognition where the Muslim interpreters discuss the ethics of *da'wah* and how to approach the non-Muslim other with solidarity and moral obligation.
25. Wiktorowicz 2005b, 227.
26. Lectures: Jurisprudence.

Many Muslims claim that things that have to do with transaction, trade, interests and things like that do not have to follow religious rulings, and only take rules regarding rituals from Islam. [...] This is totally wrong! The other extreme is those who say that a Muslim who rules with something other than the divine laws is a *kāfir*, and we need to rebel against him, blow him up, kill him. This is the Khawārij, *takfīriyun*, those who say that Muslims are non-Muslims because they do these sins.[27]

The teacher thus takes care not to automatically identify such a person as a *kāfir*. Similarly, he does not advocate the use of violence against those defined as *kuffār*. As such, he can be seen to demonstrate a more lenient attitude in comparison to many other groups that he apparently wishes to distance himself from, such as Jihadis. However, he still argues that a failure to follow the entirety of Islamic law, in all of its aspects, indicates that a person has left, or at least risks leaving, Islam.

As Muslims, we should know that the one who says that it is allowed [to use non-Islamic laws], or [that it is] equally good or better to rule with non-divine rulings, this person is not a Muslim. This leads a person out from Islam, and this is supported with the consensus of all the people of knowledge. All the people of knowledge are against that. A person who thinks that Islamic rule is better, but he has weaknesses, he takes bribes (*rishwah*), for example, and is afraid that he will lose his position as a ruler, for example through the interference of the United Nations, EU, but he still thinks that Islam is better, he will not have left Islam, as the people of knowledge have explained since the time of the *sahābah*. As ʿAbdullah ibn al-ʿAbbas [Muhammad's cousin and transmitter of several *ahādīth*, d. 688] explained, it can be big *kufr* that takes you out of Islam, or small *kufr* that does not. However, this does not make it allowed to rule with non-divine rules. But this does not mean that such a person becomes a *kāfir*, and that anyone should do terrorist actions against him, as many of the so-called Islamic groups do. If you look at them, they say that they want to apply *sharīʿah*, but they did not even begin with themselves. They are not practicing Islam as they should.[28]

A non-violent approach is clearly expressed in lectures, with the identification of others as *kuffār* being the only permissible sanction available for non- or faulty observance of Islamic law. In the above citation, we can also note how the teacher stresses the importance of members focussing on their own actions and comportment, something that reflects the views expressed above concerning *daʿwah*.

27. Lectures: Jurisprudence.
28. Lectures: Jurisprudence.

Regarding the local group, it can be said that it clearly rejects violence, considering it to be non-Islamic. The argument is made that violence has no foundation in the sources. The teachers all acknowledge that Islam and Muslims are apprehended as being violently inclined. This, they argue, is to be blamed on media representations of Muslims as terrorists and suicide attackers. Such people are condemned in the group as being non-Islamic.

> Do these things have anything to do with Islam? Answer: No! It has nothing to do with Islam. Allah did not order Muslims to become terrorists. It is not written in the Qur'an. A few people do this. And they have a faulty understanding of Islam. In Islam you are not allowed to kill innocent people. You are allowed to defend yourself, sometimes fight for justice. But that is on the battle field. The Prophet Muhammad forbade the killing of women and children, the elderly. You cannot break a branch or kill an animal without a reason. It is forbidden to kill yourself in Islam, that is *harām*. How can you blow yourself up? This is forbidden and you must avoid it. Islam is free from this. All people of knowledge today say it is forbidden. [...] And look at the different kinds of terrorists, there are not only Muslims who are terrorists. Look at George Bush. He was also a terrorist, right? But he used a different kind of way, he says there are weapons of mass-destruction. He lies. And kills hundreds of thousands of people. To get oil to his own country. Is not that terrorism? It is almost worse. Both are wrong but what he does is almost worse. What Israel does to Palestinians is also terrorism. Apartheid. Racism. Same thing. But people give it different names. You kill people in the name of democracy, or to get oil. *A'ūdhu billah* [I seek protection in Allah]! That is something very evil. There are many evil people today. And who conducts most wars today? Who causes most problems in the world? That is not Muslims. Muslims hardly have anything to say. It is the West that destroys in Africa, in Asia and so on. And this is known from colonization, that they were always there and destroyed in these countries and caused problems between people. This is also terror. Anyhow, don't let me start with politics now. But it is good if people are objective and try to differ between thing and person. It is a difference between Islam and Muslims. The majority of Muslims don't do things like this. Reject these things! We are against injustices that are in our countries, but that does not legitimize such methods that are wrong. You cannot take the law into your own hands and kill innocent people! That is wrong![29]

This citation also shows that the words 'Islam' and 'Muslim' are used to refer to different things. The distinction appears to be worthy of repetition, helping to establish who is a true Muslim and to strengthen

29.   Lecture 4: Islam.

the in-group. Moreover, this citation also shows how 'the West' is apprehended as immoral, guilty of stealing natural products from Muslims and accusing them of terrorism. The teacher maintains that the opposite is, in fact, the case—it is 'the West' that performs acts of terror.

Fuel for Hell

The teacher refers the Prophet Muhammad, who said that the one who does not follow his orders is a humiliated person. He laments, regretting that this can be seen in the Muslim world today, when Muslims attempt to imitate *kuffār*.

> It is wrong when Muslims attempt to look like *kuffār*. How and why should we imitate them? These people that Allah has described as people who are lost, in darkness, who will not be forgiven if they die as *kuffār*. A people who has Allah's curse over it! How can we want to be like them?[30]

The teacher then refers to the Qur'an: 'But whoever turns away from My reminder, surely for him (there will be) a life of deprivation, and We shall gather him blind on the Day of Resurrection' (Q 20:124).[31] The teacher speaks of the miserable state of the *kuffār*, offering their state as a warning to the participants. And, as so often, the lecture turns to warnings about Judgment day:

> We can see this in reality. Look at non-Muslims, the *kuffār*, how unhappy they are in their lives, even if it looks like they are happy considering their appearance. Look at how much anti-depressive pills they eat. Look at how much they drink and drugs they take to forget their problems. And the worst thing they know is to talk about death and the next life.[32]

The teacher speaks vividly of the angel of death who will come and take their souls. The *kuffār*, he makes clear, will scream from pain. Judgment day will arrive and then they will be thrown into the fire, which is unimaginably hot. They will wear clothes made of fire, drink boiling water, for eternity. The mildest punishment in Hell will see a man wearing burning shoes that will make his brain boil.[33] The teacher continues to warn the group members, before concluding that Islam will be victorious, regardless of the *kuffār*.

30. Lecture 1: Steadfast.
31. Lecture 1: Steadfast.
32. Lecture 1: Steadfast.
33. Lecture 1: Steadfast.

This is serious. We must wake up. Muslims must wake up and start again. We have to make *tawbah* [repentance] to Allah and take religion seriously. Do our prayers. Do what Allah wants. Keep away from *harām* [that which is forbidden]. If we don't then Allah will replace us with another people, who are better than us. [...] We as Muslims must know that the future belongs to Islam. This world will be ruled by Islam. 'They want to extinguish the light of God with their mouths, but God refuses (to do anything) except perfect His light, even though the disbelievers dislike (it)' (Q 9:32). 'He (it is) who has sent His messenger with the guidance and the religion of truth, so that He may cause it to prevail over religion—all of it—even though the idolaters dislike (it)' (Q 61:9).[34]

Engaging in the group may be seen as a form of opposition to perceived injustices, ones often framed as the subjugation and exclusion of Muslims and Islam worldwide. Yet it may also be seen as resistance to 'Western' ideologies and practices, such as capitalism and inappropriate relations between men and women, which, as we have seen, are defined as inauthentic and immoral. This sense of injustice seems to motivate the teachers to call for a change of lifestyle. Starting on the level of the individual, this change will radiate outwards, gradually helping to transform the world into a better place for all. The teacher expresses optimism that Islam *will* rule the world, bringing hope to all. In the midst of a stigmatized and oppressed presence the future looks bright. The group members are the ones who will lead humanity to the straight path, which will secure for them an eternal place in Heaven, side by side with the prophets. Such narratives may function as powerful motivators for engaging in the Salafi lifestyle as presented by the teachers.

The constant 'othering' and definitions of in-group and out-group are necessary strategies, making possible a solid group identity that motivates the participants to adhere to the teachings. The ultimate goal is to enter Paradise and to be among the righteous. The teacher recites Qur'anic verses that sum up the main attitude that he wishes to promote:

If We had prescribed for them: 'Kill one another' or 'Go forth from your homes,' they would not have done it, except for a few of them. Yet if they had done what they were admonished (to do), it would indeed have been better for them, and a firmer foundation (for them). And then We would indeed have given them a great reward from Us, and indeed guided them to a straight path. Whoever obeys God and the messenger are with those whom God has blessed: the prophets, and the truthful, and the martyrs, and the righteous. Those are good companions! (Q 4:66-69)

34. Lecture 1: Steadfast.

A *hadīth* is also recalled, concerning the *asbāb al-nuzūl*, i.e. the circumstances or historical context of revelation, where one of the *ansār* (helpers from Medina) told Muhammad that he loved him more than anybody else and that he was afraid that he would not be with him in Paradise. Muhammad did not answer his statement. However, following this episode, the Qur'anic verses 4:66–69 were revealed. Upon saying this, the teacher becomes *very* emotional and starts to sob and slows down his usually high pace of speech. He then says: 'The one who obeys Allah and his messenger, will be with them, the prophets, in the next life. And *al-siddiqīn* [the trustworthy], *al-shuhadāh* [the martyrs] and *al-sālihīn* [the righteous]. So, we find that we must obey Allah *subhānu wa ta'āla*. And if we obey Allah, then we may reach the highest levels of Paradise!'[35]

Continuously, a polarization between the in-group and others is made. Similarly, the distinction between Muslims and *kuffār* is frequently encountered, with the differences between them often set in a framework of eternity. In the following citation we also see how the teacher stresses the importance of not imitating *kuffār*. Members of the group are encouraged to do what they are created for. This will result in them entering Paradise.

> We must be proud to be Muslims. We Muslims must be convinced. We must know that we are the ones with the truth. We are right and *kuffār* are wrong. Everyone who is not a Muslim is among the *kuffār*. And all *kuffār* are wrong. All who are not Muslims are lost. Only Muslims are rightly guided. We must look at things this way as well: They shall become like us and we shall not become like them! We are right and they are wrong. So, we must be proud to be Muslims. We are the ones doing what we were created for. It is the believers that will have a happy life. It is the believers that will be honored when they die. In the grave. On Judgment day. And with Allah's *rahmah* [mercy] enter Paradise. We, as Muslims, must seek *'izza* in Islam only.[36]

This citation highlights the requirement on the participants to be proud. They must be proud to be Muslims. As historian Mark Sedgwick notes, this is a requirement that seems to be stressed in minority situations and not what you would expect to find in Muslim-majority

---

35. Lecture 1: Steadfast.
36. Lecture 1: Steadfast. The term *'izza* means 'power', but here it is used in the sense of seeking 'refuge' in God, trusting and obeying God. *'Izza* makes it possible for the believer to become 'powerful' and a steadfast Muslim, the idea being that only God is trustworthy. 'Power' should not be sought from any other source. See also Olsson 2012.

countries, where it would not really be a matter worthy of consideration.[37] In a minority setting, being proud to be Muslim may be as challenging as performing prescribed rituals. In the light of the discussion offered in the introductory comments of this study, such a situation ought not strike us as strange: Salafism may be regarded as a strategy for claiming a strong identity in a hostile surrounding.

Membership of the in-group seems to be something that constantly needs to be reassured and affirmed. This is often done by defining the surrounding society as immoral and without belief. Another strategy is also to remind the participants of how they are being oppressed by the *kuffār* and their immorality, and how they need to be patient with this. Such rhetoric serves to support a passive and patient stance. Another technique is to compare the in-group with the early Islamic era, particularly the oppression that the early Muslims experienced. The teacher comments that earlier prophets had *sabr*, patience, even when oppressed. They were alone, ridiculed, and stalked but they had patience, and this is then the prototypical behaviour requested from the participants as well. The teacher tells many stories about early Muslims who were oppressed and beaten in an attempt to make them renounce Islam, but who instead remained patient and continued to be Muslim.[38] For example, on one occasion the teacher related how Bilal was tortured for the sake of God. Bilal's heart, he said, was filled with *īmān* and so he called out the testimony of faith in Mecca. Though he was punished by his owners, he never denied his faith. When tortured, Bilal called out 'Ahad! Ahad!' (One! One!).[39] At this point the teacher began to sob. Everyone in the room seemed to hold their breath. The teacher then concluded and summarized his lecture:

> We must strive hard to reach Allah's Paradise! It is not for free! It has a price! It is surrounded with things we hate so we need patience and we need to strive to reach it! From one thousand people, only one will enter

37. Sedgwick 2012; Olsson 2012.
38. Lecture 1: Steadfast. Fawzan also stresses the importance of patience, of accepting the destiny willed by God. Fawzan 2012a, 317–340. This is returned to often and is an important part of *'aqīdah*. 'Allah does not waste the reward of the believers. He causes calamities to befall the believers for purification or multiplication of reward.' Fawzan 2012a, 346. Fawzan states that a Muslim must believe in the divine decree and that it should not be discussed. Fawzan 2012a, 370–380.
39. Bilal was a black slave who converted to Islam. He is said to have made the first call to prayer.

Paradise! So this is serious! It is not a joke! The rest! The 999! They are just fuel for Hell! So, it is time that we start to take this religion seriously! That we do our prayers! That we carry *hijab* [veil]! That we are proud to be Muslims! To do the prayer when we are supposed to! Not to be afraid of the *kuffār*! To ask Allah *subhāna wa ta'āla* to give us success! To make us steadfast in this religion! To give us understanding and knowledge![40]

Hence, says the teacher, unless participants accept and practice the teaching of the group and are proud to be Muslim, they will end up as fuel for Hell.

Differ from the Sects

In many lectures, different interpretations of Islam are thoroughly explained, then rejected. Engaging with alternative interpretations is viewed as a positive experience: 'We must know the evil to know the good. Muslims must also know what is bad in order to know the good.'[41] Having knowledge of other paths allows the Muslim to choose the right course, to avoid eternal punishment in Hell. Here, we can note that the teacher argues that the paramount danger comes from other Muslims. The danger, he says, comes from the fact that, as Muslims, they are closer to the truth. Less danger is presented by groups that are clearly different and non-Muslim, for example Christians. The Mu'tazilites are one Muslim group singled out by the teacher.[42]

Several lectures are concerned with rejecting different groups that are regarded as wrong, belonging to the out-group. Sufism and Shi'ism are criticized for leading to fragmentation among the Muslims.[43] Everyone who rejects the followers of Sunnah is severely criticized by the teachers.[44] The Shi'ites are often targeted as being completely

40. Lecture 1: Steadfast.
41. Lecture 17: Leaders 2.
42. Lecture 17: Leaders 2.
43. Sufis are rejected by Fawzan because, according to him, they do not act upon the Sunnah or Qur'an. 'They only act by their tastes and whatever they find of ecstasies, saying "We receive from Allah directly and do not receive through the path of the Messenger (*sas*) because we have reached Allah; so we are not in need of the Messenger (*sas*). [...] This is the worst of falsehood and disbelief— we seek refuge with Allah against it!"' Fawzan 2012a, 363–364.
44. Lectures: Jurisprudence. There are a number of lectures dealing specifically with different groups in history that they wish to refute, such as the Jahmiya, Sufis, Khawārij, and Shi'ites. The Shi'ites are usually called Rawāfid,

wrong, and the teacher makes an effort to explain the reasons why. Simultaneously, he informs the participants about what is the correct attitude:

> Rafīdah [i.e. Shi'ites] says that those who hate *ahl al-bayt* are *nawāsib* or *nāsibī*.[45] Why do they accuse us of hating *ahl al-bayt* [the family of Muhammad]? Fawzan says that it is because they took the *khilāfah* [the caliphate] away from *ahl al-bayt*. This is what these creeps claim. So they even say that *sahābah* are *nawāsib* [...] and that *ahl al-sunnah* is *nawāsib*! [...] What is the truth? It is *ahl al-sunnah* who loves *ahl al-bayt*! Respects them! [...] *Ahl al-sunnah* does *not* exaggerate *ahl al-bayt*![46]

The argument follows Fawzan's commentary on Barbahari's *Sharh al-sunnah*, where he explains that defaming a companion of the Prophet makes one into a disbeliever:

> whoever defames or hates them is a disbeliever in Allah; because Allah commended them, praised them and chose them to accompany His Prophet, Muḥammad (*sas*). So, the one who defames the companions or declares them as disbelievers or disparages them is a disbeliever in Allah the Exalted and Majestic; and he is a denier of Allah and His messenger (*sas*).[47]

Fawzan cites Ibn Taymiya (1263–1328) in this respect: 'Whoever defames the *khilāfah* of any anyone of these [the rightly guided caliphs], such a person is more astray than his domestic donkey.'[48]

> or Rāfidūn to enforce the negative view held on them. They also reject the Jama'at al-Tablighi. In many such lectures, if not most, they build on the *Sharh al-Sunnah* by Barbahari, using the commentary by Fawzan (Fawzan 2012a, 2012b), scholars who are among the most influential authorities in the group. The question about the Qur'an as created or eternal is returned to in several lectures. See for example Lecture 16: The 73, sects 1–3.
> 45.   The terms *nawāsib* (pl.) and *nāsibī* (s.) are used among Shi'ites in a derogatory sense, indicating that a person hates the family of Muhammad.
> 46.   Lecture 13: *nawāsib*.
> 47.   Fawzan 2012a, 201. Rejection of Shi'ah, and other groups, is frequent in Fawzan's work. See for example Fawzan 2012b, 211–217. See also Fawzan 2012b, 230–232, where he rejects Shi'ah, called Rāfidah, because they rejected Zayd bin 'Ali bin al-Husain when he refused to agree with them in abusing Abu Bakr and 'Umar. Throughout Fawzan 2012a and 2012b, there are several parts that deal with the obligation not to defame the Prophet's companions.
> 48.   Fawzan 2012a, 203. Referring to *al-'aqīdat al-wāsitiyah*.

The teacher continues to reject Shi'ites on the basis of what he considers to be the exaggeration of the status of the relatives of Muhammad. He stresses that the people of Sunnah know that the Prophet's relatives are not without fault, but that they are loved because they are related to Muhammad *and* because they had faith (*īmān*). He mentions that without faith, they would not be loved, as is the case with Abu Lahab, the uncle of Muhammad.[49]

Turning against those who promote reason or dogmatic theology, the teacher says that *ahl al-sunnah* has been accused of accepting *tashbīh*,[50] comparing creation with God. The teacher rejects this position, which he associates with Jahmiya.[51] To prove that *tashbīh* is wrong, the teacher refers to Qur'anic verses showing that nothing is like God,[52] which is foundational for the group's creed. He explains that the group confirms the attributes in the Qur'an, just like God himself does in the Qur'an. Importantly, this does not mean that the group understands God as having a body, an accusation that had been levelled by some against Salafis. Rather, he stresses that they accept what is written.[53] He also rejects the Mu'tazilah because of their focus on *'adl*, justice, when referring to God, and their rejection of *qadar*, divine predestination.[54]

---

49. Abu Lahab (d. 624) opposed Muhammad and his message and he became the leader of the Hashim clan when Abu Talib died in 620 and he withdrew the clan-protection of Muhammad, which made his life in Mecca much more difficult. Abu Lahab is cursed in the Qur'an (Q 111:1–5): 'The hands of Abu Lahab have perished, and he has perished. His wealth and what he has earned were of no use to him. He will burn in a flaming fire, and his wife (will be) the carrier of the firewood, with a rope of fiber around her neck.'

50. The term means 'closeness', and in theology it relates to ideas that God is near humanity, or similar to humanity. The opposing term is *tanzīh*, which means transcendence or distance.

51. The Jahmiya is also criticized by Fawzan in his comments on *Sharh al-sunnah*, related to a discussion on innovation and who is destined for Hell. Fawzan 2012a, 48–51.

52. See for example the verse 'There is nothing like Him' (Q 42:11).

53. Lecture 13: *nawāsib*. This literal stance appears in Fawzan 2012a, 381–385, where he states that the nocturnal trip to Jerusalem and the heavens was made by body and soul.

54. The Mu'tazilah stressed that God is above all just, and therefore human beings must have free will. Were this not the case, they argue, it would be unjust of God to punish people with Hell in the Hereafter if God had predestined their actions. In this sense, the Mu'tazilah argued against *qadar*, predestination, and did not stress God as almighty, as the Ash'arites did.

Therefore, he argues, the Mu'tazilite view on God's unity, *tawhīd*, is something completely different from what *ahl al-sunnah* believes. Another name that Mu'tazilis call *ahl al-sunnah*, the teacher argues, is *mujabbir*, or *jabriya*, because of their acceptance on *qadr*, predestination.[55] He is very critical of the Mu'tazilah, since 'they place their own intellect before understanding the texts in the right way'.[56] He also speaks about various names that the group is being called, such as Wahhabis, Madākhil or Madkhalis etc., that is, a group following a specific person. The teacher takes task with the accusation that they belong to *hizbiya*, i.e. parties or sects.[57]

> When do they use such names? [...] When you don't have anything to say! When you have no proofs! [...] To call people things... What is that? This will not change! [...] The importance is in truth and the proof. There are also those among us, even among *ahl al-sunnah*, who run around talking and doubting. They accuse others of *hizbiya* and things. We shall be careful with such things. [...] But nobody is free from this. If you wish to walk the way of the Truth you will experience problems. [...] You must be prepared for this![58]

Interestingly, regarding the use of names, we have already seen that attaching names to members of the out-group is a polemical tool employed by teachers in the local group, a means of distinguishing themselves from outsiders. Name-calling is, it seems, a common strategy of 'othering'.[59]

While unity is stressed as fundamentally important, the teacher observes that it does not exist at present. This, he argues, is because so many differing interpretations abound. The teacher refers to the Qur'an: 'Surely this community of yours is one community, and I am your Lord. So guard (yourselves) against Me!' (Q 23:53). The teacher explains that this means that unity is broken and that the various groups rejoice in their own views. He refers to Fawzan again, who criticizes the various groups today who, for example, 'proudly' publish books about their

55. Lecture 13: *nawāsib*. Jabriya designates the idea that *all* actions are dictated by God.
56. Lecture 13: *nawāsib*.
57. Madkhalis advocate segregation and withdrawal as strategies. See for example Amghar 2009. The name stems from the influential Saudi shaykh Rabi' al-Madkhali (b. 1931).
58. Lecture 13: *nawāsib*.
59. See also Wagemakers 2012 for a discussion on this strategy.

views.[60] This is seen as a punishment from God—these people rejoice even though they have no true knowledge and are lost. The 'people with the truth' will not be affected by the fragmentation and different views, the teacher holds. They are steadfast because they have true knowledge. The teacher retells the story from Sunnah wherein Muhammad said that Muslims will split into seventy-three groups.[61] This, in the teacher's thinking, is a clear reference to the realities of the contemporary era. He adds verses from the Qur'an to emphasize the importance of following the guidance from God to be saved:

> [...] If any guidance comes to you from Me, whoever follows My guidance will not go astray, nor become miserable. But whoever turns away from My reminder, surely for him (there will be) a life of deprivation, and We shall gather him blind on the Day of Resurrection (Q 20:123-124).

This choice of this text further illustrates the importance of the Hereafter in the message of the teachers.

Ahl Al-sunnah Wa Al-jamā'ah

The teachers often use the phrase *ahl al-sunnah wa al-jamā'ah* to characterize themselves as different from *ahl al-bid'ah*, 'the people of innovation'. This is, for example, the case when outlining the basic creedal foundation, where belief in one God, his prophets and books, angels, Judgment day, and predestination are included. They reject innovation. Innovation is explained as either adding or taking away something from the Sunnah. They emphasize that a Muslim must follow the entire Sunnah: 'We must follow everything, don't remove anything. Don't add anything.'[62] The teacher stresses belief in *qadar*, 'predestination', which means that God is all-knowing, that he has everything written down that he has predestined, and that he is the only creator. God knows everything about what has happened and what will happen. He knows everything about everyone, including when they will die. To

---

60. Fawzan fears that youth will be influenced by the books published by those without knowledge. 'Especially nowadays when they are published, then printed with the best print and cover and also advertised at book fairs. So these persons find that an opportunity to publicize and spread slander against the companions of the Messenger of Allah.' Fawzan 2012a, 216.
61. Lecture 9: *ahl al-sunnah*.
62. Lecture 9: *ahl al-sunnah*. This is repeated in several lectures.

prove this, he refers to the Qur'an. God is all-knowing,[63] God does what he wants[64] and he is the creator[65] and sustainer.[66] Only God can will something into being: 'But you will not (so) please unless God pleases, the Lord of the worlds' (Q 81:29).

Considering *jamā'ah*, the definition by Fawzan is followed. According to Fawzan, *jamā'ah* is the 'Muslim community that is upon the truth. [...] The followers of the truth. It does not necessarily mean that they should be many; even if it is a single person who is upon the truth, he is called a *Jamā'ah*.'[67] On the basis of this, The group defines itself as being founded upon the truth. Fawzan stresses that one must neither disagree with nor abandon *jamā'ah*. This turns out to be important for the group's view on sources and authority, since Fawzan explicates that clinging to the *jamā'ah* is founded on two matters. The first is the methodology of

63. The verses are: 'Do you not see that God knows whatever is in the heavens and whatever is on the earth? There is no secret talk of three men but He is the fourth of them, nor five men but He is the sixth of them, nor less than that, nor more, but He is with them wherever they may be. Then on the Day of Resurrection He will inform them about what they have done. Surely God has knowledge of everything' (Q 58:7); '(It is) God who created seven heavens, and of the earth a similar (number) to them. The command descends between them, so that you may know that God is powerful over everything, and that God encompasses everything in knowledge' (Q 65:12); 'We know what the earth takes away from them, and with Us is a Book (that is) keeping watch' (Q 50:4); 'Surely We—We give the dead life and We write down what they have sent forward and their traces. And everything—We have counted it up in a clear record (Q 36:12); 'Do you not know that God knows whatever is in the sky and the earth? Surely that is in a Book. Surely that is easy for God' (Q 22:70).

64. 'Do you not see that God—whoever is in the heavens and whoever is on the earth prostrates before Him, and (so do) the sun, and the moon, and the stars, and the mountains, and the trees, and the animals, and many of the people? But (there are) many for whom the punishment is justified, and whomever God humiliates, (there is) no one to honor him. Surely God does whatever He pleases' (Q 22:18).

65. 'His only command, when He intends something, is to say to it, "Be!" and it is' (Q 36:82).

66. 'God is the Creator of everything. He is guardian over everything' (Q 39:62); 'People! Remember the blessing of God on you. (Is there) any creator other than God, (who) provides for you from the sky and the earth? (There is) no god but Him. How are you (so) deluded?' (Q 35:3).

67. Fawzan 2012a, 38. See also Fawzan 2012b, 57–69.

basing everything on the Qur'an and Sunnah and not 'on the *thoughts* of a particular person nor the opinion of So-and so'.[68] Fawzan repeatedly stresses this. 'The religion is not what men view or consider as good [...]. Rather it is the religion of the people which they have innovated.'[69] Fawzan categorically rejects that there can be any in-between position: 'it is either you follow the correct religion or you follow desires; there is no third of them'.[70] Innovation is repeatedly rejected and one who innovates is rejected as Muslim: '[Sunnah] and innovation cannot co-exist except the one of them will eliminate the other. Therefore, a person cannot be an innovator and Sunni (at the same time) [...]. Both attributes cannot co-exist in him; one of them must eliminate the other. This is one of the dangers of innovation.'[71]

Fawzan's comments show how he encourages patience on behalf of the *jamā'ah*: 'Even if harm, threat, condemnation or aggression should befall him, he should be patient and endure it as long as he is upon the truth.'[72] Those who do not follow truth have gone astray and are innovators. Concerning innovation (*bid'ah*), it is defined as 'whatever is introduced into the religion that is not part of it. How will it be known that it is not a part of it? If it lacks proof.'[73] This particular citation is also commented upon in the group. The members refer to Barbahari's *Sharh al-sunnah*, specifically the *ahādīth* related to the topic of sitting (or doing something) with an innovator. The heading reads: 'If you encourage an innovator, you have helped him destroy Islam'.[74] Fawzan explains that innovation is contrary to Islam, and that becoming involved in it is a contradiction of the Qur'an and Sunnah. In Fawzan's comments, the focus on Sunnah is clearly expressed.[75] He argues that encouraging of an innovator equates to assisting in the destruction of Islam: 'because Islam

---

68. Fawzan 2012a, 40.
69. Fawzan 2012a, 63.
70. Fawzan 2012a, 66.
71. Fawzan 2012a, 78. Moreover, the group must have a leader according to Fawzan who argues that it is not permissible to meet without a leader who serves as reference. 'There is no religion except with a *Jamā'ah* and there is no *Jamā'ah* except with an *Imām*; and there is no *Imām* except by listening (to him) and obeying (him).' Fawzan 2012a, 41. This is returned to when rejecting those who disobey leaders. 'In brief, the one who does not have an *imām* is like one living in the days of ignorance. [...] lives a life of anarchy.' Fawzan 2012a, 238.
72. Fawzan 2012a, 43.
73. Fawzan 2012a, 47. For a general account of *bid'ah*, see Robson 2015.
74. Fawzan 2012b, 332.
75. Fawzan 2012b, 332–337.

is the *Sunnah* and the *Sunnah* is Islam as it had preceded'.[76] Innovators oppose God, and anyone encouraging an innovator, in any way, acts 'contrary to what is recorded in the Book of Allah and the *Sunnah*... [which is] boycotting them, hating them, distancing oneself from them and not being pleased with them since [even] smiling (at them) indicates pleasure and being delighted with them.'[77] Fawzan's comments regard those who claim to be Muslim but who are not, in his view. In response to the *hadīth*, he comments that one can in fact eat with a Jew or Christian, but not an innovator.

> This is because a Jew or Christian is well-known to be following a path and religion that opposes ours, and he is of the people of the Book. As for an innovator, he claims Islam while the Jew or Christian does not; you already know that he is a Jew or Christian. But the problem is in regard to the one who professes Islam, whom you trust and sit with and he pulls you towards evil. His danger is worse than the danger of the enemy whose enmity is clear.[78]

Fawzan explains that the phrase 'If Allah knows that a man hates a follower of innovation. He will forgive him even if his (good) deeds are few' means that it is a part of *al-walā' wa al-barā'* since there should be disassociation (*al-barā'*) from 'Allah's enemies': 'This is one of the fundamental principles of *Aqīdah*'.[79] Here we note how creed is closely associated with the program of action (*manhaj*). Fawzan equates the support of an innovator with hypocrisy, arguing that God fills the heart with faith if a person turns away from an innovator, as this is considered a part of disassociation (*al-barā'*) and will bring reward on Judgment day. Innovators should be humiliated: 'It is obligatory to humiliate them [the innovators] because Allah humiliates them. This is also part of *al-Walā'* and *al-Barā'*'.[80] Thus, Fawzan does not accept silent rejection or hatred, but rather requires active humiliation. We can note, however, that while 'active humiliation' was brought up in the group, the issue was not pressed and no explanation of what 'active humiliation' would entail if practiced was given.

---

76. Fawzan 2012b, 334.
77. Fawzan 2012b, 334.
78. Fawzan 2012a, 225.
79. Fawzan 2012b, 336.
80. Fawzan 2012b, 336.

The Saved Group

Several lectures arranged by the group also brought up the topic of the 'saved' or 'chosen', who will call others to the truth. This is an important idea for understanding the concept of the 'in-group' and the perception that it is set aside in a special, chosen, position. The 'saved' are those who are now, in this time, given the truth by God, who has promised to preserve his religion.

> You know who the *munāfiqūn* are? The hypocrites! Those who show *īmān* but hide *kufr* inside themselves. If they get the opportunity to show their evil against the truth and its people, they will do it. This we can see today. They turn according to the wind and don't know where to turn. However, considering the *'ulamā'*, they only follow the truth. So we shall not look to large numbers, the majority, and follow them. The many may be the people of evil![81]

The teacher recites a verse from the Qur'an and says that God has, with his help, allowed a small group to be victorious, and that God is with those who are patient (*al-sābirūn*):

> When Ṭālūt [Saul] set out with his forces, he said, 'Surely God is going to test you by means of a river. Whoever drinks from it is not on my side, but whoever does not taste it is surely on my side, except for whoever scoops (it) up with his hand.' But they (all) drank from it, except for a few. So when he crossed it, he and those who believed with him, they said, 'We have no strength today against Jālūt [Goliath] and his forces.' But those who thought that they would meet God said, 'How many a small cohort has overcome a large cohort by the permission of God? God is with the patient.' (Q 2:249)

The teacher also warns them that 'the one who turns between different views does not have a religion! They are the hypocrites!'[82] He then recites another verse from the Qur'an: 'wavering between (this and that), (belonging) neither to these nor to those. Whomever God leads astray—you will not find a way for him' (Q 4:143). He warns the participants that they must be careful and follow God. He mentions that people who have split and disagreed have done so because they are jealous and hateful. Such people follow their own lusts and their own wishes. He reads another verse from the Qur'an, Q 3:112, which speaks of the

---

81. Lecture 8: The Saved Group.
82. Lecture 8: The Saved Group.

'rope' from God that must be grasped. This, the teacher explains, refers to the following of the Qur'an and Sunnah.[83] The teacher says that 'if a person with no knowledge strays, he follows the wrong Islam, but there is hope! Because, if he learns about truth he can change! However, if a person leaves the truth when having knowledge, then there is no hope.'[84] He mentions the *hadīth* where Muhammad said that there will be a victorious group holding on to the truth, even though they will experience hardship until before Judgment day: 'You shall know that truth *always* remains. Allah gives some people success in following the truth, regardless of setbacks and enemies who try to destroy for them, but they will not succeed. Allah preserves Islam.'[85] He then recites another verse: 'Surely We do indeed help Our messengers and those who believe, (both) in this present life and on the Day when the witnesses arise' (Q 40:51). He stresses the fact that truth will remain and that those of the victorious group will experience hardship but must endure with patience:

> Truth remains! The people who follow the truth remain! Even though they may not be numerous at times. Allah will not let the truth disappear! But, it is obligatory for the person who wishes to follow the truth to have patience with it. And patience with what he will have to live through. What has Allah promised those who wish to follow this road? He promised them that they will experience hardship, but he will never let truth vanish.[86]

Warning them that if they turn away from God, others will take their place, he then recites another verse and says it is a very strong one:

> There you are! These (people)! You are are called on to contribute in the way of God, and (there are) some of you who are stingy. Whoever is stingy is stingy only to himself. God is the wealthy One, and you are the poor (ones). If you turn away, He will exchange a people other than you. Then they will not be like you. (Q 47:38)

83. Here, Fawzan is used as an authority. In his commentary of *Sharh al-sunnah*, he condemns those who 'follow every caller without knowing where they are heading to' (Fawzan 2012b, 38) and 'The one who sways here and there has no religion; he is a hypocrite' (Fawzan 2012b, 39), referring to the verse: 'wavering between (this and) that, (belonging) neither to these nor to those. Whomever God leads astray—you will not find a way for him' (Q 4:143).
84. Lecture 8: The Saved Group.
85. Lecture 8: The Saved Group.
86. Lecture 8: The Saved Group.

The discussion is then turned from the fear that Islam will disappear, to the risk that God will give the truth to another people: 'Don't be afraid that the religion will disappear! The danger is for *us*! If we are not steadfast! Religion will be taken away from us and given to others!'[87] The teacher again mentions that people from this group call others to Islam and in the following citation we see that the way to do it is exactly what this group claims to be doing: 'They [the victorious group] will revive the Sunnah. [...] And they will remove *bid'ah*. They return religion to what it was when it was revealed. In each time, Allah will send someone to the *ummah*, *'ulamā'*, who will restore this religion.'[88] Referring to Fawzan, this is further established. Fawzan stated that God will revive the Sunnah through the 'followers of truth':

> They will resuscitate and revive it [the Sunnah] after it has been lost and buried, this is their way. They revive the Sunnah and kill innovations. They will revive this religion until it returns to the way it was revealed to Muḥammad (*sas*). In every era, Allah raises for this *Ummah* one who revives its religion, negating it from the distortions of the extremists, the fabrication of the liars and misinterpretation of the ignorant.[89]

Earlier people were fooled by what they thought was good in this life, the teacher explains: 'The earlier nations (*umam*) were not in disagreement and split because they knew the truth or because they searched for truth. It was because they were jealous and followed their lusts and were fooled by the good in this life.'[90] He adds that 'it is obligatory that we unite behind the book of God and the Sunnah of the Prophet *sas*. Muslims must follow the truth even if it is against your lusts.'[91] He then recites the Qur'an: 'Certainly We took a covenant with the Sons of Israel, and We sent messengers to them. Whenever a messenger brought them what they themselves did not desire, some they called liars and some they killed' (Q 5:70). Following this, the teacher clarifies which direction is to be taken:

---

87. Lecture 8: The Saved Group.
88. Lecture 8: The Saved Group. Fawzan repeatedly returns to this topic as well. See for example Fawzan 2012b, 41–50, where he assures the readers that the truth shall remain, even when hardship falls upon the true believers.
89. Fawzan 2012b, 44.
90. Lecture 8: The Saved Group.
91. Lecture 8: The Saved Group.

From this we must learn. Is this only a lesson of history? No! It is a lesson that we must follow the Qur'an and the Sunnah of the Prophet and the *sahābah* and the *tābi'ūn*, even if it goes against your lusts. [...] This is good for us! This should be in our interest! But to follow our lusts hurt us in the biggest way! 'If the truth had followed their desires, the heavens and the earth and whatever is in them would indeed have been corrupted. No! We brought them their Reminder, but they turned away from their Reminder' (Q 23:71). This is a strong verse. Write it down! Look what Allah says [in it]!

In this particular lecture on the saved group, the terminology used for the in-group gives us a clear idea of how the teacher wishes the local group to be understood—as the group having the truth, the group following the Sunnah and consensus:

The group who are victorious are those who follow the Sunnah. They are the *ahl al-sunnah wa al-jamā'ah*. They are *ahl al-haqq* [The people of truth]. Those who follow truth. Those with *īmān* and who love the truth. And Allah will guide them to truth because of this. Why is a person guided to truth? Because of what he has in him of *īmān* and love for the truth. So guidance has a reason. So we pray to Allah that we will have *īmān* and love for the truth![92]

The citation shows that group perceives itself as the group following the truth, as well as the shared view that if a person is a believer, he or she will be guided. Being guided is, then, another proof of one's belonging to the victorious group.

Foam of the Sea

Another lesson making use of a *hadīth* saw the teacher shed light on the present weak state of Muslims. The words of Muhammad are given:

The people [*umam*] will soon summon one another to attack you as people when eating invite others to share their dish. Someone asked: Will that be because of our small numbers at that time? He replied: No, you will be numerous at that time: but you will be scum and rubbish like that carried down by a torrent, and Allah will take fear of you from the breasts of your enemy and last enervation into your hearts. Someone asked: What is *wahn* (enervation), Messenger of Allah (*sas*): He replied: Love of the world and dislike of death.[93]

92. Lecture 8: The Saved Group.
93. From sunnah.com, with slight modifications. Abu Dawud, *hadīth* no. 4297, accessed April 14, 2014.

The teacher tells the participants that the time will come when the non-Muslims, the *kuffār*, will fight against the Muslims because of their weak state. This *hadīth* is described as a revelation, because it speaks about the future, which only God knows. The teacher says that the *kuffār* are split, but that they manage to unite around the fight against Muslims. He says that the *'ulamā'* explain that the *hadīth* shows that the Muslims have something that the *kuffār* want, and he explains that it is above all oil. The *'ulamā'* say that it will be easy for the *kuffār* to 'eat from the plate', because the Muslims are weak, like 'the foam of the sea'. This part of the *hadīth* is deemed important because it shows that the strength of Muslims is not their numbers but their *taqwā*, their fear of God. He rhetorically asks how many times a small group has been victorious, with the help of God. He refers to the Qur'an and the battle of Hunayn, where the *sahābah* assumed they would be victorious because of their large numbers, but they lost: 'Certainly God has helped you on many (battle) fields, and on the day of Ḥunayn, when your multitude impressed you but was of no use to you at all, and the earth was too narrow for you, despite its breadth, and you turned back, retreating' (Q 9:25).[94]

The only way to gain victory is said to be to practice Islam: 'If we give victory to Allah, through practicing Islam, then Allah will grant us victory. So it is wrong that Muslims trust large numbers, money et cetera. [...] The priority is to have *'īmān* [faith].'[95] The teacher stresses that quality is more important than quantity, 'just like the Swedes say'.[96] He mentions in this regard that there are really embarrassing translations in books and on websites. Furthermore, he criticizes Muslims who consider what the majority do when deciding what is right. They should follow the Sunnah instead, he argues, referring to the well-known *hadīth* on the saved group: 'The Prophet said that the Muslims will split in 73 groups. Only one will be saved from Hellfire. The rest are lost.'[97] The Muslims are said to have weakness in their hearts because of the love of this life (*dunya*) and fear, or hate, of death. It is described as the illness afflicting the Muslims today. Reference is made to Albani's explanation

---

94. Lecture 6: The Contemporary Situation.
95. Lecture 6: The Contemporary Situation.
96. Lecture 6: The Contemporary Situation.
97. Lecture 6: The Contemporary Situation. This topic is the focus of several individual lectures and also returned to in lectures not specifically dedicated to this subject. It is often based on *Sharh al-sunnah*. Lecture 16: The 73, sects 1–3. In these lectures, the teacher stresses that those who are saved will go to Paradise, even if only one person is saved in the end. The saved one follows the true path, which is the path of the Prophet and the *sahābah*. They are the

of this *hadīth*, namely that its purpose is not that we should accept this situation, but rather that we should avoid the causes for the situation. The teacher says that this *hadīth* is proof that we must leave the love for this world and fear of death, and that the only remedy is to follow Islam and to avoid innovations. 'Not through demonstrations and revolts, but to return to Islam. [...] It is not a new Islam. We already have it in front of us.'[98] The teacher reads part of a verse in order to show that Muslims must change themselves first in order to get God's help: 'Surely God does not change what is in a people, until they change what is in themselves' (Q 13:11). He argues that the *kuffār* cannot be blamed for their state. They must first ask themselves about the reasons for this state and find the cure. He refers to Ibn al-Qayyim (1292–1350), the student of Ibn Taymiyah, who said that this situation will not persist, since, as the Prophet himself had made clear, Islam will spread East and West and enter each house. 'There is hope!' Hence, the teacher concludes, Muslims will be victorious. He reminds the group of the Prophet's teaching that there will always be a victorious group in his *ummah* until Judgment day. The teacher calls this group 'the strangers' and 'the saved group',[99] which are seemingly used as self-designations.

One lecture specifically refers to a *hadīth* that is often called the *hadīth* of the strangers, *hadīth al-ghurabā'*, where Muhammad said: 'Islam began as something strange; and it will return as something strange. Paradise is for the Strangers.' When asked who these strangers were, Muhammad replied: 'Those who forbid evil when people become corrupt'.[100] The teachers refer to the group as the strangers, on the basis of this *hadīth*, in the sense of those who forbid evil. However, in one particular lecture, the teacher also relates this to a feeling of estrangement that Muslims may experience while living in the Western world, or among other Muslims belonging to the out-group.

<hr>

jamā'ah. Here, also Fawzan is used as a source. See Fawzan 2012b, 72–80 on the sources of innovation and the 73 sects. Here, he states that there are four foundations to all the sects: the Shi'ah, the Qadariya, Khawārij, and Murji'ah. This is returned to in Fawzan 2012b, 285–288.

98. Lecture 6: The Contemporary Situation.
99. Lecture 6: The Contemporary Situation.
100. Lecture 11: The Strangers. The *hadīth* is from Muslim, *kitāb al-ʾīmān*. Fawzan also refers to this in his rejection of using analogies in matters of creed. 'They rectify themselves and rectify what people have corrupted. These are the strangers. Why were they named the strangers? This is because those who oppose and challenge them are many; so they are the strangers in their home towns and among their contemporaries.' Fawzan 2012a, 468.

As a Muslim in this country [Sweden], or in the Western world at large, you can feel like a stranger. People look at you. Laugh at you. You are criticized in the media. At work. At school. Because of your religion. [...] The Muslim may feel like a stranger when he sticks to his religion. Among Muslims, you may also feel like a stranger, when you stick to the Sunnah of the Prophet sas. People look upon you. Call you things, because you follow the Prophet Muhammad. It is from the Sunnah, that the people who stick to the truth will always be few, compared to people of falsehood.[101]

The importance of building an Islamic society is stressed as the means of countering this feeling of strangeness. The way to do that is to worship God, something about which they already received guidance:

They [the prophets] came to correct the wrong faith of people, and their faulty *akhlāq* [virtue, morality]. [...] The last Prophet was Muhammad sas. He was sent to a people at a very low level. They worshiped idols, stones. [...] They were not developed. They were analphabets. They were under-developed. [...] Allah chose Muhammad among them to become a Prophet. [...] He was alone against all of humanity. [...] Then the Prophet could spread Islam over the Arabic peninsula. [...] He made them into the best of people, who worshiped the one God, with good *akhlāq*.[102]

The teacher cites the *hadīth* in which the Prophet mentions that the Muslims will be like the foam on the sea, regardless of their high numbers. He again refers to *ahl al-hadīth* and *ahl al-sunnah* as the people who stick to the Sunnah. He also mentions that they are *ta'ifāt al-mansūra*, the 'victorious group'.[103] The teacher draws upon a saying by Ahmad ibn Hanbal, commenting on a question about the people of *hadīth* and the saved group, in order to establish who they are and to convince the participants that they belong to the saved group. This builds on Fawzan's comments on Barbahari's *Sharh al-Sunnah*, where Fawzan argues: 'Do not go past the *Hadīth* and the people of *Hadīth* for they are upon the truth, they are the Saved Sect. When *Imām* Ahmad was asked: "Who are the saved sect?" He said: "If they are not the people of *Hadīth*, I do not know who they are."'[104] Fawzan also defined the saved group (*firqat al-nājiyah*) as those who follow Muhammad and his companions' 'creed, worship, dealings, characters and manners'.[105]

---

101. Lecture 11: The Strangers.
102. Lecture 10: *ummah*.
103. Lecture 10: *ummah*.
104. Fawzan 2012b, 258.
105. Fawzan 2012a, 58, 252–254.

Obeying Leaders

In a series of lectures, based on the well-known Shafi'i jurist al-Nawawi (1234–1277) as a source, the teacher informs the participants about the demand to obey leaders. It is stressed that Nawawi is ranked among *ahl al-sunnah*, but it is simultaneously stressed that he made mistakes concerning divine names and attributes.[106] Despite this, the teacher argues that since Nawawi did a lot of work for Sunnah he should nevertheless be respected. The teacher notes that this is a case that proves that it is not enough simply to pick up a book and read it—one must also turn to those with knowledge:

> To study these works, you have to study with someone with good *'aqīdah*. [...] You cannot just get the books and read them. You must study with the people of knowledge from *ahl al-sunnah wa al-jamā'ah*. [...] They [Nawawi and ibn Hajar][107] should not be called *ahl al-bid'ah*. There is a difference between them [*ahl al-bid'ah*] and, for example, Nawawi. We have been ordered to take what is true and leave what is wrong. But regarding them, they are a part of *ahl al-sunnah*.[108]

106. The names, or attributes, of God are words used to refer to God. They are often called the 99 names of God, but there is no agreed-upon list of these names. The names describe God as, for example, the compassionate, the merciful, the provider, and the creator. How to understand these names or attributes has been a source of conflict within Islamic theology, for example between the dogmatic theological groups Mu'tazilah and Ash'ariyah and their argument about how to understand the speech of God, the Qur'an. In the case of Nawawi, the teacher does not explain what mistakes he made during this lecture and I did not hear about it again. However, Nawawi is often connected to *tawfīdh*, meaning that the attributes were relegated and not explained. The attributes ought not to be taken literally due to the risk of anthropomorphism. This is regarded as a form of *ta'tīl*. The issue was not, to my knowledge, elaborated further in the group and when I attempted to discuss it with some of the others who heard the lecture, there seemed to be no interest in it. However, looking at the opinion of other Salafi-oriented scholars, this opinion on Nawawi is repeated. See for example a question regarding Nawawi and Ibn Hajar and a collection of answers from, among others, Bin Baz and Fawzan, on the website http://islamqa.info/ar/107645.
107. Ibn Hajar was, like Nawawi (773–852/1372–1448), a Shafi'i scholar. He was Egyptian and authored many works on *ahādīth*.
108. Lecture 17: Leaders 1.

This citation also shows that care is needed when calling people innovators. Having enough knowledge is crucial. The teacher informs the group that the examples of Barbahari and Ahmad ibn Hanbal confirmed that *ahl al-sunnah* should obey leaders. He refers to *mihnah* as one case that illustrates this in practice, specifically Ahmad ibn Hanbal's refusal to revolt against the leaders. Even when a non-Muslim becomes leader over Muslims, revolt is not the solution. The teacher argues that it is for the *'ulamā'* to decide what is best for Muslims, not just anyone. Only if the Muslims are *capable* of replacing a ruler committing *kufr* may they do it; otherwise, they must not. In that case, the *kufr* must first be proven (*burhān*) by religion. That interest is being charged, that people are committing sins, that oppression is being experienced, that disagreeable things are happening—none of this is enough to justify revolt: open *kufr* must be taking place.[109] Thus, we see how the teacher goes about stressing that the participants must obey the leaders and not revolt. In this sense, we can see the promotion of a passive stance that should only be changed when the leaders commit *kufr*, and that must also be proven by the *'ulamā'*. This, the teacher makes clear, is not something that an ordinary person can decide upon.[110]

The teacher repeatedly states that this is nothing new, that it was already explained in detail by the Prophet and the *'ulamā'*, and that it still applies today. Because Nawawi reports what people said regarding these questions he is used as a source, in spite of the mistakes he is considered to have made regarding the divine attributes.[111] The teacher stresses the obligation to obey leaders: 'When a leader sins, we shall hate what he does, but still obey!'[112] He also argues that this is the will of God, emphasizing that the unity of Muslims is essential: '*Sharī'ah* has closed this door. To protect the leaders. This is to unite the Muslims. Because fragmentation leads to bad religion and bad *dunya!*'[113] This also follows the arguments proposed by Fawzan, who, in his comments on *Sharh al-sunnah*, establishes the same view. However, the teacher explains that Fawzan speaks about Muslim rulers. Based on my observations, it can

---

109. Lecture 17: Leaders 2.
110. Fawzan also addresses the obligation to obey regarding prayer. He even states that if the leader is a Jahmi, then members should still pray behind him, but repeat the prayer. Fawzan 2012b, 159. He also states that one cannot take up arms against a leader, claiming it is part of enjoining good and forbidding evil. Fawzan 2012b, 184. Both *dalīl* and *burhān* are used to designate 'proof'.
111. Lecture 17: Leaders 2.
112. Lecture 17: Leaders 3.
113. Lecture 17: Leaders 3.

be said that the group does not make comment about whether they would include non-Muslims, for example the Swedish prime minister, in among their leaders.[114]

Fawzan states that to obey the leader (*imām*) is to follow the Sunnah.

> Fighting the leader is not a part of the established *Sunnah* from the Prophet (*sas*). [...] There is no *Ḥadīth* in the *Sunnah* that indicates the permissibility of fighting the Muslim leader even if he is sinful, oppressive, and unjust or embezzles wealth. [...] This does not mean that the leader should not be advised (if he errs). Rather, he should be advised secretly, between him and the one advising.[115]

Fawzan warns that disobedience to the leaders may lead to chaos and anarchy, which may pave the way for enemies that will lead to the ruin of Islam, a situation in which nobody is in a position to implement the law.[116] The remedy to such a situation, according to the teacher, is knowledge:

> The cure is knowledge! Muslims must have knowledge to change the situation. We have to correct ourselves, our families, our areas and our countries. Don't think you can do it because you have a lot of feelings for Islam, *hamās*, because that only leads to more problems. It will never lead to a solution for Muslims. It only causes more problems. The solution is to gain more knowledge. To learn what Islam says.[117]

In this manner, the teacher manages to distinguish who is a true Muslim, who belongs to the in-group, from those outside of it.[118]

114. Fawzan also explains that a leader should be appointed by *ahl al-hall wa al-ʿaqd*, which means legal scholars, and the rest of the people should accept their decision. This was the case when Abu Bakr was appointed caliph. The second way is that the leader appoints his follower, as was the case when Abu Bakr appointed ʿUmar. The third way is when a Muslim prevails over others and becomes their leader, as was the case after the death of Yazid, when ʿAbd al-Malik bin Marwan bin al-Hakam took over the affairs and became the new leader. See Fawzan 2012a, 220–226. The leader is called *imām*, which indicates that he is also to be a religious leader, and Fawzan expands on the rights of the ruler and the obligation to obey him. See Fawzan 2012a, 227–251. In several informal conversations with participants, Fawzan's rejection of *takfīr* against Muslim leaders was often brought up.
115. Fawzan 2012a, 241.
116. Fawzan 2012a, 242.
117. Lectures: Jurisprudence.
118. Lectures: Jurisprudence.

The teacher also refers to the last sermon of Muhammad, in which he stressed the need to fear God, to listen to and obey the rulers, to stick to his Sunnah, and to watch out for innovation. The teacher explains that fearing God (*taqwā*) means to do what God has ordered and to stay away from what he has forbidden. To listen to and obey the leaders means that each nation needs a leader in order to prevent chaos. He argues that the Prophet has explained in detail how Muslims should behave towards their leaders: 'Of course not if they order you to do a sin! But in all other aspects we obey. We don't revolt against our leaders! [...] As long as he establishes prayer!' He also mentions that there is fragmentation today, just as in the past, and that the solution for this is to follow the Sunnah of Muhammad and the *sahābah* and to avoid innovation.[119]

> Because the way of Allah is one and not many! The truth is one way, not many ways! Everyone cannot be right. There are those who say: 'It doesn't matter, as long as we are Muslims and recite the confession of faith, then we are together. It doesn't matter.' These people worship graves. Those blow themselves up. 'No problem. We are all together.' These condemn Abu Bakr. Those 'Umar. They say that they are best. 'No problem! We are together!' No! That does *not* work! Two things that contradict each other cannot be together! The way of Allah is one way![120]

Simultaneously, the teacher also reminds the group of Fawzan's comments about those who do not obey the leader (*imām*) because of his sins being equated to Khawārij. Rejecting Khawārij is, as we have seen, considered to be an obligation, and, not surprisingly, the local group rejects Khawārij. Khawārij are rejected by Fawzan too, because of their revolt against the leaders and their declarations about others being disbelievers. This is considered to be extremism. 'Excessiveness means addition to religion—i.e. addition of things to what is ordained in refuting evil.'[121] Fawzan states that when Khawārij (of today) are not in power, they should be left alone and given advice. However, if they attain power, fighting them is an obligation, in order to prevent their

---

119. Lecture: 73 Sects: 3.
120. Lecture: 73 Sects: 3. This follows Fawzan's comments to *Sharh al-sunnah*: 'The way of Allah is one. [...] the straight path is one. There is no diversity in it. You will not lose forever if you follow it.' Fawzan 2012a, 94.
121. Fawzan 2012a, 236. This does not mean that Fawzan holds that leaders who sin should be obeyed. He expands on this matter in Fawzan 2012a, 247–251, where he states that leaders should be obeyed, but if a command is wrong, that should not be followed.

evil. Fawzan's views on this are clear: 'They should not be fought on the basis that they are disbelievers. Rather, they should be fought on the basis of being Muslims who have revolted and transgressed against Muslims.'[122] However, we can note that the group does not elaborate on this. This may be because they are not currently in a position that would make lengthy discussion relevant.

A discrete approach to leaders is stressed, based on the example of the Prophet. The local teacher says in one lecture that anyone wishing to give advice to a leader should do so discretely and at a distance from the rest of the group. The Prophet advised discretion. Members of the group are not to criticize openly or to preach about points of contention. To do so would be comparable to actions of the Khawārij, who are rejected because of their use of *takfīr* and revolt against leaders.

> To preach about this, is from the Khawārij. Who are they? That is a lesson on its own, [...] but *shaykh al-islām* Ibn Taymiyah said they were the first to conduct *takfīr* on Muslims because of what they regarded as sins. Because of this [*takfīr*] they made the blood of Muslims *halāl* to take. This was exactly how the Prophet described them. They kill the Muslims and leave the others. Another thing is that they revolt against the leaders. And that they openly speak badly about them when preaching. The Prophet warned against them, that they are the dogs of Hell, young and stupid. The Prophet said that wherever you meet them, kill them, or fight them, and you shall be rewarded on Judgment day. [...] The point is that it is from the *ʿaqīdah* of Khawārij to revolt against the leaders.[123]

The teacher argues that when there is a problem, they shall be referred to those in power: Muhammad when he was alive, *ahl al-sunnah* after his death, and following them the leaders. He justifies this with a verse from the Qur'an:

> When any matter comes to them concerning security or fear, they divulge it. But if they were to refer it to the messenger and to those (who have) the command among them, those who investigate (such things) would indeed have known (about) it. If (it were) not (for the) favor of God on you, and His mercy, you would indeed have followed Satan, except for a few (of you). (Q 4:83)

---

122. Fawzan 2012a, 244.
123. Lecture 17: Leaders 3.

Another verse is brought up, offering additional support:

> You who believe! Obey God, and obey the messenger and those (who have) the command among you. If you argue about anything, refer it to God and the messenger, if you believe in God and the Last Day. That is better and fairer in interpretation. (Q 4:59)[124]

This is also relevant for the issue of *jihād*. Fawzan states that *jihād* is only legitimate when ordered by the *imām*, the Muslim leader. Furthermore, it must be well organized and it must follow Islamic rulings. He too turns against those who disobey this rule, since it would cause upheaval:

> But if chaos gets into it [*jihād*], then it becomes destruction as its harm becomes more than its benefit; [...] This issue is not one of disorderliness where one of the callers to *Fitnah* leading the extremists, radicals or ignorant people who do not know that he leads them to destruction and says: 'we are fighting in the cause of Allah!' This is considered as harm to Islam and Muslims. This is not *Jihād*; [...]. Whatever exceeds its limits changes to its opposite.[125]

From this, we can conclude that the advocated stance toward political leaders is rather passive. 'Silent hatred' is a suitable strategy for a group such as the one I observed, a group living as minority Muslims in Sweden. By adopting this position, the group avoids confrontation with political authorities.

Emigration

The teacher warns the participants, especially the young, to be careful about what and who they listen to, and he rejects those he calls 'activists'. Problems, he warns, 'shall not be referred to the activists! They shall not be referred to those who base themselves on feelings and lack of understanding, screaming slogans that they have! They will just bring ruin! They will ruin and fragment the *ummah!*'[126] He laments that the youth has left the people of knowledge; the only ones from whom insight and understanding can be gained. In the following citation, the teacher clearly rejects those who advocate violent *jihād*, and argues that the participants must not 'join a group':

124. Lecture 17: Leaders 1.
125. Fawzan 2012a, 228.
126. Lecture 17: Leaders 3.

The Islam we have today is not the same as when Allah revealed it. My advice to the students is not to speak to others in order not to be confused, but to speak to the people of knowledge. A sickness today is that the young swiftly accept new opinions. And not listen to *salāfah*. Especially when it comes to *jihād*. [...] The advice is to turn to the people of knowledge and to start to gain a correct *'aqīdah*. Then to study Islam from the true sources and persons who have studied and have a correct understanding of *al-islām*. Muslims must first unite! Otherwise they will fight against an enemy and then they will fight among themselves. Everyone must have the same *manhaj* and understanding! [...] Leave all groups and live on your own! This does not mean to isolate yourself, but it means that you shall not join a group![127]

In this lecture, attention is turned to the youth element present. The teacher tells young members not to be fooled and to occupy themselves with things that they do not understand. He repeats that the sources he mentioned during the lectures are clear and to be followed:

Stick to them! Practice them! Then knowledge will come in the future! You are not obliged to do more than what Allah demands! Study! Study! Study! Keep away from groups who lead you astray! Follow the *'ulamā'*! Don't take knowledge from whoever![128]

In speaking about the 73 groups, the teacher argues that *ahl al-sunnah* do not make *takfīr* (excommunication) on others. He asks the participants if the *hadīth* means that all groups who do not belong to the saved group are *kuffār*. The teacher answers the question himself:

This does not mean that all of these groups are *kuffār*. Some are! But not all of them! This does not mean that they will be in Hell forever, but that they are threatened by the Fire, depending on how much they leave the truth behind. So, *ahl al-sunnah* does not make *takfīr* on them, only when there is a proof that they have left religion. Otherwise, they are just concerning this question on *takfīr*. They are just in calling someone a *kāfir*. This is not easily done. And they do not do *takfīr* unless there is proof that he has committed *kufr*. Then, shaykh Fawzan says something very important. They [*ahl al-sunnah*] do not hurry in this question [calling someone *kāfir*]. This is something that the *'ulamā'* talks about a lot. [...] They also say that it is not permissible for someone without knowledge to say that somebody is a *kāfir*. [...] The one without knowledge shall remain

127. Lecture 17: Leaders 2.
128. Lecture 17: Leaders 2.

silent and not speak up in these questions! Another important thing is that we don't do *takfīr* on a person that has committed *kufr*. First, he must understand that it is *kufr*.[129]

Furthermore, the issue of segregation is constantly present in the local group. Evidently some members of the group experience problems while living among the *kuffār* in non-Muslim Sweden. Muslims, if they have the possibility, are encouraged to emigrate to a Muslim-majority country. Such a course of action, the teacher maintains, would help them be steadfast Muslims:

> Keep away from bad places. Places where sinners gather, such as bars or festivals. And, for example, also this country [Sweden]. Because, if you have the chance you shall *inshallah* move to a Muslim country because that will help you to be steadfast in your religion.[130]

Thus, the participants are recommended to emigrate, to make a *hijrah*, to leave Sweden for a Muslim-majority country. In the meantime, however, they are encouraged to follow the program of action as laid out by the teachers of this puritan Salafi group. As the preceding discussion has hopefully shown, political passivity and segregation are key strategies enabling the participants to live as steadfast Muslims in their current 'impure' environment. This is a strategy that might rightly be called 'sunnisized self-minoritization', wherein the everyday lives of the participants are affected in detail if they choose to follow the ideology promoted by the local teachers. The teachers occupy a position that sees them functioning with sacred authority, serving as intermediaries between the *'ulamā'* and revelation and the participants in the Swedish local setting.[131]

Final Comments

The group elaborates on the theme of themselves being the chosen or saved group. They are the ones 'with the truth', destined for Paradise—as long as they walk the straight path. Those not belonging to the in-group are *kuffār*. This criticism is directed to non-Muslims and Muslims alike.

---

129. Lecture 16: The 73, sects 3.
130. Lecture 1: Steadfast. See also Olsson 2014.
131. See Gugler 2011, who uses the term 'Sunnaization' to designate the striving to let Islam influence all aspects of life, in a similar manner to the local group of this study. See also Svensson 2012.

Those Muslims who are too concerned with *dunya*, with materialism, being Westernized, have an ambiguous position and it is doubtful whether they are really regarded as Muslims. Islam and Muslims are held to be two different things, just like religion and culture. What Muslims claim to do or say may have nothing to do with true Islam, according to this group. The group builds up a notion of being the saved group, and advocates a strategy for preserving their steadfastness in Islam that is founded on the imitation of the Sunnah at all times. They promote a passive attitude towards (though perhaps against) leaders. Leaders should be obeyed and not revolted against. The group advocates a lenient attitude towards calling others *kuffār*. This is something only those with knowledge can do. In terms of the group's own terminology, those in a position to identify *kuffār* have 'first-level authority'. In this way, the group leaders attempt to convince the participants not to enjoin in violent activities, but rather to be passive and to make sure they inform themselves about the dangers, gaining what is considered to be true knowledge from those who have it. They are to avoid joining groups containing 'activists'. Thus, the teacher emphasizes that the best strategy for those living in Sweden as a part of *ahl al-sunnah* is to avoid places where sinners gather. Friends are to be chosen from the in-group. If possible, Muslims should emigrate and leave Sweden for a Muslim-majority country where it will be easier to live a steadfast life in Islam. Sweden is an immoral and unbelieving society, and the minority Muslims living there should avoid contact with the *kuffār*. As we have seen, avoidance is the method, together with silence and segregation, non-violence, and an apolitical passive stance. This results in a 'sunni-sized self-minoritization'.

Epilogue

As the introduction to this study showed, the contemporary Swedish setting can be characterized as modern, upholding an idea of secularization where religion should be kept private. This is challenged today, and many argue that religion should occupy more space in society. Conversely, some maintain that religion already occupied too much ground and must be removed from the social sphere. The debate is heated, with critical remarks on religion principally concerning Islam and Muslims. Among Muslims, several interpretative stances can be observed. One is a more liberally inclined stance, advocating integration and democratic values. Another position is more 'fundamentalist', and has been defined as Salafism in this study. Salafism can be analyzed as a reaction against the surrounding society. In the context of Muslim-minority societies, many young people have turned, and continue to turn, to a Salafi-oriented Islam. In some cases, this seems to be mainly in terms of appearance and dress codes. In some groups, we can note that science and logic are promoted. This is coupled with the active giving of street-*da'wah* among non-Muslims in an effort to gain converts. In some cases, Salafis reject missionary activities in public space and do not actively engage in conversion work. Instead, they promote segregation and attempt live as pious Muslims, welcoming those who approach them. Salafism can be understood as a counter-movement, a movement of opposition, that seeks to combat immorality and capitalism. Salafism is also perhaps characterized by a fear of taking more place/space, since the awareness of the ideal of secularization and privatization of religion is strong. Salafis also appear to have a keen appreciation of Islamophobic attitudes, something that is used in the promotion of social segregation. Importantly, however, the drive among some Salafis to 'hide' may in fact serve to increase their visibility, and to fuel criticism and accusations of upholding a non-integrative stance and promoting non-democratic values.

The group that has been in focus in this study is marginal in Sweden and also among the various Swedish Islamic interpretations and practices that exist. There are of course various subjective apprehensions on what constitutes marginal and core. The group I observed is marginalized when considered in a larger national setting. It is 'minor-itized'. However, the group conforms to a different understanding of its marginalization. The members see themselves as occupying the centre; they are the ones who will enter Paradise. They are members of the victorious and the saved group. They are the strangers who walk the straight path to Paradise when the Muslim majority is like the foam of the sea. It is perhaps not really correct to describe this marginalization as a choice, but the participants seem to think of it that way. In many cases, the situation in Sweden may have contributed to marginalization being the preferred option. It may be that Swedish society is such that it is difficult for people to feel as though they can actively participate in the public space in society. A feeling of exclusion may not be limited to Salafi Muslims.

One likely reason for the appeal of fundamentalism is the socio-economic conditions that bring about segregation, where dissociation from mainstream culture can be understood as a strategy to reclaim a stigmatized identity. In such a setting, the disadvantages that partici-pants experience may be turned into something positive. Such reactive identity formations may also be caused by the surrounding society's hostility towards Islam and Muslims, which makes Islam stand out as a significant point of identification. Here, ethnicity and culture may be downplayed and a focus on a universalistic Islam comes to the fore, which in turn appears as a political ideology that 'explains' the situation of the participants in a historical context with eternity as a time-frame. Salafism affirms the self and rejects the surrounding society. Salafism may be seen by participants as personally empowering, offering a salvific interpretation and means of practicing of Islam. In this sense, the apparent growth of Salafism in Western Europe may be associated with a desire among participants to transform themselves into superior humans with direct access to truth. This is a radically different position as compared to feeling humiliated and marginalized. Participants are the avant-garde, but consider themselves to be part of the chosen group, which may be a psychological remedy to feelings of malcontent and exclusion. Hence, it can be understood as a psychological solution to the minority situation, where Salafism helps explain the situation and give guidance towards the future.

Even though the empirical data show that the group does not advocate the development of a political consciousness, preferring instead to focus on correction of faith and practice, it can be said that participants do attempt to bring about an Islamic consciousness that, if put into effect, would lead to an Islamic world order. A main aim of the group seems to be to articulate a 'new' form of life in the immoral and unbelieving Sweden. They wish to motivate action (*manhaj*), to establish codes of behaviour and ethics that appear as marginal and strange to most Swedes, including Swedish Muslims. To practice 'new' forms of life means, to members of the group, to live and practice the Sunnah, which appears as a vision of a holistic Islam put into practice. They stress that Muslims must accept the situation in Sweden patiently, even though this may be hard at times. Living in a Muslim-minority context is considered a test, one that requires patience and a need to constantly remember God and the Hereafter, which is all that really matters, in the long run, to members of the group. The 'core framing tasks' help to define the strategy, diagnosing the condition that needs to be remedied, which is the preoccupation with *dunya*, worldly matters, through Westernization, materialism, and the immorality that surrounds the participants. The group laments a decline of Islamic values globally, but also an increase of values related to consumer culture, and non-Islamic ideals, values, and lifestyles. The group promotes an ideal of an active piety through personal salvation, emotions, and issues of identity in a situation that sees them living in a specific minority situation. This kind of focus on piety is a multifaceted phenomenon. It concerns issues related to the problematic question of how to live and regard oneself as an authentic Muslim following 'true Islam' while in the midst of a hostile and immoral society. Throughout the lectures I observed, the teachers outlined a solution to the problematic condition, one which sees Muslims returning to 'the straight path' and following the program of action as defined by them.

The interpretation of Islam that constitutes the empirical material gathered for this study wishes to reform individuals according to an Islamic model or system, which by extension is supposed to lead to a reformation of the Muslim *ummah*, the (idea of the) 'community of Muslims'. In a manner of speaking, the group wishes to create a 'new' Islamic consciousness that can meet the challenges of modernity and the minority situation that they experience. From the perspective of the group, it is rather a striving to restore an original or authentic Islamic consciousness. Moreover, the rationale to motivate support and collective action must be understood in the timeframe of eternity, since those walking the straight path are destined to enter Paradise. Everyone else is fuel for Hell.

Some key issues stemming from insider Salafi terminology are as important in this group as in other Salafi-oriented groups and constitute the foundation for the program of action. One key aspect is the focus on *tarbiya*, education, which is a main part of the group's activities. This is mainly expressed as a form of *da'wah*, call to Islam. The teaching illuminates views on authority formed around a strict hierarchy focussed on what sources to use and who is allowed to teach. The local teachers are on an 'intermediate' level, while certain *'ulamā'* are considered to be the main authorities and the participants. Those who attend lectures occupy the 'lowest' level of the hierarchy. Group members should listen to the teaching and gain more knowledge; eventually, they too may reach the 'intermediate' level of knowledge—or perhaps even the highest, since this position is open to everyone, being solely dependent on the attainment of knowledge.

This study has not focussed heavily on *'aqīdah*, the dogmatic teaching, which constitutes the foundation for the worldview of the group. The teaching in this respect is similar to most Salafi-oriented groups, stressing the unity of God and the obligation not to associate anybody or anything with God (*shirk*). This teaching has implications for the view on *manhaj*, program of action, which has been highlighted in this study. It includes, for example, ethics but also *da'wah*, and how Salafis view reform (*islāh*). As this study illustrates, there is an ideal among contemporary Salafis that one must seek the good life through ethical means. The abstract knowledge presented by the teachers must moreover manifest itself in practices, notably rituals and imitation of the Sunnah, and it may also include a social commitment.

The view on hermeneutics and epistemology has been analyzed in order to establish what interpretative stance the group advocates. The apprehension that we can note within the group of an uncritical imitation of earlier Islamic interpretations and also of Westernization is caused by a sense of loss—the loss of what is regarded as the authentic Muslim self. We can observe how there is a polarization between Islam and the West, or materialism. Islam must be made relevant in order to make Muslims become practicing Muslims and to gain new converts. It is notable that the teachers call the participants to cultivate an Islamic lifestyle that should be manifested in good behaviour in general and in observing obligatory religious rituals. However, their entire lives can be regarded as 'ritualized'. Salafism is 'embodied' in dress codes, and 'style' is very important. The focus on ethical character traits is also a part of the 'ritualization' of the everyday lives of Salafis, and it has direct effects on what they can do and where. Practical behaviour, such as going to work and school, may be difficult when trying to avoid the unbelievers (*kuffār*). In some cases this means that participants are recommended to choose on-line courses and to change their jobs.

We can note how the theology and core rituals conform to a mainstream Sunni Islam, and in this sense there is nothing 'new' or unexpected. However, their idea of authenticity is always in focus, and through the emphasis on the need for authenticity they construct a certain view on sacred authority and loyalty. Their insistence on imitating the Prophet and the pious predecessors may place them in a further stigmatized position, one in which they may be considered odd and as 'too' Muslim, compared to other Muslims.

One important aspect of the group's work is to establish clear boundaries of the in-group and the out-group. The group members' view of themselves as morally superior underlies group identity and supports a division of people into 'us' and 'them'. This leads them to devote a lot of time to presenting who the 'others' are and what makes them wrong. However, the group does not advocate violence but rather a passive stance and an isolation from that which does not constitute true Islam according to the teaching. Their ethical outlook underlies how they view their bodies, the surrounding society, and their relationship to it and the people there, defined as out-group. Notably, group members do participate in selected societal institutions, such as marriage, studying, and having a profession. Still, they struggle to maintain a distance to the morally corrupt society where they live, to maintain spiritual and moral purity. It is a moral vision connected to social activism, but political quietism. It is a theological stance requiring loyalty to the past, upholding socio-moral values, where they appear as custodians of tradition. Here, the Prophet and the pious predecessors are presented as moral paragons. Their mode of conduct can be referred to as 'Traditionist resistance', which includes self-denial of criticism, advocating moral chastisement through *al-amr bī al-ma'rūf wa nahy 'an al-munkar*. However, in Hanbali thought, and in this Salafi group, the political side to it is gone. It now only concerns 'correcting' people in general, not the political leadership. We have seen how group members insist on the obligation to obey leaders, though no explanation of how to relate to Swedish laws was encountered. Considering 'correction', group members are focused on correcting themselves first, before then successively widening out the correction to include friends and family.

As the introduction to this study made clear, there is a 'core' to Islam, which is revelation. Divergent opinions of how revelation should be approached exist, and the local group strives hard to show how it represents 'authentic' Islam. Tradition always changes and those who claim to defend a tradition also change it. As 'internal critics', the group feels able to criticize other interpretations and practices of Islam. We can note that, in this group, the Sunnah is the main source of authority and authenticity. In using Sunnah, they can claim legitimacy and reject others who do not agree to their views, including the juridical schools. In this way, the Sunnah becomes a strong locus for identity and authority, where the teachers are on the highest local level of authority due to their knowledge of the Sunnah. This use of Sunnah is an expression of the importance of the 'core' of Islam that has the sacred texts function as markers of identity and authenticity.

Returning to the discussion on tradition and authenticity that was given at the outset of this study, it can be restated that, in a manner of speaking, all traditions are 'invented' since no tradition is unchanging. However, the *notion* of a continuous tradition may function as a strong marker of identity and authenticity, and this too implies an 'invention' of tradition. The idea of an 'invented tradition' does not have to do with real or factual continuity with a tradition, and it is not a matter of attempting to establish a 'false consciousness'. In the case of the Salafi group in focus, the notion of tradition is rather one of trying to identify and revive a once-lost tradition, and to imitate it in a new historical situation. Hence, to this group, 'tradition' is more about reestablishing the 'golden past', which may or may not have existed as a fact. This, however, is not a relevant question for academic scholars to probe into. What is important here is to analyze how it is perceived, or construed, and how it is argued that it should be performed in the present situation. It is not a notion of practicing an unchanged tradition therefore. Rather, it is a lamentation of the loss of a tradition. It is an attempt at its revival or reform (*islāh*), where tradition, understood in a wide sense as the 'golden past', is ideologically used as a source of legitimacy and inspiration. Thus, the use of history and tradition can be regarded as a symptom of felt problems which provokes a need to 'return to the beginning' and to revive the 'golden past'. The interpretation of Islam presented in this study can thus be understood as a symptom of how a minority group experiences its position. It is a reaction to perceived injustices on a global scale, where capitalism and immorality is rejected. Yet it is also a need located in the group's local context. The material studied has also shown how 'tradition' has been used to legitimize certain actions and to establish group cohesion. The notion of this 'golden past' is a symbol of struggle, where the Sunnah is the focal point and at the centre of combatting viewpoints.

However, the past is gone. The sacred tradition does not exist in real life any longer. There is no continuity, only rapture. What the group aims for is a return to the beginning. Or, differently expressed, they aim for the beginning to return, via their active assistance. The Sunnah is the link to the sacred past now vanished, a past which may be retrieved through imitation of the Sunnah corpus and the example of the pious predecessors. The teachers who transmit tradition to the participants seemingly choose their topics and textual sources in order to create a sense that the recreation of the sacred past is a possibility, even in a minority situation. This is a notable aspect of the understanding of tradition among many revivalist groups, of various leanings, which may provoke critical comments from those who speak of continuity of tradition. Such expressions also draw our attention to the outsider view of such strivings to be 'false'. In the group, tradition is vested with authority, and the teachers, as custodians and transmitters of tradition, in their turn become vested with authority. The teachers function as leaders of the group in their search for the golden past now vanished and their campaign to revive it and ensure a place in Paradise constituting 'the chosen group'.

Many Muslims today, regardless of where they live, are not content with what an imitation of the juridical schools would give them. Imitation is not enough to meet their needs and solve their problems. Muslims in a minority situation may, in fact, consider imitation of juridical schools to be problematic, and thus feel the need to creatively understand and practice Islam in new contexts. Therefore, new approaches to Islam emerge along with new attitudes to sources and methods of interpretations. What is characteristic of a Salafi approach is a return to the sources with a literal stance, avoiding metaphorical interpretation and individual reasoning. Islam is sometimes presented as not in contradiction to logic and reason, as seen for example in the comment above on Islamization of knowledge. This has developed and gained an increasing popularity among Muslims, and we saw above that the Salafi group studied alludes to it as well, however briefly. This shows how Islam is historically situated and constantly changing. The Western 'enlightenment demand' of reason may have affected interpreters to strive for a presentation of religion as being rational and compatible with reason. This may be particularly important for Muslims living in the Western world, but is also a popular trend in countries dominated by Muslims. The relation between faith and reason has not been a major problem in Islamic philosophy.[1] Islam can be interpreted as a faith based on reason, and there are several verses in the Qur'an that may be used

---

1.   Oliver Leaman held that philosophers 'saw their faith in Islam as a rational enterprise'. Leaman 1999, 21.

to support such a view. The Islamization of science is considered proof of the divinity of the Qur'an. There also seems to be a need in many groups to explain why the gender roles that are promoted are truly equal, contrary to what secular feminists may argue. The focus may therefore be negotiated and changed depending on the contextual needs, and interpretative stances may vary depending on which topic is in focus. Considering that *da'wah* material is propaganda material, aiming to reach a specific audience, this ought not to surprise us. Reflecting the studied group, it can be said to strive for the literal following of the Qur'an and Sunnah, and to promote a certain amount of reasoning, notably analogical reasoning, *qiyās*, to be used. Aside from this, however, the use of logic or opinions is not allowed.

We have also seen how the group relates to the juridical communities, whose views and methods were questioned and whose imitation was rejected. This is somewhat surprising, since we can clearly detect an affinity with Hanbalism. This, I would conclude, is due to the reliance on Hanbali jurists as sources of authority of the highest level of knowledge. What we can notice in the local group is, however, a different kind of imitation, one which does not refer to *taqlīd*, or the imitation of a juridical school or a person, but rather *ittibā'*, in the sense of imitating the Prophet and the pious predecessors. As such, the Hanbali fundamentalist stance is not rejected outright, but rather understood differently based on the requirement to approach the sources directly and to imitate the moral paragons of the first generations. That which does not conform to this interpretative stance within the juridical schools is rejected.

This study has shown that the project of this puritan Salafi group results in a 'sunnisized self-minoritization'. This is a strategy whereby the local teachers, claiming a position of sacred authority, function as intermediaries between the *'ulamā'* and revelation and the participants in the Swedish local setting. Through the local teachers, the 'truth' is transmitted and those who want to reach a place in Heaven are motivated to comply with the program of action, thus constructing a messianic utopia.

Glossary

ahl al-hadīth, the people of the *hadīth*, people who follow the *hadīth*
ahādīth, see *hadīth*
al-amr bi al-ma'rūf wa nahy 'an al-munkar, to command the right and forbid the wrong
                (legal term)
akhlāq, ethics, character traits
'aqīdah, creed, content of faith

bid'ah, innovation

dalīl, proof
da'wah, call to Islam, mission
dhikr, remembering God
du'ā', voluntary prayer, supplication
dunya, world; the material world

fatwa, pl. fatāwa, legal opinion
al-firqat al-nājiyah, the saved group
fitnah, upheaval
fiqh, jurisprudence
fiqh al-aqalliyāt, minority jurisprudence

hadīth pl. ahādīth, tradition; report of a deed or saying by Muhammad
hijrah, emigration

'ibādāt, rituals and related practices
ijmā', consensus (legal term)
ijtihād, legal reasoning
'īmān, faith
inshallah, If God wants
ittibā', following or imitating

jihād, struggle

khayr, the good
kāfir, pl. kuffār, unbelievers; infidels
kufr, unbelief; infidelity

madhhab, pl. *madhāhib*, the jurisprudential schools
manhaj, program of action
mashallah, what God wants
mu'amalāt, transactions between people (legal term)

niyyah, intention

qiyās, analogy (legal term)

sadaqah (charity)
sahābah, the early Muslim community who met Muhammad
al-salaf al-sālih, the pious predecessors
salla Allāh 'alayhi wa sallam, May Allah exalt and bring peace upon him
sas, see *salla Allāh 'alayhi wa sallam*
sharī'ah, the Islamic law
shirk, to associate someone or something with God; the major sin
sīrah, biography
sirāt al-mustaqīm, the straight path
subhāna wa ta'āla, Glorified and exalted be He (God)
sunnah, custom, tradition, example, of the Prophet
swt, see *subhāna wa ta'āla*

tābi'ūn, the followers of the *sahābah*
tā'ifat al-mansūrah, the victorious group
takfīr, excommunication
taqlīd, imitation, adhering to the juridical schools
tarbīya, education
tawhīd, unity, monotheism
tawbah, repentance

'ulamā', s. *'ālim*, religiously learned people of knowledge
ummah, the Muslim community

wājib, obligatory (legal term)
al-walā' wa al-barā', allegiance and disavowal (legal term)

ya'ni, I mean, it means

zīnā', extramarital relations

Bibliography

Abou El Fadl, Khaled. 2001. *Speaking in God's Name: Islamic Law, Authority and Women.* Oxford: Oneworld.

Abrahamov, Binyamin. 1998. *Islamic Theology: Traditionalism and Rationalism.* Edinburgh: Edinburgh University Press.

Abu-Rabi', Ibrahim M. 2004. *Contemporary Arab Thought: Studies in Post-1967 Arab Intellectual History.* Sterling, VA: Pluto Press.

Adang, Camilla. 2002a. Belief and Unbelief. In *Encyclopaedia of the Qur'ān*, edited by Jane Dammen McAuliffe, 1:218–226. Washington, DC: Georgetown University Press.

Adang, Camilla. 2002b. Hypocrites and Hyprocisy. In *Encyclopaedia of the Qur'ān*, edited by Jane Dammen McAuliffe, 2:468–472. Leiden: Brill.

Agrama, Hussein Ali. 2010. Ethics, Tradition, Authority: Toward an Anthropology of the Fatwa. *American Ethnologist* 37(1): 2–18.

Amir-Moezzi, Mohammad Ali. 2002. Heresy. In *Encyclopaedia of the Qur'ān*, edited by Jane Dammen McAuliffe, 2:420–421. Leiden: Brill.

Amghar, Samir. 2007. Salafism and Radicalisation of Young European Muslims. In *European Islam: Challenges for Public Policy and Society*, edited by Samir Amghar, Amel Boubekeour, and Michael Emerson, 38–51. Brussels: Centre for European Policy Studies.

Amghar, Samir. 2009. Ideological and Theological Foundations of Muslim Radicalism in France. In *Ethno-Religious Conflict in Europe: Typologies of Radicalisation in Europe's Muslim Communities*, edited by Michael Emerson, 27–50. Brussels: Centre for European Policy Studies.

Ammerman, Nancy T. 2007. Studying Everyday Religion: Challenges for the Future. In *Everyday Religion: Observing Modern Religious Lives*, edited by Nancy T. Ammerman, 219–238. Oxford: Oxford University Press.

Anderson, Benedict. 2006/1983. *Imagined Communities.* London & New York: Verso.

Asad, Talal. 1986. *The Idea of an Anthropology of Islam.* Washington, DC: Center for Contemporary Arab Studies, Georgetown University Press.

Asad, Talal. 1993. *Genealogies of Religion: Discipline and Reasons of Power in Christianity and Islam.* Baltimore: Johns Hopkins University Press.

Asad, Talal. 2003. *Formations of the Secular: Christianity, Islam, Modernity.* Stanford, CA: Stanford University Press.

Asad, Talal. 2006. Responses. In *Powers of the Secular Modern: Talal Asad and his Interlocutors*, edited by David Scott and Charles Hirschkind, 206–241. Stanford, CA: Stanford University Press.

Atharia Website: http://athariyah.webs.com/thesavedsect.htm, accessed January 11, 2012.

Ibn al-Athir. 1965–1966. *al-Kāmil fī al-ta'rīkh, ta'līf, 'Izz al-Dīn Abi al-Ḥassan Abi al-Karam Muḥammad bin Muḥammad bin 'Abd al-Karīm bin 'Abd al-Wāhid al-Shabtānī al-ma'rūf bi Ibn al-Athīr.* 13 vols. Beirut: Dar Sadir li al-tiba'ah wa al-Nashr.

Atran, Scott. 2010. *Talking to the Enemy: Violent Extremism, Sacred Values, and What it Means to be Human.* London: Allen Lane.

Atran, Scoot. 2014. Jihad's Fatal Attraction. *The Guardian.* Published September 4, 2014, accessed November 16, 2015.

Bangstad, Sindre. 2011. The Morality Police Are Coming! Muslims in Norway's Media Discourses. *Anthropology Today* 27(5): 3–7.

Bayat, Asef. 2007. *Making Islam Democratic: Social Movements and the Post-Islamist Turn.* Stanford, CA: Stanford University Press.

Berglund, Jenny. 2010. *Teaching Islam: Islamic Religious Education in Sweden.* Münster: Waxmann.

Berkey, P. Jonathan. 2001. *Popular Preaching and Religious Authority in the Medieval Islamic Near East.* Seattle & London: University of Washington Press.

Bin Baz. Ruling on Smoking and Using Hookah. http://www.alifta.net/Search/ResultDetails.aspx?languagename=en&lang=en&view=result&fatwaNum=&FatwaNu mID=&ID=4553&searchScope=14&SearchScopeLevels1=&SearchScopeLevels2=&highL ight=1&SearchType=exact&SearchMoesar=false&bookID=&LeftVal=0&RightVal=0&si mple=&SearchCriteria=allwords&PagePath=&siteSection=1&searchkeyword=1041111 11107097104#firstKeyWordFound, accessed September 28, 2015.

Boubekeur, Amel. 2007. Political Islam in Europe. In *European Islam: Challenges for Public Policy and Society,* edited by Sarmir Amghar, Amel Boubekeour, and Michael Emerson, 14–37. Brussels: Centre for European Policy Studies.

Brown, Daniel. 1996. *Rethinking Tradition in Modern Islamic Thought.* Cambridge: Cambridge University Press.

van Bruinessen, Martin. 2007. *Producing Islamic Knowledge: Transmission and Dissemination in Western Europe.* London: Routledge.

Bunt, Gary R. 2009. *iMuslims: Rewiring the House of Islam.* Chapel Hill: University of North Carolina Press.

Caeiro, Alexandre. 2010. The Power of European Fatwas: The Minority fiqh Project and the Making of an Islamic Counterpublic. *International Journal of Middle East Studies* 42: 435–449.

Cesari, Jocelyne. 2004. *When Islam and Democracy Meet: Muslims in Europe and in the United States.* New York: Palgrave macmillan.

Cesari, Jocelyne. 2005. Ethnicity, Islam, and les banlieues: Confusing the Issues. Published online November 30, 2005. http://hia.squarespace.com/storage/Ethnicity%20 Islam%20and%20les%20banlieues%20-%20Confusing%20the%20Issues%20J.Cesari. pdf, accessed November 2, 2012.

Cesari, Jocelyne. 2009. Islam in the West: From Immigration to Global Islam. *Harvard Middle Eastern and Islamic Review* 8: 148–175.

Cesari, Jocelyne. 2010. Introduction. In *Muslims in the West after 9/11: Religion, Politics and Law,* edited by Jocelyne Cesari, 1–5. New York: Routledge.

Cook, David. 2005. *Understanding Jihad.* Berkeley & Los Angeles: University of California Press.

Cook, Michael. 2000. *Commanding Right and Forbidding Wrong in Islamic Thought.* Cambridge: Cambridge University Press.

Cook, Michael. 2003. *Forbidding Wrong in Islam.* Cambridge: Cambridge University Press.

Cooke, Miriam. 2002. Multiple Critique: Islamic Feminist Rhetorical Strategies. In *Postcolonialism, Feminism and Religious Discourse*, edited by Laura E. Donaldson and Kwok Pui-Lan, 142–160. New York & London: Routledge.

Daun, Holger, and Geoffrey Walford, eds. 2004. *Educational Strategies among Muslims in the Context of Globalization: Some National Case Studies.* Leiden: Brill.

de Koning, Martijn. 2012. The 'Other' Political Islam: Understanding Salafi Politics. In *Whatever Happened to the Islamists? Salafis, Heavy Metal Muslims and the Lure of Consumerist Islam*, edited by Amel Boubekeur and Olivier Roy. New York: Columbia University Press.

Devin, R. Springer, James L. Regens and David N. Edger. 2009. *Islamic Radicalism and Global Jihad.* Washington, DC: Georgetown University Press.

Dogan, Güney. 2012. Moral Geographies and the Disciplining of Senses among Swedish Salafis. *Comparative Islamic Studies* 8(1–2): 93–112.

Droge, Arthur J. 2013. *The Qur'ān: A New Annotated Translation.* Sheffield: Equinox.

Duderija, Adis. 2010. Constructing the Religious Self and the Other: Neo-traditional Salafi manhaj. *Islam and Christian-Muslim Relations* 21(1): 75–93.

Duderija, Adis. 2011. *Constructing a Religiously Ideal 'Believer' and 'Woman' in Islam.* New York: Palgrave Macmillan.

Eickelman, Dale. 1978. The Art of Memory: Islamic Education and its Social Reproduction. *Comparative Studies in Society and History* 20(4): 485–516.

Eickelman, Dale F., and Jon W. Anderson, eds. 2003. *New Media in the Muslim World: The Emerging Public Sphere*, 2nd ed. Bloomington: Indiana University Press.

Eickelman, Dale F., and James Piscatori. 1996. *Muslim Politics.* Princeton: Princeton University Press.

El Shamsy, Ahmed. 2008. The Social Construction of Orthodoxy. In *The Cambridge Companion to Classical Islamic Theology*, edited by Tim Winter, 97–117. Cambridge: Cambridge University Press.

Al-Fahad, Abdulaziz. 2004. From Exclusivism to Accommodation: Doctrinal and Legal Evolution of Wahhabism. *New York University Law Review* 79(2): 485–519.

Fattah, Hala. 2003. 'Wahhabi' Influences, Salafi Responses: Shaikh Mahmud Shurki and the Iraqi Salafi Movement, 1745–1930. *Journal of Islamic Studies* 14(2): 127–148.

Fawzan, Salih b. 2012a. *Sharḥ as-Sunnah*, Vol. 2, by Abu Muhammad al-Hasan bin 'Ali bin Khalaf Barbahari with Commentary by the Noble Shaykh Dr. Salif bin Fawzan bin 'Abdullah al-Fawzan. Birmingham: Dar Makkah International.

Fawzan, Salih b. 2012b. *Sharḥ as-Sunnah*, Vol. 2, by Abu Muhammad al-Hasan bin 'Ali bin Khalaf Barbahari with Commentary by the Noble Shaykh Dr. Salif bin Fawzan bin 'Abdullah al-Fawzan. Birmingham: Dar Makkah International.

Fawzan, Salih b. n.d. 'Fatwa against Hymns and Theater'. http://www.darulhadith.com/v2/anashid-och-skadespel-i-islam/, accessed September 28, 2015.

Fierro, Maribel. 1992. The Treatises against Innovation (kutub al-bida'). *Der Islam* 69(2): 204–224.

Fishman, Shammai. 2006. *Fiqh al-Aqalliyyat: A Legal Theory for Muslim Minorities.* Research monographs on the Muslim World, Hudson Institute.

Gaffney, Patrick D. 1994. *The Prophet's Pulpit: Islamic Preaching in Contemporary Egypt.* Berkeley: University of California Press.

Gallab, Wael Philip. 2015. Modes of Anti-Orthodoxy: Historical Contextualism, Radical Critique, and Qur'anism in Comtemporary Egypt (1980–2010). Dissertation, Oslo University.

Gauvain, Richard. 2013. *Salafi Ritual Purity: In the Presence of God.* London & New York: Routledge.

Gellner, Ernest. 1992. *Postmodernism, Reason and Religion.* London: Routledge.

Gerle, Elisabeth. 1999. *Mångkulturalism för vem? debatten om muslimska och kristna friskolor blottlägger värdekonflikter i det svenska samhället: om Sverige i förändring.* Nora: Nya Doxa.

Griffel, Frank. 2000. *Apostasie und Toleranz im Islam: Die Entwicklung zu al-Ghazālīs Urteil gegen die Philosophie und die Reaktionen der Philosophen.* Leiden: Brill.

Gugler, Thomas K. 2011. Making Muslims Fit for Faiz (God's Grace): Spiritual and Not-So-Spiritual Transactions Inside the Islamic Missionary Movement Dawat-E Islami. *Social Compass* 58(3): 339–345.

Gustafsson, Kristina. 2004. *Muslimsk skola, svenska villkor: konflikt, identitet & förhandling.* Dissertation, Lund University.

Hallaq, Wael B. 2001. Apostasy. In *Encyclopaedia of the Qur'ān*, edited by Jane Dammen McAuliffe, 1:119–127. Leiden: Brill.

Hawting, Gerald R. 2002. Idolatry and Idolaters. In *Encyclopaedia of the Qur'ān*, edited by Jane Dammen McAuliffe, 2:475–480. Leiden: Brill.

Haykel, Bernard. 2009. On the Nature of Salafi Thought and Action. In *Global Salafism: Islam's New Movement*, edited by Roel Meijer, 33–57. London: Hurst & Co.

Hefner, Robert W., and Muhammad Qasim Zaman, eds. 2007. *Schooling Islam: The Culture and Politics of Modern Muslim Education.* Princeton, NJ: Princeton University Press.

Hernroth-Rothstein, Annika. 2014. A Local Story of Global Jihad: For Sweden, the War on Terror Is too Close for Comfort. *Commentary* 138(4): 31–34.

Hirschkind, Charles. 2005. Cassette Ethics: Public Piety and Popular Media in Egypt. In *Religion, Media, and the Public Sphere*, edited by Birgit Meyer, 29–51. Bloomington: Indiana University Press.

Hjärpe, Jan. 1997. What Will Be Chosen from the Islamic Basket? *European Review* 5(3): 267–274.

Hobsbawm, Eric. 2013a (1983). Introduction: Inventing Traditions. In *The Invention of Tradition*, edited by Eric Hobsbawm and Terrence Ranger, 1–14, Cambridge: Cambridge University Press.

Hobsbawm, Eric. 2013b (1983). Mass-Producing Traditions: Europe, 1870–1914. In *The Invention of Tradition*, edited by Eric Hobsbawm and Terrence Ranger, 263–307. Cambridge: Cambridge University Press.

Holger, Daun, Åsa Brattlund and Salada Robleh. 2004. Educational Strategies among some Muslim Groups in Sweden. In *Educational Strategies among Muslims in the Context of Globalization: Some National Case Studies*, edited by Daun Holger, 187–207. Leiden: Brill.

Hurvitz, Nimrod. 2002. *The Formation of Hanbalism: Piety into Power.* London: RoutledgeCurzon.

Islamqa Website. http://islamqa.info/ar/107645. 'Mawqif *'ulamā'inā* min al-hāfidhayn ibn Hajar wa al-Nawawi, rahimahummā Allāh'. Question 107645, accessed September 28, 2015.

Jacobsen, Christine M. 2005. The Quest for Authenticity: Islamization amongst Muslim Youth in Norway. In *European Muslims and the Secular State*, edited by Jocelyne Cesari and Seán McLoughlin, 155–168. Hampshire & Burlington: Ashgate.

Jacobsen, Christine M. 2011. *Islamic Traditions and Muslim Youth in Norway.* Leiden & Boston: Brill.

Karlsson Minganti, Pia. 2007. *Muslima. Islamisk väckelse och unga kvinnors förhandlingar om genus i det samtida Sverige.* Stockholm: Carlssons Bokförlag.

Karlsson Minganti, Pia, and Ingvar Svanberg. 1995. *Moskéer i Sverige: en religionsetnologisk studie av intolerans och administrativ vanmakt.* Uppsala: Svenska kyrkans forskningsråd.

Kepel, Gilles. 1994. *Jihad: The Trail of Political Islam.* London: I.B. Tauris.

Khalidi, Tarif. 2009. *Images of Muhammad: Narratives of the Prophet in Islam across the Centuries.* New York: Doubleday.

Kooi-Ching Tong, Joy, and Bryan S. Turner. 2008. Women, Piety and Practice: A Study of Women and Religious Practice in Malaysia. *Contemporary Islam:* A Special Issue of Contemporary Islam on Piety 2(1): 41–59.

Krämer, Gudrun, and Sabine Schmidtke. 2006. Introduction: Religious Authority and Religious Authorities in Muslim Societies. In *Speaking for Islam: Religious Authorities in Muslim Societies,* edited by Gudrun Krämer and Sabine Schmidtke, 1–14. Leiden: Brill.

Lacroix, Stéphane. 2009. Between Revolution and Apoliticism: Nasir al-Din al-Albani and his Impact on the Shaping of Contemporary Salafism. In *Global Salafism: Islam's New Movement,* edited by Roel Meijer, 58–80. London: Hurst & Co.

Landolt, Hermann. 2005. Walāyah. In *Encyclopedia of Religion,* edited by Lindsay Jones, 2nd ed. Vol. 14. Detroit: Macmillan Reference USA, 2005. 9656-9662. Gale Virtual Reference Library. Web. November 16, 2015. URL http://go.galegroup.com/ps/i.

Larsson, Göran. 2005. Muslimer i Sverige. In *Det mångreligiösa Sverige: ett landskap i förändring,* edited by Daniel Andersson and Åke Sander, 447–490. Lund: Studentlitteratur.

Larsson, Göran. 2006. *Muslimerna kommer: tankar om islamofobi.* Göteborg: Makadam.

Larsson, Göran. 2009. Muslimer och islam. In *Det mångreligiösa Sverige - ett landskap i förändring,* edited by Daniel Andersson and Åke Sander, 463–520. 2nd ed. Lund: Studentlitteratur.

Larsson, Göran. 2011. Islam and Tattooing: An Old Question, a New Research Topic. *Scripta Instituti Donneriani Aboensis* 23: 237–256.

Larsson, Göran. 2014a. *Islam och muslimer i Sverige—en kunskapsöversikt.* Stockholm: Nämnden för statligt stöd till trossamfund.

Larsson, Göran. 2014b. Towards a Sociology of the Quran: A Reading of Q 4:34. In *Micro-Level Analysis of the Quran,* edited by Håkan Rydving, 147–167. Uppsala: Acta Universitatis Upsaliensis.

Larsson, Göran, and Mårten Björk. 2015. *Globala konflikter med lokala konsekvenser: Översikt om utresandeproblematiken.* Myndigheten för samhällsskydd och beredskap. https://www.msb.se/RibData/Filer/pdf/27618.pdf, accessed September 28, 2015.

Larsson, Göran, and David Thurfjell. 2013. *Shiamuslimer i Sverige: en kortfattad översikt.* Stockholm: Nämnden för statligt stöd till trossamfund.

Lauzière, Henri. 2010. The Construction of Salafiyya: Reconsidering Salafism from the Perspective of Conceptual History. *International Journal of Middle East Studies* 42(3): 369–389.

Leaman, Oliver. 1999. *A Brief Introduction to Islamic Philosophy.* Malden, MA: Polity Press.

Lewisohn, L. Taḳwā. In *Encyclopaedia of Islam,* edited by P. Bearman, Th. Bianquis, C.E. Bosworth, E. van Donzel, and W.P. Heinrichs. 2nd ed. Brill Online, 2015. Reference. Stockholm University Library, November 16, 2015. http://referenceworks.brillonline.com/entries/encyclopaedia-of-islam-2/takwa-COM_1457. First appeared online: 2012. First Print Edition: isbn: 9789004161214, 1960–2007.

Lincoln, Bruce. 2003. *Holy Terrors: Thinking about Religion after September 11.* Chicago: University of Chicago Press.

Lincoln, Bruce. 2005. Theses on Method. *Method and Theory in the Study of Religion* 17(1): 11–17.

MacIntyre, Alasdair. 1988. *Whose Justice? Which Rationality?* Notre Dame: University of Notre Dame Press.

Mahmood, Saba. 2005. *Politics of Piety: The Islamic Revival and the Feminist Subject*. Princeton & Oxford: Princeton University Press.

Martin, Richard C., and Abbas Barzegar. 2010. Formations of Orthodoxy: Authority, Power, and Networks in Muslim Societies. In *Rethinking Islamic Studies: From Orientalism to Cosmopolitanism*, edited by Carl W. Ernst and Richard C. Martin, 179–202, Columbia: University of South Carolina Press.

Martin, Richard C., and Mark R. Woodward. 1997. *Defenders of Reason in Islam: Mu'tazilism from Medieval School to Modern Symbol*. Oxford: Oneworld.

Mamdani, Mahmood. 2004. *Good Muslim, Bad Muslim: America, the Cold War, and the Roots of Terror*. New York: Pantheon Books.

March, Andrew F. 2009a. Sources of Moral Obligation to non-Muslims in the 'Jurisprudence of Muslim Minorities' (Fiqh al-aqalliyāt) Discourse. *Islamic Law and Society* 16: 34–94.

March, Andrew F. 2009b. *Islam and Liberal Citizenship*. Oxford & New York: Oxford University Press.

Marlow, Michael. 2013. Social interaktion med djinner enligt västafrikanska mandinko i Stockholm. *Chaos: Skandinavisk tidskrift for religionshistoriska studier* 60: 189–209.

McGuire, Meredith B. 2008. *Lived Religion: Faith and Practice in Everyday Life*. Oxford: Oxford University Press.

Meijer, Roel. 2009. Introduction. In *Global Salafism: Islam's New Religious Movement*, edited by Roel Meijer, 1–32. London: Hurst.

Metcalf, Barbara D. 1996. New Medinas: The Tablighi Jama'at in America and Europe. In *Making Muslim Space in North America and Europe*, edited by Barbara D. Metcalf, 110–127. Berkeley: University of California Press.

Moberg, Jessica. 2013. Piety, Intimacy and Mobility: A Case Study of Charismatic Christianity in Present-day Stockholm. Dissertation. University of Gothenburg.

Olsson, Susanne. 2008. Apostasy in Egypt: Contemporary Cases of hisbah. *The Muslim World* 98(1): 95–115.

Olsson, Susanne. 2009. Religion in the Public Space: 'Blue-and-Yellow Islam' in Sweden. *Religion, State and Society* 37(3): 277–289.

Olsson, Susanne. 2014. Proselytizing Islam—problematizing 'Salafism'. *The Muslim World* 104(1–2): 171–197.

Olsson, Susanne. 2012. A Hijra within. *Comparative Islamic Studies* 8(1–2): 71–92.

Olsson, Susanne. 2015a. *Preaching Islamic Revival: 'Amr Khaled, Mass Media and Social Change in Egypt*. London: I.B. Tauris.

Olsson, Susanne. 2015b. *Minority Jurisprudence in Islam: Muslim Communities in the West*. London: I.B. Tauris.

Olsson, Susanne. 2017. Shiah as Internal Others – A Salafi Rejection of the 'Rejecters'. *Islam and Christian-Muslim Relations* 28(4): 409–430. http://dx.doi.org/10.1080/09596 410.2017.1318545.

Olsson, Susanne, and Simon Sorgenfrei. 2011. Svensk religionskritisk diskurs. *DIN. Tidskrift for religion og kultur* 3–4: 82–98.

Olsson, Susanne, and Leif Stenberg. 2015. Engaging the History of Religions—from an Islamic Studies Perspective. *Temenos* 51(2): 201–225.

Otterbeck, Jonas. 1998. The Baltic Tatars: The First Muslim Group in Modern Sweden. In *Cultural Encounters in East Central Europe*, edited by Karin Junefelt and Malin Peterson, 145–53. Stockholm: Swedish Council for Planning and Coordination of Research.

Otterbeck, Jonas, and Pieter Bevelander. 2006. *Islamofobi: en studie av begreppet, ungdomars attityder och unga muslimers utsatthet.* Stockholm: Forum för levande historia.

Pickthall, Muhammad M. 2006. *The Meaning of the Glorious Quran: An Explanatory Translation.* New Delhi: USB Publishers' Distributors Pvt. Ltd.

Pierre Vogel Website. http://www.pierrevogel.de/, accessed November 5, 2012.

Poljarevic, Emin. 2012. In Pursuit of Authenticity: Becoming a Salafi. *Comparative Islamic Studies* 8(1–2): 139–164.

Poljarevic, Emin. 2016. Locating the Event Horizon of Salafi Activism. *The Muslim World.* 106: 145–55

Ranstorp, Magnus, and Josefine Dos Santos. 2009. *Hot mot demokrati och värdegrund: en lägesbild från Malmö.* Stockholm: CATS, Center for Asymmetric Threat Studies.

REDCo. *Religion in Education: A Contribution to Dialogue or a Factor of Conflict in Transforming Societies of European Countries (REDCo).* http://www.redco.uni-hamburg.de/web/3480/3481/index.html, accessed February 26, 2009.

Riesebrodt, Martin. 1993. *Pious Passion: The Emergence of Modern Fundamentalism in the United States and Iran.* Berkeley: University of California Press.

Riesebrodt, Martin. 2000. Fundamentalism and the Resurgence of Religion. *Numen* 47(3): 266–287.

Rispler, Vardit. 1991. Toward a New Understanding of the Term bid'a. *Der Islam* 68(2): 320–328.

Roald, Anne Sofie. 1994. Tarbiya: Education and Politics in Islamic movements in Jordan and Malaysia. Dissertation, Lund University.

Robinson, Francis. 2009. Crisis of Authority: Crisis of Islam? *Journal of the Royal Asiatic Society* 3(19): 339–354.

Robson, James. 2015. Bid'a. In *Encyclopaedia of Islam,* edited by P. Bearman, Th. Bianquis, C.E. Bosworth, E. van Donzel and W.P. Heinrichs, 2nd ed. Brill Online. Stockholm University Library, September 28, 2015. http://referenceworks.brillonline.com/entries/encyclopaedia-of-islam-2/bida-SIM_1393.

Roy, Olivier. 2004. *Globalized Islam: The Search for a New Ummah.* New York: Columbia University Press.

Salvatore, Armando. 2007. *The Public Sphere: Liberal Modernity, Catholicism, Islam.* New York: Palgrave Macmillan.

Schielke, Samuli. 2010. Second Thoughts about the Anthropology of Islam, or How to Make Sense of Grand Schemes in Everyday Life. *ZMO working papers,* no. 2.

Schwartz, Benjamin E. 2007. America's Struggle against the Wahhabi/Neo-Salafi Movement. *Orbis* 51(1): 107–128.

Sedgwick, Mark. 2012. Introduction: Salafism, the Social, and the Global Resurgence of Religion. *Comparative Islamic Studies* 8(1–2): 57–70.

Sikand, Yoginder S. 1988. The Origins and Growth of the Tablighi Jamaat in Britain. *Islam and Christian-Muslim Relations* 9(2): 171–192.

SST. 2013. *SST rapport 2013: Ledarskaps- och kompetensutveckling för trossamfundens ledare.* Stockholm: SST.

Staten och imamerna. Religion, integration, autonomi: betänkande (Sverige Imamutbildningsutredningen) (SOU 2009:52). http://www.regeringen.se/content/1/c6/12/73/17/851006b1.pdf. Stockholm: Fritze.

Steinberg, Guido. 2009. Jihadi-Salafism and the Shi'is: Remarks about the Intellectual Roots of anti-Shi'ism. In *Global Salafism: Islam's New Movement,* edited by Roel Meijer, 107–125. London: Hurst.

Stenberg, Leif. 1996. *The Islamization of Science: Four Muslim Positions Developing an Islamic Modernity*. Lund Studies in History of Religions 6, Stockholm: Almqvist & Wiksell International.

Sunnah.com Website: sunnah.com, accessed February 10, 2014.

Svensson, Jonas. 2000. *Women's Human Rights and Islam: A Study of Three Attempts at Accommodation*. Lund Studies in the History of Religions, Dissertation, Lund University.

Svensson, Jonas. 2012. Mind the Beard! Deference, Purity and Islamization of Everyday Life as Micro-factors in a Salafi Cultural Epidemiology. *Comparative Islamic Studies* 8(1–2): 185–210.

Sveriges Radio Website. http://sverigesradio.se/sida/artikel.aspx?programid=83&artikel=6098603, accessed November 16, 2015.

SVT Website. http://www.svt.se/nyheter/regionalt/vast/har-ar-21-aringen-bakom-skolattacken, accessed November 16, 2015.

Turner, Bryan S. 2008. Introduction: The Price of Piety. Contemporary Islam: A Special Issue of *Contemporary Islam on Piety* 2(1): 1–6.

Valliere, Paul. 2005. Tradition. In *Encyclopedia of Religion*, edited by Lindsay Jones, 13:9267–9281. 2nd ed. Detroit: Macmillan Reference USA, Gale Virtual Reference Library. Web. January 21, 2014.

Van Doorn-Harder, Nelly. 2006. Teaching and Preaching. In *Encyclopaedia of the Qur'an*, edited by Jane Dammen McAuliffe, 5:205–231. Leiden: Brill.

Voll, John O. 1997. Sultans, Saints, and Presidents: The Islamic Community and the State in North Africa. In *Islam, Democracy, and the State in North Africa*, edited by John P. Entelis, 1–16. Bloomington & Indianapolis: Indiana University Press.

Waardenburg, Jacques. 2002. *Islam: Historical, Social and Political Perspectives*. Religion and Reason 40. Lausanne, Berlin & New York: W. de Gruyter.

Wagemakers, Joas. 2008. Framing the 'Threat to Islam': Al-wala' wa al-bara' in Salafi Discourse. *Arab Studies Quarterly* 30(4): 1–22.

Wagemakers, Joas. 2009. The Transformation of a Radical Concept: Al-wala' wa-l-bara' in the Ideology of Abu Muhammad al-Maqdisi. In *Global Salafism: Islam's New Movement*, edited by Roel Meijer, 81–106. London: Hurst.

Wagemakers, Joas. 2012. 'Seeders' and 'Postponers'? An Analysis of the 'Khawarij' 'Murji'a' Labels in Polemical Debates between Quietists and Jihadi-Salafis. In *Contextualising Jihadi Thought*, edited by Jevaan Deol and Zaheer Kazmi, 145–164. London: Hurst.

Waldman, Marilyn Robinson. 2005. Sunnah. In *Encyclopedia of Religion*, edited by Lindsay Jones, 13:8852–8855. 2nd ed. Detroit: Macmillan Reference USA, Gale Virtual Reference Library. Web. April 16, 2014.

Wehr, Hans. 1994. *A Dictionary of Modern Written Arabic (Arabic-English)*, 4th ed., considerably enl. and amended by the author. Student ed. Urbana, IL: Spoken Languages Services.

Wiktorowicz, Quintan. 2001. *The Management of Islamic Activism: Salafis, the Muslim Brotherhood, and State Power in Jordan*. New York: State University of New York Press.

Wiktorowicz, Quintan. 2003. Introduction: Islamic Activism and Social Movement Theory. In *Islamic Activism: A Social Movement Theory Approach*, edited by Quintan Wiktorowicz, 1–33. Bloomington: Indiana University Press.

Wiktorowicz, Quintan. 2005a. *Radical Islam Rising: Muslim Extremism in the West*. Lanham, MD and Oxford: Rowman & Littlefield.

Wiktorowicz, Quintan. 2005b. The Salafi Movement: Violence and the Fragmentation of Community. In *Muslim Networks from Hajj to Hip Hop*, edited by Miriam Cooke and Bruce B. Lawrence, 208–234. Chapel Hill: University of North Carolina Press.

Wiktorowicz, Quintan. 2006. Anatomy of the Salafi Movement. *Studies in Conflict and Terrorism* 29(3): 207–239.

Wilson, Bryan R. 1992 (1990). *The Social Dimensions of Sectarianism: Sects and New Religious Movements in Contemporary Society*. Oxford: Clarendon Press.

World Value Survey, cultural map. http://www.worldvaluessurvey.org/WVSContents.jsp, accessed September 16, 2015.

Zaman, Muhammad Qasim. 2002. *The Ulama in Contemporary Islam: Custodians of Change*. Princeton, NJ: Princeton University Press.

Zaman, Muhammad Qasim. 2012. *Modern Islamic Thought in a Radical Age: Religious Authority and Internal Criticism*. Princeton, NJ: Princeton University Press.

Index

Lightning Source UK Ltd.
Milton Keynes UK
UKHW011959120419
340965UK00003B/59/P

9 781781 793398